Imagining Extinction

Imagining Extinction: The Cultural Meanings of Endangered Species

Ursula K. Heise

The University of Chicago Press :: Chicago and London

Ursula K. Heise is the Marcia H. Howard Chair in Literary Studies in
the Department of English and the Institute of the Environment and
Sustainability at the University of California, Los Angeles.

The University of Chicago Press, Chicago 60637
The University of Chicago Press, Ltd., London
© 2016 by The University of Chicago
All rights reserved. Published 2016.
Printed in the United States of America

Chapters 1 and 2 first appeared in different form in German in *Nach der
Natur: Das Artensterben und die moderne Kultur* (Berlin: Edition Unseld,
2010), © Suhrkamp Verlag AG. Reprinted by permission.

25 24 23 22 21 20 19 18 17 16   1 2 3 4 5

ISBN-13: 978-0-226-35802-4 (cloth)
ISBN-13: 978-0-226-35816-1 (paper)
ISBN-13: 978-0-226-35833-8 (e-book)
DOI: 10.7208/chicago/9780226358338.001.0001

The University of Chicago Press gratefully acknowledges the generous
support of the University of California, Los Angeles, toward the
publication of this book.

Library of Congress Cataloging-in-Publication Data

Names: Heise, Ursula K., author.
Title: Imagining extinction : the cultural meanings of endangered
    species / Ursula K. Heise.
Description: Chicago ; London : The University of Chicago Press, 2016. |
    Includes bibliographical references and index.
Identifiers: LCCN 2015045699 | ISBN 978-0-226-35802-4
    (cloth : alk. paper) | ISBN 978-0-226-35816-1 (pbk. : alk. paper) |
    ISBN 978-0-226-35833-8 (e-book)
Subjects: LCSH: Extinction (Biology) | Endangered species. |
    Extinct animals.
Classification: LCC QH78 .H45 2016 | DDC 576.8/4—dc23 LC record
    available at http://lccn.loc.gov/2015045699

♾ This paper meets the requirements of ANSI/NISO Z39.48-1992
(Permanence of Paper).

For Jon, with love

Contents

Illustrations

Acknowledgments

Books have more authors than appear on the front page. Many of them tend to be listed on the last few pages: the sources, models, influences, and conversation partners across times, places, and texts that an argument has emerged from. Others deserve gratitude beyond and outside their written work. I've been lucky enough to have had many outstanding "coauthors" of both kinds.

I have benefited immensely from my colleagues and students working in the environmental humanities at Stanford University and the University of California, Los Angeles, over the past ten years, some of whom have since moved on to other institutions: Allison Carruth, Jessica Cattelino, Elizabeth DeLoughrey, Justin Eichenlaub, Susanna Hecht, Heather Houser, Helga Leitner, Donald S. Maier, Anahid Nersessian, Eric Sheppard, Vasile Stănescu, Rob Watson, and Richard White. Vas Stănescu gave detailed feedback on chapter 4, for which I am particularly grateful. Conservation biologists at both Stanford and UCLA inspired my work and helped it along—warm thanks to Gretchen Daily, Paul and Anne Ehrlich, and Bradley Shaffer.

Many friends, colleagues, and fellow environmentalists from around the world have inspired, corrected, and sharpened my argument, provided additional references, and given me the opportunity to discuss parts of my research with their communities: Stacy Alaimo, Etienne Benson, Hannes Bergthaller, David Bialock, Brett Buchanan, Guillermina De Ferrari, Greg Garrard, Catrin Gersdorf, George Handley, Steven Hartman, Dolly Jør-gensen, Finn Arne Jørgensen, Bernhard Malkmus, Jorge Marcone, Neill Matheson, Sylvia Mayer, Mario Ortiz Robles, Kate Rigby, Deborah Bird Rose, Scott Slovic, Heather Sullivan, Patrick Swenson, Alexa Weik von Mossner, Sabine Wilke, Cary Wolfe, and Masami Yuki. In the spring of 2012, the members of the Environmental Humanities Workshop at the University of California, Davis, especially Julie Sze and Mike Ziser, of-fered very helpful comments on chapter 2. The workshop on endanger-ment at the Max Planck Institute for the History of Science in the summer of 2012, organized by Fernando Vidal and Nélia Dias, provided valuable feedback on chapter 4—special thanks to Julia Adeney Thomas for her detailed comments. The work of the Extinction Studies Group has been an inspiration and a model throughout the writing of this book.

Four referees for the University of Chicago Press were extraordi-narily generous and helpful in their comments on the manuscript. Two of them I can only thank anonymously. Peter Kareiva and Thom van Dooren have been generous far beyond the call of duty in offering de-tailed comments and corrections. It goes without saying that all remain-ing errors are mine.

An earlier version of chapter 1 appeared in the journal *Configurations* 18.1–2 (2010), 49–72 (copyright 2011 by Johns Hopkins University Press and the Society for Literature and Science), and is here reprinted in an expanded and updated version with the permission of Johns Hop-kins University Press. My first book on the contemporary extinction cri-sis, *Nach der Natur: Das Artensterben und die moderne Kultur*, appeared in 2010 with the German publisher Suhrkamp. Heinrich Geiselberger, the editor, made that book a much better one than it would have been without his comments, and *Imagining Extinction*, whose first two chap-ters loosely resemble the beginning of *Nach der Natur*, benefited over the long term from his support.

I am grateful to Isabella Kirkland and Joel Sartore for allowing me to use some of their paintings and photographs in this book, and to Adam Johnson and Tom Kealey for granting me permission to use images from the graphic novel *Virunga*, which a group of Stanford undergraduates created with their guidance.

The generosity of the John Simon Guggenheim Foundation in 2011–12 allowed me to complete a good deal of research and launch the writ-ing of *Imagining Extinction*. Stanford University enabled me to work on biodiversity databases with the Digital Humanities specialist Elijah

Meeks, to whom I owe warm thanks for his expertise, dedication, and patience. Dave Shepard helped me to continue this work at UCLA. An invitation to spend two months at the University of Umeå in 2011 and 2012 allowed me to discuss the first chapters of the book with the community of environmental and digital humanists there and to do further research. The sustained intellectual and institutional support of the Chair of the Department of English at UCLA, Ali Behdad, and the Dean of Humanities, David Schaberg, has been crucial for completing this book, and I have benefited greatly from Marcia Howard's inspiring intellectual presence and generosity. A grant from the Mellon Foundation for a Sawyer Seminar on the Environmental Humanities in 2014–15 provided the means for a continuous conversation with a dedicated group of humanists and social scientists from the University of California and many invited guests from universities in the United States and around the world that allowed me to revisit and rethink various parts of the book.

A lively multispecies community of birds, tortoises, and fish inside and outside of our home in Venice has helped remind me of the purpose of environmental scholarship, of why we care for other species and how they matter to us and we to them. In the midst of these scaly, leathery, and feathery presences, Jon Christensen has been my constant companion and has helped me manage their sometimes noisy and impetuous demands on our time and attention. His passion for nature, for writing, and for the weird things people do with both, his sharp eye for evidence and argument, his finely tuned editorial skills, his patience in talking me through low moments, and his sense of humor and unfailing optimism have been my lifeline in navigating the research, drafts, presentations, revisions, and technicalities from beginning to end. Without him, this book could not have been written.

Introduction: From the End of Nature to the Beginning of the Anthropocene

Extinctions in a Bag

The Muji store I walked into in a Hong Kong shopping mall in November 2010 had all the usual hallmarks of this Japanese retail chain: housewares, furniture, and clothing designed with clean minimalism, muted colors, and elegant functionality. Mujirushi Ryōhin, whose Japanese name 無印良品 translates as "No Brand Quality Goods," has made a brand name out of the refusal to brand, a logo of "no logo." It caters to upper-middle-class longings for the return to a simple life in the midst of urban complexity, with an emphasis on quality, minimalism, recycling, and reduced waste. Not that everybody sees the charm—a German friend of mine once referred to Muji dismissively as "the Japanese Ikea"—but its appeal is widespread enough that the chain now has stores all over East Asia, western Europe, and North America.

During the Christmas season, Muji departs from its basic principle, which is always sticking to the same lineup of goods so customers can easily replace lost or broken parts, and offers more unique gift items. That year, among wooden toys, tin robots, and delicate stationery, a pile of small linen drawstring bags with the words "Extinct Species" printed on them drew my eye. Each contained a set of ten small wooden animals, carved toy replicas of ten extinct species from around the world (fig. 1), whose Latin names were indicated along with their place of origin on a delightfully Japanocentric paper map (fig. 2).

I bought several of these bags—I had begun to be interested in endangered and extinct species several years before—without being sure for whom, exactly, this would turn out to be an appropriate gift. I had repeatedly given dinosaur-related presents to friends' children who were at the age when a dinosaur obsession seems well-nigh inescapable. But these toy animals seemed too simple and unspectacular by comparison, and more sinister in their implication: after all, these were all species for whose extinction, unlike that of the dinosaurs, humans were directly or indirectly responsible. What does it mean to give a set of extinct- species toys to a kid to play with or to an adult to enjoy aesthetically, I wondered? Why do we produce and consume replicas and images of endangered and extinct species as commodities, and with what effects? Do they draw attention to an urgent environmental crisis or, on the contrary, trivialize it? Do they use an everyday object slyly to alert us to the problem, or do they help to integrate biodiversity loss into everyday routines to the point where it does not seem disastrous or even extraordinary anymore? In the years that followed, as I continued to research this book, and as I read popular science books, novels, and poems about endangered species, watched documentaries, and looked at photographs, paintings, and Internet art, these questions returned to me again and again.

Why do we care about nonhuman species at risk? In asking this question, *Imagining Extinction* departs from the usual emphasis of popular or academic books on endangered species, which typically seek to convince their readers that the current biodiversity loss is a major crisis, that we do not care enough collectively, that we need to care and do more to rescue species at risk, and that readers should participate in this concern and contribute to conservation efforts. I believe these are valid and important objectives—and there are hundreds of books and documentary films, thousands of photographs, and tens of thousands of essays, articles, and websites that aim to do exactly these things. The sheer volume of texts and images concerning particular endangered species or the general panorama of biodiversity loss has by now turned into so large-scale a phenomenon that it deserves the attention of cultural scholars.

Driven by a growing interest in animals and plants, both domestic and wild, I began to read books and watch films about endangered species around 2005. The broad consensus of these works was that at the turn of the third millennium, humankind likely faces a mass extinction of a kind that has occurred only five times before in the 3.5 billion years

FIGURE 1 Set of "Extinct Species" toy figures, Mujirushi Ryōhin (2010). Author's photograph.

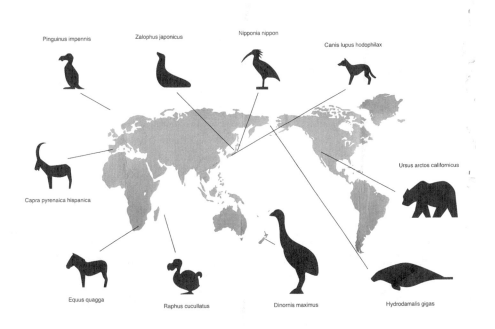

FIGURE 2 Map accompanying Mujirushi Ryōhin's "Extinct Species" toy figures (2010). Author's photograph.

of life on Earth, but this time it would be due to human impact. Years of rather depressing research turned up dozens of works whose titles typically featured phrases like "The Last X," "The Search for Y," or "The Race to Save Z." One anthology of poems hailed with the ominous title *The Dire Elegies: 59 Poets on Endangered Species of North America*. Most of these books and films combined apocalyptic portrayals of the future of wildlife with, usually, one or two more optimistic sections at the conclusion that pointed to successful conservation efforts and exhorted readers to become involved.

The formula quickly became too familiar to remain inspiring in and of itself, although I did come to admire more and more the deep commitment and intense effort that was evident in these works. Rather than the imperative that we should care, the fact that we evidently do care a great deal, even if our concern may not at present suffice to save many animal and plant species at risk, imposed itself more and more as the central question for thinking about why conservation matters and how it might be fostered. The omnipresence of endangered species—from chocolate wrappers at the supermarket and stuffed animals in museum stores to pictures on yearly calendars and extensive news coverage of newborn polar bears and dead panda cubs, and from the films of David Attenborough to Lee Hyla's classical composition about the ivory-billed woodpecker—highlights just how sustained an interest cultural communities in various nations already have in certain endangered species, if not in all of them. Individuals, organizations, and corporations, even some of those whose practices contribute to habitat destruction and species extinction, invest significant amounts of money in conservation efforts.

Many of the books, essays, and films tell personal and moving stories about how the writer or filmmaker became aware of the plight of threatened species; how encounters with this or that majestic, spectacular, bizarre, or pitiful animal triggered an emotion and a concern that turned into the vocation to fight on its behalf; how journeys around the globe revealed the magnitude of the crisis and what difficulties emerged in the attempt to mitigate it. From my perspective as a textual and cultural scholar, what is most interesting about these works is not so much their uniquely personal content as the elements that repeat themselves across many stories and the means they use to convince readers with quite different experiences to share the concern expressed in them. How, when, and why do we invest culturally, emotionally, and economically in the fate of threatened species? What stories do we tell, and which ones do we not tell, about them? What do the images that we use to represent them reveal, and what do they hide? What kind of awareness, emotion, and action are such stories and images meant to generate? What broader cultural values and social conflicts are they associated with?

The central thesis of this book is that however much individual environmentalists may be motivated by a selfless devotion to the well-being of nonhuman species, however much individual conservation scientists may be driven by an eagerness to expand our knowledge and understanding of the species with whom we co-inhabit the planet, their engagements with these species gain sociocultural traction to the extent that they become part of the stories that human communities tell about themselves: stories about their origins, their development, their identity, and their future horizons. These human stories that frame our perception and relation to endangered nonhumans are the subject matter of this book. Such stories, directly or indirectly, explain why we care, not just as individuals but as communities or cultures. This is not to deny the important role that passionate individuals have played in science and conservation and will no doubt continue to play, but to focus on the larger narratives that enable individuals' efforts to resonate with larger social networks. Public engagement with endangered species depends on these broader structures of imagination, and individuals' paths to conservationist engagement become meaningful for others only within these cultural frameworks. Ultimately, I will argue that biodiversity, endangered species, and extinction are primarily cultural issues, questions of what we value and what stories we tell, and only secondarily issues of science.

The writer Jon Mooallem, in his quasi-anthropological study of conservationists, has likened current efforts to manage wildlife in the United States to "a surreal kind of performance art": "We train condors not to perch on power lines," he writes. "We slip plague vaccine to ferrets. We shoot barred owls to make room in the forest for spotted owls. We monitor pygmy rabbits with infrared cameras and military drones. We carry migrating salamanders across busy roads in our palms" (2013, 2). Everyone from high school kids and retirees to the Cornell Lab of Ornithology and the Army Corps of Engineers participates willingly in elaborate maneuvers to give endangered animals one last stab at survival. We expend enormous labor and capital to save polar bears, whose habitat is melting away and who may be interbreeding with northward-migrating grizzlies; we guide whooping cranes with planes on hundreds of miles of migration to summer habitats that may well be engulfed by rising sea water in the foreseeable future, as Mooallem highlights. Even though these efforts are often undertaken in the name of nature and the restoration of wild things that used to be, they more closely resemble a collective construction of alternative natures that obeys cultural impulses more than scientific ones.

Studying the imaginative webs that surround endangered species will, I hope, be helpful in thinking about conservation and its public face in the future. But it also shows some of the crucial ways in which animals and, more rarely, plants and other organisms, are cultural tools and agents in humans' thinking about themselves, their communities, their histories, and their futures. Understanding the ways in which relationships to other species already form part of our self-understanding will be useful in developing the forms of multispecies justice and multispecies cosmopolitanism I discuss at the end of the book as possible models for rethinking humans' place in what we have come to call the Anthropocene.

Nature at Risk

The roots of environmentalism in general and contemporary perceptions of endangered species in particular lie in the decades around the turn of the nineteenth century, when Western societies' perception of nature underwent a seismic shift. For most of the preceding millennia, nature had been both the principal resource and a major threat to human well-being. Even as it provided humans with the basic raw materials and foodstuffs for survival, nature also put them constantly at risk. Heat, cold, storms, floods, droughts, earthquakes, fires, predators, poisonous plants, and diseases all forced human communities to struggle with nature, at the same time that soil, water, climate, animals, plants, and other organisms enabled them to go on living and to develop a richly varied inventory of tools and practices by which to make use of their environment and ward off its dangers.

In the face of the first wave of sustained industrialization around 1800, a perception that had only occasionally surfaced in earlier centuries began to make itself felt as a new cultural dominant: the sense that humans were endangering nature on a grand scale, rather than the other way around. Nature, it seemed, was deteriorating under the impact of modern society and might vanish entirely in another generation or two. This sense of nature at risk catalyzed the emergence of movements and societies for the protection of nature at the end of the nineteenth century, led to the rise of modern environmentalist movements between the 1960s and the 1980s, and shapes current fears about a range of ecological crises, including climate change, ocean acidification, and biodiversity loss. Exactly what causes nature to go from bad to worse has varied in cultural

perception over time and region, as have the consequences of nature's decline. The enclosure of the commons, the construction of railroads, and
deforestation worried nineteenth-century advocates for nature in Europe
and North America; population growth, urbanization, and environmental toxins moved to the forefront in the 1960s; ozone depletion and biodiversity loss dominated environmental discussions in the 1980s, along
with the connections between colonialism, racism, and environmental
degradation in the 1980s and 1990s; and over the past decade, climate
change and its connections to neoliberal forms of capitalism have over-
shadowed all other environmental concerns in public debate and have led
to the most alarming forecasts for the coming century.

Whatever the concrete ecological crises at hand, modern environmentalists, like their nineteenth-century forebears, have tended to rely on a
similar story template: the idea that modern society has degraded a natural world that used to be beautiful, harmonious, and self-sustaining and
that might disappear completely if modern humans do not change their
way of life. In postcolonial societies, this story often contrasts an indigenous, ecologically grounded past with the degradation of nature European imperialism has brought about. Environmentalism inside and outside of recognizable social movements and organizations has relied on
such "declensionist" narratives, as historians and literary critics call them.
In these stories, the awareness of nature's beauty and value is intimately
linked to a foreboding sense of its looming destruction. Environmentalist
writers and thinkers have skillfully mobilized literary and aesthetic concepts and genres such as the sublime, the picturesque, pastoral, apocalyptic narrative, and what one critic has called "toxic discourse" about
polluted landscapes and deformed bodies so as to convey a sense of a
precious, beautiful, and fragile natural world at risk (Buell 2001, 30–54).

This sense that humans—in particular, modern and colonial humans
and the ways of life they have developed in Western societies over the
past two centuries—put nature at risk has not only aesthetic but also
considerable political power. As Raymond Williams's classic *The Country and the City* (1973) showed in some detail, the idea that humans used
to live in a more harmonious relationship with nature just a generation
or two ago is not mere nostalgia, but also a powerful anchoring point for
both political authority and resistance. For environmentalists, this story
template offered an important critique of more dominant narratives
about social, economic, and technological progress, and as such it was
able to attract a variety of political forces that were opposed to certain
aspects of modernization. From Thoreau's ambivalence toward the construction of the railroad to the countercultures of the 1960s and current

protests in the global south against the role of northern societies in generating global warming, to pick just three examples, advocacy on behalf of a natural world at risk has been linked to—and has arguably derived a good deal of its power from—broader opposition to the shape modern society has been taking. Regret, mourning, and melancholy over aspects of nature that were degraded or lost in modernization processes, as I will discuss in more detail in chapter 1, turn into more than personal emotion in this context, as public grief over what most societies have not normally considered worth mourning becomes an act of political resistance.

The End of Nature

In our own historical moment, the environmentalist rhetoric of decline has come to a head in the cultural meme of the end of nature, the idea that nature such as we have understood it since the Romantic age has disappeared. When researchers, writers, or activists claim that nature has vanished, they do not mean, of course, that natural processes such as plant growth, seasonal variation, and decay no longer happen. Neither do they mean only that certain landscapes or species have disappeared, although such disappearances form part of the process. Rather, what they propose is that nature in the sense of a domain apart from human intention and agency no longer exists. This idea has been most forcefully articulated by the environmental author and activist Bill McKibben. In his book *The End of Nature* (1989), one of the first books to ring the alarm about climate change for the nonscientific public, McKibben argues that climate change, aside from its material consequences, has also brought about the end of nature as modern society conceived of it: "We have changed the atmosphere, and thus we are changing the weather. By changing the weather, we make every spot on earth man-made and artificial. We have deprived nature of its independence, and that is fatal to its meaning. Nature's independence is its meaning; without it there is nothing but us" (58). And he laments: "We have ended the thing that has, at least in modern times, defined nature for us—its separation from human society" (64). Almost a quarter of a century later, with the consequences of climate change far more visible globally and far more present in public debates, McKibben has given this idea a new, science-fiction-style twist that I will discuss in greater detail in chapter 6. In a book with the oddly spelled title *Eaarth: Making a Life on a Tough New Planet* (2011), he argues that "the world hasn't ended, but the world as we know it has—even if we don't quite know it yet. We imagine we still live on that old planet. . . . It's a different place. A different planet. It needs a new name.

Eaarth" (2–3). Consequently, McKibben proposes, humans today face a challenge similar to the one confronting settlers on an alien planet that in some ways resembles Earth, but whose global ecology is palpably different and will require new ways of life.

Environmental scholars such as Leo Marx and Richard White have argued that defining nature as in principle separate from humans turns it into an abstract, metaphysical concept with serious limitations for understanding how humans—and, for that matter, other species—actually inhabit material environments (Marx 2008, 19; White 2011, 119). The study of how human communities have inhabited nature in different cultures over time has led other environmental researchers to agree with McKibben's sense that traditional approaches to nature and its conservation are no longer quite in sync with the environments we currently confront. But quite a few of them arrive at this conclusion by way of arguments that are diametrically opposed to McKibben's. The idea that environmentalism should seek to protect natural ecosystems from human interference and, where possible, return them to what they were before modern (especially European) humans disrupted them is becoming harder to sustain as evidence mounts that indigenous peoples around the world have reshaped their environments far more extensively and over longer time periods than was previously thought. Environmental anthropologists, geographers, and historians have shown that in Australia, Latin America, and North America, landscapes that European settlers perceived as "wildernesses" untouched by humans had in fact been altered by indigenous societies for millennia before their arrival.

The Australian historian Bill Gammage, for example, has shown that Aboriginal peoples extensively managed their land through fire, vegetative cycles, and water flows for thousands—quite possibly tens of thousands—of years before they were displaced by Europeans (2011). Charles Mann, in his books *1491* (2005) and *1493* (2011), synthesizes parallel research for Central and South America that points to much denser populations and much more intensive land usage in the pre-Columbian ages than was previously documented, some of it "agroforestry" of a kind unknown and unrecognizable to Europeans. Even the Amazon rainforest, it emerges, was by no means just the domain of scattered tribes of hunter-gatherers but was partly cultivated and domesticated.[1] Analogous studies of North America have also revealed regimes of fire management that date back millennia (Pyne [1982] 1997, 2003). The wilderness

---

1. For a detailed study of the Amazonian rainforest in this context, see Hecht and Cockburn ([1990] 2010).

European settlers in North America initially feared and later came to embrace as they began to think of their new continent as "nature's nation," it turns out, was often purchased at the price of ignoring or understating the impact of the indigenous societies that had preceded them (Cronon 1995).

Moreover, precisely at the time when McKibben published his elegy for nature, the Indian sociologist Ramachandra Guha argued that American environmentalists' emphasis on the conservation of untouched landscapes ran against the interests of environmentalists in the developing world. Barely recognized by environmentalists in the global north as engaged in the protection of nature, many communities in developing regions struggle to continue their own sustainable uses of resources against the destructive practices of corporations and organizations based in industrialized nations (Guha 1989). Together with the Catalan scholar Joan Martínez-Alier, who had extensively researched such movements in Latin America, Guha sought to persuade European and North American environmentalists that they needed to acknowledge "varieties of environmentalism" other than those grounded in the reverence for pristine landscapes (Guha and Martínez-Alier 1997). Against the background of historical and political arguments such as these, the idea of nature as Bill McKibben and other North American environmentalists have defined it increasingly appears as, at best, a retrospective misperception and, at worst, a misconstruction of the historical context and ecological impact of Euro-American colonial ventures. Nature never really was separate from human society; it appeared untouched only to those who did not know, or did not want to know, how much indigenous peoples had transformed it long before Europeans' arrival. This is not to deny the very different kind of impact that colonial societies had on their natural environments compared to that of the civilizations that preceded them, or that precolonial societies can in some cases offer models for how to coinhabit places with other species. But it does mean that whatever baseline for a desirable nature the environmentalist movement sets for itself needs to be chosen from different cultural models and preferences rather than grounding itself simply on the idea of minimal human presence and impact.

Beyond the End of Nature: New Environmentalisms

In view of this historical evidence as well as humans' pervasive impact in the contemporary age, some environmentalist organizations have begun to shift their focus. The biologist Peter Kareiva, former scientific director of the world's largest conservation society, the Nature Conservancy, for example, has suggested that environmentalists should move away from the idea that they need to protect nature from human impact. Instead of dwelling on stories of decline, environmentalists should acknowledge that nature is largely domesticated and should actively shape its human uses: "There really is no such thing as nature untainted by people. Instead, ours is a world of nature domesticated, albeit to varying degrees, from national parks to high-rise megalopolises. . . . Instead of recounting gloom-and-doom statistics, it would be more fruitful to consider the domestication of nature as the selection of certain desirable ecosystem attributes, such as increased food production, with consequent alteration to other ecosystem attributes that may not be desirable" (Kareiva et al. 2007, 1866). Other biologists have begun to study what they call the "novel ecosystems" that result from human interventions in and subsequent abandonment of particular ecosystems (Hobbs, Higgs, and Hall 2013), and they have suggested that environmental science may need to reenvision its own task in terms of "intervention ecology," the deliberate design of future ecosystems, rather than the more conventional "restoration ecology" (Hobbs et al. 2011). The science writer Emma Marris has popularized these ideas with a similar metaphor of domestication in her tellingly entitled book *Rambunctious Garden: Saving Nature in a Post-Wild World* (2011). Over the past few years, such attempts to reenvision environmentalism in the context of a pervasively domesticated natural world have begun to overlap with discussions around the concept of the Anthropocene, as I will show in detail in chapter 6.

Moving beyond established decline narratives to a new, future-oriented conceptualization of environmentalism is clearly no easy task in the United States, and not just because quite a few environmentalists themselves resist the shift.[2] Whatever the shortfalls may be of environmentalists' gloomy forecasts and nature nostalgia, they have, since the 1960s, set in motion social movements that have sprung up around the globe, changed political and legal landscapes, and provoked far-reaching cultural transformations. Changing the basic concepts and story lines that have mobilized millions of people across different continents runs the risk of weakening environmentalism's cultural and political power—a danger that is quite apparent in Ted Nordhaus and Michael Shellenberger's calls for rethinking environmentalism. From initial limited critiques in the years around 2004–5 of the political strategies

2. The German biologist Josef H. Reichholf makes a similar point for environmentalism more generally (2008, 211).

the environmentalist movement had adopted, they have in recent years moved to a relentless boosterism of modernization and technological progress that leaves no room for considering how the missteps and disasters of the past might be kept from repeating themselves: "The solution to the unintended consequences of modernity is, and has always been, more modernity—just as the solution to the unintended consequences of our technologies has always been more technology" (Nordhaus and Shellenberger 2011, 18). Their arguments often end up reverting to the unqualified, relentlessly anthropocentric narrative of progress that environmentalism set out to question, intellectually and politically, in the first place.

The question that the tension between these divergent new strands of environmentalism raises, then, is whether and how it might be possible to move environmentalism beyond the stereotypical narrative of the decline of nature without turning it into progress boosterism. What affirmative visions of the future can the environmentalist movement offer, visions that are neither returns to an imagined pastoral past nor nightmares of future devastation meant to serve as "cautionary tales"? What new ways of conceptualizing the relationship between humans and nonhuman species might an environmentalist perspective rely on, beyond saving nature only as a resource for humans or, conversely, privileging nature in itself to the point where human aspirations become secondary? How can environmentalism accommodate especially the aspirations of those communities who have already been stymied by colonialism or poverty? Now that the notion of "nature" itself has become tenuous ground, what might be the foundation for a new kind of environmentalism?

Rethinking Biodiversity and Endangerment

Imagining Extinction was written against the background of these questions about the future of environmentalist thought and politics. Clearly, the narrative of nature's decline under the impact of modernization is an important framework within which we need to understand the interest in biodiversity loss: endangered animal species—and, more rarely, plants, corals, and fungi—derive a part of their perceived value and beauty from their rarity and the larger crisis in our relation to nature that their endangerment points to. The elegiac and tragic modes in which endangered species are often portrayed in film, photography, and writing are meant to convey this general sense of decline, of sweeping losses of life, diversity, knowledge, and beauty. However effective these modes of storytelling and image-making may have been, it is also clear, at this point, that conservationists will need to complement or even replace them with other kinds of stories. As in environmentalist communication in general, stories and images of decline go only so far. Is it possible to acknowledge the realities of large-scale species extinction and yet to move beyond mourning, melancholia, and nostalgia to a more affirmative vision of our biological future? Is it possible to move beyond the story templates of elegy and tragedy and yet to express continuing concern that nonhuman species not be harmed more than strictly necessary?

In pursuing these questions about environmental cultures of risk, I assumed initially that the science on species extinction in general and the current mass extinction of species in particular was fairly straightforward. The cultural filtering, transformation, and re-creation of that science in image and narrative would be the most interesting aspects to a scholar in the humanities, I thought. But I was wrong. Much about the science is extremely complex, indeterminate, or unknown. And if our perception of species at risk is founded on scientific research, it is equally clear that a good deal of the science is shaped by underlying cultural assumptions, in many cases by the same stories about the decline of nature that have shaped our ecological culture at large. For this reason, the project broadened from its primary objects of study—the books, films, photographs, websites, and other aesthetic artifacts that are the standard material of literary and cultural analysis—to include quite different objects such as biodiversity databases, Red Lists of endangered species, and endangered species laws. All of them, I came to understand, are expressions of our collective concern over threats to nonhuman species, even though they are channeled through quite different cultural forms and social institutions. Analyzing these different genres and artifacts contributes to a fuller understanding of what makes us collectively care about the well-being of nonhuman species, but it also helps us see what kinds of stories and genres might be more successful at generating this concern than others.

In asking specific questions such as why species go extinct, how we know what endangers them, why we care about some endangered species and not others, and what means we choose to express our concern, I also saw myself forced to confront the broader questions I have outlined here about how we envision nature and what stories we tell about its relationship to human culture. Coffee-table books, TV documentaries, and endangered species laws are all in different ways shaped by such broader narratives, and these objects themselves contribute to perpetuating or subtly changing the stories. What we think about endangered species and the current wave of biodiversity loss is difficult to separate from the broader concern over the decline of nature and the positive valuation, over the past three decades, of both biological and cultural diversity. It turned out, then, that questions about endangered species and mass extinction, and about how they come to form part of our cultural life, are also questions about environmentalism more broadly understood with which the movement is currently struggling. In this way, *Imagining Extinction* is meant as a contribution to the ongoing conversation about the future of environmentalist thought.

The six chapters of the book move along an arc from concrete cultural engagements with endangered species in the first three chapters to broader political and philosophical reflections in the last three. The first three chapters examine how our interest in endangered species has manifested itself over the past few decades in cultural artifacts, in global biodiversity databases, and in endangered species laws, whereas the last three engage with the tensions between conservation and animal welfare advocacy, between conservation and the environmental justice movement, and with the role of conservation in ongoing debates over the Anthropocene.

Chapter 1, "Lost Dogs, Last Birds, and Listed Species: Elegy and Comedy in Conservation Stories," focuses on the wide range of fictional and nonfictional texts, photographs, film documentaries, musical compositions, and artistic websites that portray endangered species. The majority of them, this chapter shows, rely on the genre templates of elegy and tragedy to portray well-adapted animal species at risk or those that have already vanished through no fault of their own. Many of the species that are singled out for attention function as symbolic shorthands for more encompassing stories about a particular nation's history of modernization and its changing relationship to the natural world, or about broader misgivings regarding the planetary consequences of modernization, as the cases of the dodo, the Honshu wolf, the ivory-billed woodpecker, the huia, the passenger pigeon, the thylacine, and the gray whale demonstrate. Such stories are both galvanizing and problematic: the nostalgia they generate has often successfully mobilized support for conservation and for critiques of modernization, even as it has made the understanding of ecosystem functioning more difficult and forward-looking perspectives more inaccessible. Only occasionally has conservationist writing mobilized the resources of comedy, a genre that offers an alternative model for thinking about biodiversity. Comedy emphasizes contingency and improbable modes of survival over predictability and extinction and thereby opens up different cognitive and emotional attachments to the lives of other humans as well as nonhuman species.

Chapter 2, "From Arks to ARKive.org: Database, Epic, and Biodiversity," focuses on global biodiversity databases as a cultural medium that relies not on the framework of elegy but on that of epic and encyclopedia. Databases such as ARKive.org, the Catalogue of Life, the Encyclopedia of Life (EoL), the Global Biodiversity Information Facility, the International Nucleotide Sequence Database Collaboration, and the International Union for the Conservation of Nature's (IUCN's) Red List of Threatened Species, all Internet-based biodiversity archives, aspire to catalog all known species, and some of them emphasize endangered ones. Most of them function as metadatabases in the sense that they rely on information transferred from other, more specialized databases and invest varying degrees of effort into the integration of these sources. Drawing on media theorists who have approached databases as not just administrative and scientific tools, but as a cultural medium of their own in the digital age, this chapter seeks to understand global biodiversity databases as a contemporary form of ecological epic. This may seem like a counterintuitive claim at first sight, since databases typically lack the elaborate narrative structures that made epic so compelling a way of accounting for the premodern world. Yet some biodiversity databases include lengthy narrative entries on some species, and their metadata and classification schemata are in some cases clearly shaped by story templates that also appear in more properly aesthetic ways of engaging with biodiversity loss. "From Arks to ARKive.org" links the environmental and the digital humanities in its exploration of databases as ecological epic. This chapter engages in some detail with the IUCN's Red List of Threatened Species, a database that is often used in national and regional efforts to establish Red Lists and formulate laws for the protection of endangered species. Chapter 2 also seeks to show how the database aesthetic has inflected texts and artworks about endangered species, from the novels of Lydia Millet and the installations of Maya Lin to Isabella Kirkland's paintings and Joel Sartore's collections of photographs.

Chapter 3, "The Legal Lives of Endangered Species: Biodiversity Laws and Culture," approaches current laws for the protection of animals and plants from the comparative perspective that I pursue throughout this book. Many nations around the globe, as well as subnational states and supranational organizations such as the European Union, have passed such laws over the past half century. These laws share a few elements but derive from quite divergent national histories of engagement with nature at risk. In the laws of the United States and Germany, the history of the nation and national identity are interwoven with the concern for the conservation of endangered species in the United States and, in

Germany, for cultural landscapes, including their biodiversity. The European Union, unable to rely on a unique tradition for formulating the concern for biodiversity across its more than two dozen member nations, replaces the German rhetoric of "landscapes" with that of "habitats" and species, seeking at the same time to invoke a shared scientific approach and to create a sense of a shared patrimony in its conservation directives. In contrast, Bolivia, South America's poorest country, has reinvented itself over the past decade with a new constitution and laws that invoke humans' relation to "Mother Earth," the "Pachamama" of indigenous cosmologies, to empower both traditional communities and the modern state to pursue a holistic form of development that will diminish poverty and ecological degradation at the same time. Fraught with tensions and practical difficulties, these laws are nevertheless an ambitious attempt to reconceive biodiversity conservation within the broader goal of building a just and equitable society. Highlighting the divergent cultural histories and current goals of contemporary laws about biodiversity and endangered species also shows why it is difficult to compare the effectiveness of laws that tell quite different stories about what is politically at stake in conserving nonhuman species. Biodiversity laws clearly demonstrate just how much conservation is at bottom a product of the cultural imagination rather than just of scientific investigation.

   Chapter 4, "Mass Extinction and Mass Slaughter: Biodiversity, Violence, and the Dangers of Domestication," shifts the discussion of endangered nonhumans and their legal status to a different conceptual level. In the 1970s, environmentalists and advocates for animal welfare sometimes fought side by side, for example in the struggle against the harvesting of furs from baby seals in Alaska and Canada. Today, the two movements continue to share a concern for the well-being of nonhuman species, but their ideological commitments and targets for political action differ quite sharply. Environmentalists usually fight on behalf of wild species, including animals, plants, and other organisms, and they approach these species with the larger goal of ensuring the continued health of ecosystems. In the process, they sometimes accept the necessity of eradicating introduced species so as to save native ones. Animal welfare and animal rights advocates, by contrast, focus on individuals rather than species, on animals to the exclusion of other kinds of organisms, and for the most part on domesticated animals and those used in research and entertainment. From the 1980s onward, environmentalist and animal welfare advocates have at times been sharply critical of each other, engaging in conflicts that T. C. Boyle's novel *When the Killing's Done* (2011) insightfully fictionalizes. At the same time, philosophers have sought to reconcile the two perspectives. My analysis seeks not so much to reconcile as to understand the different approaches to modernity and domestication that shape the two movements. Where environmentalists have located the danger of modernization in an excessive domestication of nature that leads to species extinction, animal welfare advocates have been critical of the incomplete or misguided domestication that results in factory farming. Since environmentalists over the past decade, as I pointed out earlier, have increasingly adopted the idea of domestication as a way of thinking about a planetary ecology that has been pervasively reshaped by humans, animal advocates' warnings about the dangers of domestication are becoming newly relevant to environmentalist thought.

If animal welfare advocates at times accuse environmentalists of not caring enough about animals, environmental justice advocates have sometimes reproached mainstream environmentalists for caring too much about animals and plants and not enough about disempowered humans. Chapter 5, "Biodiversity, Environmental Justice, and Multispecies Communities," engages the conflict between the concern for other humans and the concern for nonhumans that confrontations over environmental justice and biodiversity conservation have generated. The analysis of three texts, Cuban novelist Mayra Montero's *Tú, la oscuridad* (1995); the Stanford Graphic Novel Project's collectively authored graphic narrative *Virunga* (2009), edited by Adam Johnson and Tom Kealey; and Bengali author Amitav Ghosh's *The Hungry Tide* ([2005] 2006), traces different narrative templates that shape stories about the encounter of endangered humans and endangered animals: confrontations of scientific stories from the global north with indigenous knowledge from the global south; of literature with orature; of state power with the power of international corporations, NGO's, and subnational resistance movements; and the divergent symbolic meanings that different endangered species and communities hold in the cultural imagination. The emergent framework of "multispecies ethnography" as it has been developed by anthropologists over the past decade to highlight the shaping agency of nonhuman species in human societies, I argue, offers some of the conceptual tools for understanding such stories. It also offers a conceptual and political framework for rethinking environmental justice as "multispecies justice," reaching across differences of culture as well as of species.

Chapter 6, "Multispecies Fictions for the Anthropocene," takes these reflections one step further to environmentalist visions of the planetary future. The idea that we now live on a planet that humans have transformed even in its most basic structures, summed up in the concept of the

Anthropocene, draws on tropes of terraforming that are a staple of science fiction, itself a mode of epic complementary to the database. Not only do works of environmental nonfiction draw increasingly on themes and narrative strategies of speculative fiction, but the Anthropocene itself can usefully be understood as a science fiction trope. The idea that our own planet has already been pervasively terraformed has led to similarly futuristic projects of "de-extinction," the re-creation of extinct species by means of DNA extracted from fossils or museum specimens and cutting-edge biotechnology. These scenarios and their conception of human species agency have theoretically crystallized in discussions following historian Dipesh Chakrabarty's influential theses on the consequences of climate change for history and social theory. The debate about Chakrabarty's "negative universalism" highlights the difficulties of arriving at a collective "we" that might jointly engage with nonhuman species. But it also foregrounds, I argue, the urgent need for a cosmopolitanism that does not take for granted anything about humans as a biological species but instead constructs versions of the human in a careful and painstaking, cross-cultural process of assembly in both its technological and its political meanings. These issues are worked through in speculative fiction itself, especially Orson Scott Card's *Ender* series, which quite explicitly moves from humans' extermination of other species to a vision of multispecies contracts, constitutions, and communities on other planets, thereby contributing to the imaginative and narrative possibilities—the multispecies fictions—of a cosmopolitanism that works through such assemblies toward multispecies justice.

1

Lost Dogs, Last Birds, and Listed Species: Elegy and Comedy in Conservation Stories

1. How We Learned to Start Worrying and Love Endangered Species

Cultural anxieties about vanishing nature over the past two hundred years have typically focused on places and species. The concern to conserve places began to take legal and political shape in the nineteenth century with the creation of national parks, nature reserves, and wilderness areas in a variety of countries, efforts that continued throughout the twentieth century. The concern over vanishing species took longer to manifest itself institutionally, legally, and culturally. Three important turns in the knowledge and perception of species endangerment and extinction led up to the emergence of conservation movements and the concern with biodiversity loss that we are familiar with today: the discovery of extinction as a biological and historical process, fears concerning the extinction of individual species in the contemporary age that are often tied up with anxieties over the consequences of modernization and colonization, and insights into the historical importance of mass extinctions that generated the scenario of another mass die-off of species in the present.

Extinction is so ordinary and pervasive an occurrence in the history of life on Earth that we tend to take the concept for granted today. Yet it took the discovery of geologic time scales, the unearthing of prehistoric fossils, and the emergence of Darwinian theory in the nineteenth century to make extinction part of modern societies' cultural horizons. The Christian belief in a natural world created by divine mandate made the idea implausible that God would let creatures he had gone to the pain of creating simply vanish. Once geologists opened up previously unimagined depths of past time in the early nineteenth century, ideas about Earth's age and history began to shift. But even the discovery of fossils clearly belonging to creatures that geologists had never seen alive took some time to translate into the insight that these creatures had actually vanished, rather than inhabiting a remote continent where European and North American scientists had not yet had the occasion to see them. Once the reality of extinction had been broadly accepted and dinosaur bones were discovered, a wave of fascination with these prehistoric creatures swept Britain and the United States in the 1860s and 1870s.[1]

In the second half of the nineteenth century, the idea that species extinction had not merely occurred in the deep time of natural history but could occur in the present gradually gained acceptance. The decline of species such as the bison and the passenger pigeon attracted widespread public attention in the United States in the late nineteenth century (Barrow 2009, 78–134). From the 1920s on, conservationists of various stripes, often focused in a colonial manner on the preservation of wildlife in Africa for big-game hunting, began to establish committees and associations in Europe and the United States dedicated to the protection of endangered species. Conservation, in this context, built on game protection and forestry as they had developed under imperial rule. The possible extinction of big-game species added a new dimension and urgency to these preservation efforts (Adams 2005, 19–42).

In the 1970s and 1980s, evolutionary scientists such as David Raup and Jack Sepkoski began to emphasize the historical importance of large-scale mass extinctions over the gradual, one-by-one extinctions of individual species as a crucial factor in shaping the development of life on Earth. Periods of mass extinction function according to a different logic than ordinary evolution, in that they drive large numbers of species to extinction regardless of their adaptations. The best known of the five mass extinction events known to science occurred 65 million years ago,

---

1. Mark Barrow's *Nature's Ghosts* (2009) delivers a minutely detailed account of the historical development and institutional crystallizations of the concern over endangered species, mostly focused on the United States. See also Kolbert (2014, 23–91) for a popular-scientific narrative of the discovery of extinction in the nineteenth century in France and Britain.

when a meteorite hit Earth and led to the demise of the dinosaurs as well as 80 percent of the species then existing: this was not a consequence of bad genes but bad luck, as Raup emphasizes. Bad luck for the reptiles, that is—good luck, by contrast, for mammals, whose subsequent evolution, including that of homo sapiens, was enabled by the disaster (Raup 1991; Jablonski 1993; Sepkoski 2012, chap. 9). Biologists such as Norman Myers, Paul Ehrlich, and E. O. Wilson argued that such abrupt evolutionary change might yet again be taking place in the contemporary age—but for the first time, mass extinction might be triggered by human activities (Myers 1979; Ehrlich and Ehrlich 1981; Wilson 2002). In the 1980s, endangered species and the threat of such a mass extinction in the contemporary age turned into a defining environmentalist concern, just as the term *biological diversity* and its short form, *biodiversity*, came into widespread use. It led to the Convention on Biological Diversity (CBD) at the Rio Earth Summit in 1992 and the declaration by the United Nations of 2010 as an International Year of Biodiversity and 2011–20 as the Decade on Biodiversity. In public debates, the threat of mass extinction now often features as one of several global ecological crises, right behind climate change in the urgency of action it requires.

According to Darwinian theory, extinction and adaptation are, of course, normal components of evolutionary processes that have taken place during all of the 3.5 billion years of biological life on Earth. Genetic changes that arise randomly in biological organisms create handicaps or advantages for certain individuals and populations as they interact with a complex network of other species and configurations of soil, water, climate, and vectors of disease. Dynamic processes of ecological change lead to the increase of some plant or animal species and the decrease or extinction of others at what biologists refer to as the "background rate," which is computed either as the number of species that go extinct in a particular number of years, in Million Species Years, or as the time intervals during which species survive (Lawton and May 1995). Some of the extinct species may be succeeded by differently adapted daughter species. But currently, biologists estimate that we may be losing species at about 50 to 500 times the background level. If one adds to this figure species that may have gone extinct but whose status is not known with certainty, the extinction rate rises to 100 to 1,000 times the background level, though the exact numbers are in dispute among biologists themselves.[2] What is not

2. See the exchange in the journal *Science* in 2013: the original article by Costello, May, and Stork (2013a), followed by responses by Laurance (2013) and by Mora, Rollo, and Tittensor (2013), and a reply by Costello, May, and Stork (2013b).

in dispute is the general trend toward higher extinction rates; neither are its causes, mainly habitat destruction, invasive species, pollution, human population growth, and overharvesting (the list is sometimes abbreviated HIPPO). Climate change may become an additional factor driving extinctions in the future. While most extinctions over the past five hundred years have been limited to island ecosystems, they have now spread to continents, in a sign of deepening crisis (Wilson 2002, 50; Baillie, Hilton-Taylor, and Stuart 2004, xxi–xxii).

Mass extinctions are extremely rare; they have occurred only five times previously in the 3.5 billion years of life on Earth and have never before been triggered by human agency. Each time, biodiversity took millions of years to return to precataclysmic levels.[3] If we are currently undergoing a sixth mass extinction, it may entail a large-scale biological and ecological transformation whose consequences are difficult to predict. They include the possible collapse of some ecosystems, the destruction of some of the basic foundations of food and energy economies, the disappearance of medical and other resources for the future, and the disappearance of important cultural foundations and assets. Such cataclysmic portrayals of past and future species extinctions are common currency in biodiversity discourse. Less catastrophic consequences, such as increases in local biodiversity, range expansion for certain species, hybridization, and the emergence of new species, are rarely mentioned, presumably because biologists and environmental advocates fear that they might make the crisis appear less serious to a public that does not usually delve into scientific detail.

But even when we focus on those dimensions of biodiversity that *are* commonly discussed, it is striking how often public debate, including scientists' own summaries of their knowledge, leaps over complexities, uncertainties, and open questions. The story template according to which nature in general and biodiversity in particular has done nothing but deteriorate under the impact of modern societies is mostly taken for granted, and details that do not unambiguously fit into this narrative tend to be underemphasized or left out. The narrative template is made to work in the context of species endangerment and extinction through a pervasive logic of what biologists usually call proxy and literary scholars call synecdoche—the part standing in for the whole. Such proxy procedures

---

3. Recent research on the mass extinction in the Late Permian, during which 80 percent of marine genera and possibly 90 percent of species in general disappeared, suggests that at least some taxa may have recovered more speedily than previously assumed (see Brayard et al. 2009).

link different scales and different levels of abstraction in the scientific arguments, and they also enable the interpretation of biological changes as indicative of cultural transformations. As I will show in this chapter and throughout this book, the cultural logic of extinction discourses lies in their function as powerful tools for criticizing or resisting modernization and colonization; so powerful, in fact, that scientific arguments themselves are inflected by this logic. Biodiversity discourses revolve at bottom around these cultural values and narratives, which are crucial to take into account in any consideration of the future of conservation.

Let me explain what I mean by the "proxy logic" of discourses about endangered species and biodiversity. This logic works by a series of referrals whereby certain kinds of species are taken as a shorthand for all species. Species serve as proxies for ecosystems and biodiversity. And biodiversity itself becomes a measure for what we value about nature as well as, more indirectly, about ourselves, so that biodiversity loss comes to be felt and understood as a sign of something that we lost in the course of modernization and/or colonization—the "we" referring to national, regional, or indigenous communities in different contexts. There is nothing in principle wrong with interpreting observations about natural change in this way, either scientifically or culturally. But it is important to remain aware of the substitutions that are made and what they involve at each step, so that the narrative that emerges at the end does not appear as falsely inevitable, but as one possible story. Taking into account other measures and substitutions opens up the possibility of different stories we might tell about how biodiversity is currently changing—and how our communities are changing.

As is obvious to anyone who has seen or bought one of the innumerable commodities that revolve around endangered species—chocolate bars, calendars, tote bags, T-shirts—or who has watched documentaries, read books, or attended lectures about the extinction crisis, the species that are usually selected to signal the crisis tend to belong to a fairly narrow set. The species or groups of species that are portrayed are almost always animals, while plants, which are equally affected by extinction, receive almost no attention. Among the animals, large mammals such as gorillas, tigers, bears, pandas, whales, and white rhinos, and birds, particularly beautiful ones such as raptors, parrots, and colorful songbirds, are the preferred objects of coverage, while reptilians, amphibians, and fish are mentioned far less frequently. Among invertebrates, only photogenic butterflies—particularly, in recent years, the monarch butterfly, which has generated a whole advocacy movement of its own—occasionally come into view; taxa such as worms, crabs, fungi, and bacteria usually remain invisible.

There are some good reasons why scientists might want to focus on some species at the expense of others. So-called keystone species occupy crucial positions in the food web; without them many other species would also be endangered, and it may therefore be more important to conserve those species than others.[4] The health or decline of "indicator species" can sometimes help to diagnose the status of the ecosystems they inhabit. Focusing conservation efforts on "umbrella species" can help preserve habitat that is also used by many other species. But this kind of selectiveness does not lead to what conservationists themselves often call, half humorously and half disdainfully, "charismatic megafauna" or, more neutrally, "flagship species," animal types whose appeal to the broad public makes them good tools in campaigns to raise public awareness and funds for conservation issues.

Many conservationists view these species with ambivalence. The focus on a single species that is selected for its obvious anthropomorphic qualities or its aesthetic appeal blocks from view other species, lacking those qualities, that may be more endangered or more crucial for ecosystemic functioning. It is doubtful that charismatic species by themselves can generate any real public understanding of how ecosystems work and what threatens their functioning. And yet, such "taxonomic bias" is not limited to the nonexpert public. Conservation science itself shows preferences in its objects of study that broadly parallel public biases: The 2008 edition of the most comprehensive Red List, that of the International Union for the Conservation of Nature (IUCN), indicates that all of the 5,488 known mammal and 9,900 bird species have been evaluated for their endangerment status; but of 30,700 known species of fishes, only 3,481 have been assessed; of 950,000 insect species, 1,250; of 12,838 fern species, 211, and of 30,000 species of fungi, just one (Hilton-Taylor et al. 2008, 17, table 1; cf. chapter 2 of the current volume).[5] A recent study that focused on changes in rates of extinction concluded that the evidence indeed pointed to an ongoing mass extinction—but the study limited itself to vertebrates because of "data deficiencies" regarding other species (Ceballos et al. 2015). In both the expert and the nonexpert spheres,

4. The notion of "keystone species" was introduced in 1966 by the biologist Robert Paine, who researched the impact of starfish on sea urchins, mussels, and crabs. For a detailed discussion of the varied criteria that go into species conservation decisions, see Perlman and Adelson (1997, especially chaps. 2–4), and the essays collected in Kareiva and Levin (2003).

5. These numbers have changed over time, and the IUCN is keen to include understudied taxa in its purview; but for the time being, the bias persists.

then, attention focuses above all on birds and mammals as proxies for understanding the welfare of species at large.

If we move from charismatic megafauna in biodiversity discourse to the role of species more broadly understood, other complications arise. Biological diversity ranges from genetic diversity to species and ecosystem diversity, and not all biologists are convinced that species are the best category for organizing conservation efforts. Some of them believe that the conservation of populations, geographically specific groups of a particular species, is more decisive for maintaining ecosystem services. "If the population of spruce trees in the canyon upstream from your house in Colorado is cut down, its flood protection service will be lost. That the same species of spruce has abundant populations elsewhere will be of little consolation as you struggle to keep your head above water while riding your house downstream," biologists Paul and Anne Ehrlich quip (2004, 52–53). By the same token, if bees were to disappear everywhere except in Italy, the species itself would not be extinct, but the consequences for agriculture would be catastrophic.[6] "Indeed, it would theoretically be possible to lose no more species diversity at all and yet, because of declines in population diversity, suffer such a steep decline in ecosystem services that humanity itself would go extinct," the Ehrlichs argue (2004, 53). From this perspective, the focus on the conservation of species needs to be complemented by a close analysis of their geographical and ecological distribution.[7]

The species concept itself raises other problems. Species have been classified in terms of Linnaean taxonomy since the eighteenth century, yet contemporary biology has proposed a variety of different definitions. The most famous is undoubtedly Ernst Mayr's "biological" species concept, which defines species in terms of their reproductive isolation, that is, the mating and reproductive behavior by means of which one species distinguishes itself from others. "Phylogenetic" definitions, by contrast, understand species as communities of the same evolutionary lineage that disappear when all their organisms die or when new species evolve from them. "Morphological" species definitions refer to physical characteristics that enable the distinction of different species and overlap sometimes, but not always, with evolutionary species definitions. Some of these species definitions are more applicable to some organisms than

6. Paul Ehrlich, personal conversation, December 15, 2009.
7. For more detailed discussions of population diversity, see Hughes, Daily, and Ehrlich (1997, 2000); Luck, Daily, and Ehrlich (2003).

others: the biological species concept, for example, is difficult to use for species that do not reproduce sexually and for fossil species whose mating behavior is unknown. The morphology and reproductive behavior of bacteria are so different from those of other taxa that biologists often recur to a "physiological" species concept based on metabolic processes. The rise of molecular genetics and genomics, in turn, has opened up new possibilities for the definition of species.[8] Taxonomy, which had become a dusty and somewhat disdained subdiscipline in biology, has reemerged as an innovative area of research, partly because of the biodiversity crisis, but its new prominence has served only to highlight the lack of consensus regarding species definitions.[9] Debates among biologists about species boundaries are often highly technical, but the questions they address are far from merely academic. Most laws and policies protecting endangered species presuppose at least an approximate consensus on the species concept to define what is to be preserved: a particular morphological type, a reproductive group, an evolutionary line, or a genome?

Difficulties surrounding the definition of species are compounded by the fact that the number of species currently inhabiting Earth is unknown. About 1.8 million species, about half of them insects, have been identified and scientifically classified, and several large-scale database projects are currently under way to make knowledge about these species accessible on the Internet for researchers and conservationists (cf. chapter 2). Even this much is by no means a simple task, since for historical and political reasons, not all data about already known species are readily available. But estimates of the total number of species on Earth are even more tenuous; they range from a low of 3 million to a high of 100 million, with typical estimates ranging between 10 and 40 million species. "The median of the estimates is a little over 10 million, but few experts would risk their reputations by insisting on this figure or any other, even to the nearest million," E. O. Wilson observes (2002, 14).[10] The divergence is in part due to very different assessment methods for different geographical areas and taxa. No matter what the definitive number might be, it is clear that humans know only a fraction of existing species, and very likely species are constantly going extinct that humans have not had a chance to encounter and name.

8. For a detailed analysis of the history and recent developments of the species concept, see Wilkins (2009).

9. For a survey of the history and recent developments in taxonomy, see Wheeler (2008).

10. See the discussion of the total species number problem in May (1989).

Yet this limit on current knowledge also entails, paradoxically, that even though we live in an age of mass extinction, the number of species is steadily increasing. The number of known species, that is: Wilson points out that, contrary to popular belief, the discovery of new species is a common occurrence, to the point where in some taxa such as insects, specialists can barely keep publications current with the new discoveries. He foregrounds that he himself has identified 341 new ant species in addition to the 10,000 already known ones, and that even in such well-explored taxa as flowering plants and birds, new species are constantly being added to the record (2002, 16–17). Some of the newly discovered species are so rare that they are almost immediately added to existing Red Lists. The rapid pace of new discoveries derives from some of the same reasons that also cause biodiversity loss itself, such as the spread of human populations into previously unsettled areas (Angier 2009). But it remains a fact that even as the number of existing species is likely declining, the number of known species is rapidly increasing.[11]

It is possible to argue, of course, that the total number of species is irrelevant for the problem of mass extinction. If a large enough number of species is threatened that entire ecosystems are at risk, it may seem pointless to ask for knowledge that is in practice extremely hard to come by. In a metaphor that is often repeated in the literature on species extinction, this would be tantamount to asking how many books are archived in a library that is on fire. But this argument leaves two important aspects out of consideration. In terms of historical comparison and the stories we tell about nature's ascent or decline, total species numbers are a part of the picture. If it is difficult to ascertain such a number for the present, the task is even more challenging for periods in the past, which in turn makes it more difficult to assess unambiguously the upward or downward trends in biodiversity. And even if one approaches biodiversity as essentially an inventory of evolutionary information, as the library metaphor suggests, it is hardly beside the point to ask what proportion of the total information is at risk. All the more so if the library is not burning down by accident but because humans use the books to heat their homes. Such is indeed the case in some parts of the world when one traces the library

---

11. The 2013 controversy in the journal *Science* that I alluded to earlier (see note 2) in fact took its point of departure precisely from an attempt to assess how extinction processes might conflict with attempts to count all of Earth's species, though the debate segued into the question of current extinction rates.

metaphor to its final implication, that human beings destroy habitats to survive themselves.[12]

Total species numbers also inflect biodiversity debates in terms of the scale that they refer to. The tenor of many popular-scientific and creative engagements with endangered species is that the loss of a species is also an irreversible loss in the breadth and depth of human experience. From fairly general books such as Robert Michael Pyle's *Thunder Tree: Lessons from an Urban Wildland* (1993) and Richard Louv's *Last Child in the Woods: Saving Our Children from Nature-Deficit Disorder* (2005), which lament the "extinction of experience" in future generations' diminished exposure to the diversity of nature, all the way to works specifically concerned with endangered species, such as Mark Walters's *Seeking the Sacred Raven*, about the Hawaiian crow, disappearing species are associated with a narrowing of human experience and culture. Yet while local biodiversity has decreased in some places, especially island ecosystems, it has exponentially *increased* in many places as commerce and travel ferry microorganisms, plants, and animals ever more easily around the globe, intentionally and unintentionally (Sax and Gaines 2003). These global movements are the long-term consequence of what the environmental historian Alfred Crosby famously called the "Columbian exchange" of animal and plant species after Europeans' colonization of the Americas ([1972] 2003). Following the logic that derives human environmental well-being from local experience, this should contribute to an enhanced rather than a diminished range of encounters with nature. Conservationists would argue that we pay for the increase in local biodiversity with a decrease in global biodiversity, as the same "cosmopolitan species" take root across the world and displace native species, becoming, in fact, indistinguishable from native species for local human inhabitants, who simply perceive them as part of their natural surroundings. From this perspective, a commitment to global biodiversity conservation requires the kind of investment in abstractions and statistics that is considered part of our alienation from nature in other environmentalist perspectives.[13]

---

12. For a somewhat different analysis of the library metaphor, see Esa Väliverronen and Iina Hellsten (2002, esp. 235–237).

13. Temporal horizons also play a role in this understanding of the current state of nature. Whenever biologists and journalists refer to the current biodiversity loss as the sixth mass extinction in the history of life on Earth, their intention is to characterize it as an irreparable catastrophe. But after each of the previous mass extinctions, biodiversity did eventually return to or even exceed precataclysmic numbers of species, though the species involved changed. Without such upheavals—the demise of the dinosaurs, for example—Homo sapiens would not have been able to evolve to its current state. Admittedly, this process took many millions of years each time, a time horizon that is irrelevant

The other reason why local biodiversity increases are not often discussed in debates over species loss is that the increase is usually due to introduced species. Some of these, it is true, can become invasives that significantly diminish overall species numbers over time: often-quoted examples include the impact of the Nile perch on native cichlid species in Lake Victoria, the disappearance of native bird species from the island of Guam after the accidental introduction of the brown tree snake, *Boiga irregularis*, and the biodiversity reduction in Australia after the introduction of cats and rabbits. But as biologists themselves have pointed out, the invasives among introduced species tend to be the exception rather than the rule. Most introduced species disappear quickly or end up coexisting with native species. Nevertheless, conservation, especially in settler societies with a colonial history, such as Australia and the United States, has for a long time set the state of ecosystems before the arrival of Europeans as the ideal goal of restoration. From this perspective, species introduced later do not count as part of the biodiversity that matters. This orthodoxy, however, has been increasingly contested among scientists themselves over the past decade; while prominent conservation biologists such as Daniel Simberloff (2013) continue to argue for the importance of eradicating or diminishing nonnative species, other biologists, such as Mark Davis et al. (2011) and Ken Thompson (2014), have sought to shift the emphasis of conservation to the current ecological functioning of a species rather than its geographic origin. "Most human and natural communities now consist both of long-term residents and of new arrivals, and ecosystems are emerging that never existed before. It is impractical to try to restore ecosystems to some 'rightful' historical state," Davis et al. argue (2011).[14]

Species, then, routinely function as proxies for biodiversity in expert as well as public debates about current ecological crises. But what a species is, which species are counted, which ones are considered important enough to receive in-depth attention, and how local and global species numbers should be compared are all matters of debate even among conservation scientists (see Grenyer et al. 2006). The notion of biodiversity

---

to the concerns of humankind today. So it makes good sense to downplay this fact in current discussions of species loss. But quite a few of the popular-scientific essays and books on the subject attempt to dissuade their readers from a narrowly anthropocentric perspective. Given this context, it is not clear why current humans' horizon of expectation should invariably function as the absolute yardstick by which to measure biodiversity and its future.

14. See also Fred Pearce's popular-science book on advocacy for nonnatives, *The New Wild: Why Invasive Species Will Be Nature's Salvation* (2015).

itself is no less complex, as it is hard to define and measure precisely. It pertains at the level of the ecosystem, of the species, and of subspecies variation and can be considered in terms of richness (the number of different elements at a particular level), evenness (the question of how equitable these elements are), and heterogeneity (the divergence in forms and functions of the elements that make up the diversity) (Balvanera et al. 2013). Bare numbers of different species in an ecosystem can only give an incomplete picture of its biodiversity: the question of how genetically different these species are also matters for conservation efforts, as does their ecological functionality. The understanding of how biodiversity relates to ecosystem services is still patchy (Cardinale et al. 2012; Balvanera et al. 2013).[15]

Beyond such practical problems of accounting for biodiversity, one of its central difficulties lies in the way the concept blends ecological facts with value judgments. Why is a world with more species and ecosystems better than a world with fewer? Clearly, the cultural cachet that the concept of "diversity" has accreted over the past half century in a variety of social spheres is hard to disentangle from the scientific arguments. Following this logic, "biodiversity" itself has often come to stand as a proxy for what we value about "nature." The science studies scholar David Takacs showed in the 1990s how part of the value of the biodiversity concept derives from the idea that scientific research on biodiversity might generate ethical guidelines, which would in turn confer considerable political power on such research. Many biodiversity scientists are also impassioned conservationists, so that "objective" research and "subjective" engagement are not always as clearly separable as some (though by no means all) scientists claim. Indeed, some biologists overtly refer to a "moral imperative" that drives them to make their insights public and to translate them into social and political principles (Takacs 1996, 337). The moral philosopher Donald S. Maier, much more recently, has delivered a detailed and scathing analysis of the reasoning that underlies most arguments about biodiversity: "Instead of a solid edifice, I found a chimera. I was stunned that I could not find a single argument that does not have serious logical flaws, crippling qualifications, or indefensible assumptions" (2012, 2). Maier's comprehensive, five-hundred-page analysis lays bare the logical flaws in common arguments about biodiversity in great detail. If these shortfalls must be painful to conservationists who seek to ground their ventures on solid scientific and logical foundations, however, they also

---

15. For an in-depth philosophical analysis of the biodiversity concept, see Maclaurin and Sterelny (2008).

highlight that the cultural and political power of certain environmentalist kinds of reasoning derives precisely from metaphorical superimpositions and narrative associations that do not obey strict logic. As this and subsequent chapters will show, the value of endangered species in particular and biodiversity in general is anchored at least as much in cultural narratives as in scientific facts.

My argument so far has focused on biodiversity as humans encounter it in the natural world. Yet humans alter nature not only by putting other species at risk and causing their extinction, but also by creating new forms of biodiversity. Through fire, hunting, fishing, agriculture, horticulture, pet-keeping, and medicine, humans have wittingly or unwittingly created an abundance of new variants and subspecies, as well as a few species. Millennia of domestication have generated innumerable new kinds of plants, for example, as the thousands of currently existing apple, orchid, and rice varieties demonstrate. The use of gene technologies may accelerate and multiply such diversity in the future. But humans also alter species indirectly and unintentionally. Our harvesting of certain fish, for example, provides an evolutionary advantage for other fish with characteristics we find less desirable. Our struggle against weeds by means of herbicides and against bacteria by means of antibiotics leads to the emergence of resistant varieties, even as the original target species sometimes disappear.

It is true, of course, that human-generated biodiversity is not exempt from decline: scientists, historians, farmers, and consumers have recently become increasingly concerned about the loss of historical varieties because of industrial-style agribusiness with its attendant standardization. The creation of fourteen hundred seed banks worldwide is testimony to a concern for preserving human-created biodiversity, some of which is itself endangered. But the possibility of such seed banks itself foregrounds that human interventions in nature can by no means be characterized as invariably destructive of biodiversity.[16] Yet biodiversity counts, whether of species or subspecies, typically do not include domesticated species, just as nonnative species are often discounted as part of local biodiversity, especially in urban settings.

Accounts of species extinction in popular science and the media, therefore, frequently depend on concepts that are less firmly defined than nonscientists tend to assume, and statements about increases and decreases of biodiversity are often less nuanced than they deserve to be in terms of the

16. For detailed explorations of these issues, see Nazarea (1998), Palumbi (2001) and Pollan ([2001] 2002).

taxonomic levels and the spatial and temporal scales they are able to address confidently. In the same vein, limits of knowledge and uncertainties that are addressed in the scientific literature often disappear in public discussion. To say this does not at all imply that the problem of biodiversity loss is just a product of biased environmental rhetoric. Many animal and plant species are undoubtedly at risk, and it is equally incontestable that humans bear the responsibility for most of these risk scenarios. But what this implies for the future of nature, and what particular communities should do in response, cannot be determined without understanding how these communities understand biodiversity, its decline, and its possibilities for the future; what kind of nature they would ideally like to live in; and what trade-offs they are willing to accept in order to achieve it. These questions can be answered only by looking at the stories about species loss that are told in different cultural contexts, which typically cast vanishing or extinct species as proxies for broader changes a community has experienced in processes of modernization and colonization, and which often articulate a more or less explicit critique of these processes.

2. *Species Elegies, the Power of Mourning, and the Critique of Modernity*

Over the past half century, growing awareness of species loss has translated into a profusion of popular-scientific books, travel writing, novels, poems, films, documentaries, photographs, paintings, murals, musical compositions, and websites. Some of these works focus on the fate of an individual species or taxon, while others engage with the global panorama of decreasing biodiversity. Many of these works deploy the genre conventions of elegy and tragedy in such a way that the endangerment of a particular species comes to function as a synecdoche for the broader environmentalist idea of nature's decline as well as for the stories that communities and societies tell about their own modernization. With mass extinction as a backdrop, these stories trace the endangerment or extinction of a particular species as part of the cultural history of modernity. More specifically, narrating the endangerment of culturally significant species becomes a vehicle for expressing unease with modernization processes or for an explicit critique of modernity and the changes it has brought about in humans' relation to nature. Understanding endangered species from a cultural perspective, therefore, means understanding their function in these narratives.

Many of the numerous books about the presumed "sixth mass extinction" rely on one or another variant of the narrative in which nature itself deteriorates or vanishes as a consequence of modernization or colonization. They sometimes focus on a single species, for example George Schaller's *The Last Panda* ([1993] 1994), Peter Matthiessen's *Tigers in the Snow* (2000) on the Siberian tiger, Tony Juniper's *Spix's Macaw* (2002) on a rare Brazilian parrot, and Joel Greenberg's *A Feathered River across the Sky: The Passenger Pigeon's Flight to Extinction* (2014), the latest in a long list of works on the extinction of the passenger pigeon. Others describe a group of species, such as the extinct birds Chris Cokinos evokes nostalgically in *Hope Is the Thing with Feathers: A Personal Chronicle of Vanished Birds* (2000), the trumpeter swans, Siberian cranes, and whooping cranes that David Sakrison follows on their migrations in *Chasing the Ghost Birds: Saving Swans and Cranes from Extinction* (2007), or the grizzlies, wolves, and whales that William Stolzenburg mourns in *Where the Wild Things Were: Life, Death, and Ecological Wreckage in a Land of Vanishing Predators* (2008). The most encompassing books portray biodiversity loss as a global ecological, economic, social, and philosophical problem, as Diane Ackerman does in *The Rarest of the Rare: Vanishing Animals, Timeless Worlds* (1995), Richard Leakey and Roger Lewin in *The Sixth Extinction* (1995), David Quammen in *The Song of the Dodo: Island Biogeography in an Age of Extinctions* (1996), Beverly Peterson Stearns and Stephen C. Stearns in *Watching, from the Edge of Extinction* (1999), Scott Weidensaul in *The Ghost with Trembling Wings: Science, Wishful Thinking, and the Search for Lost Species* (2002), E. O. Wilson in *The Future of Life* (2002), Terry Glavin in *The Sixth Extinction: Journeys among the Lost and Left Behind* (2006), Jeff Corwin in *100 Heartbeats: The Race to Save the World's Most Endangered Species* (2009), Melanie Challenger in *On Extinction: How We Became Estranged from Nature* (2011), Lothar Frenz in *Lonesome George oder Das Verschwinden der Arten* (Lonesome George or the disappearance of species; 2012), and Elizabeth Kolbert in *The Sixth Extinction: An Unnatural History* (2014). Many of these books take the form of global travelogues that paint appalling pictures of human misery and poverty, of governmental mismanagement and corruption, and of population growth, colonialism, and corporate exploitation. In these narratives, some people kill off the world's endangered species to eke out a living on the economic margins; others kill on an industrial scale and for large-scale profit; and yet others engage in activities that never targeted the endangered species but eliminate it as a side effect to some other cultural, economic, or political pursuit. In the vision that underlies most of these books, only a last-ditch large-scale conservation effort can save future generations from having to live in an utterly impoverished and homogenized natural world, with the plant and animal abundance of the past a mere memory to be visited in museums and viewed in documentaries.

Often, these stories of decline seek to mobilize readers' emotions through the lament, melancholy, and mourning that are characteristic of elegy (traditionally, a poem commemorating the death of a beloved person) and, in a different way, of tragedy (conventionally, the story of the inevitable and partly undeserved fall of a person of high social standing; in its modern sense, the meaningless and undeserved death of innocent victims). The psychoanalyst Sigmund Freud famously distinguished between mourning as a completed act of grieving and melancholy as the unfinished mourning that displaces itself onto other objects. But whereas Freud saw melancholy as a pathological state that ultimately needs to be overcome, contemporary thinkers have sought to redeem it. Mourning for people or things that are not usually considered worthy of such emotion and publicly expressing melancholia, they argue, can in and of itself turn into an act of political resistance.[17] Philosopher Judith Butler, for example, has noted that during the HIV/AIDS crisis of the 1980s and 1990s, public opinion made it difficult for partners of deceased AIDS victims to express their grief. Similarly, in the aftermath of the 9/11 attacks, public mourning for the American victims became part of the nation's recovery from the trauma it had suffered, whereas reminders of the victims of American foreign policy abroad were at times treated as tantamount to acts of treachery. For this reason, Butler claims, "we have to consider the obituary as an act of nation-building" (2004, 34). Literary critics Jahan Ramazani and Clifton Spargo, in *Poetries of Mourning* (1994) and *The Ethics of Mourning* (2004), have similarly examined the power of mourning and elegy for signaling distinctions between who or what is worthy of our collective moral consideration, and who or what is not.

Because of these social implications, mourning where society sees nothing worthy of grief can become an explicitly political act. "Melancholia is not only a denial of the loss of a beloved object," sociologist Catriona Mortimer-Sandilands has argued, "but also a potentially politicized way of preserving that object in the midst of a culture that fails to recognize its significance" (2010, 333). The environmentalist narrative of nature's decline has frequently served to express exactly such political emotions. En-

17. In the study of affect and emotion as it has evolved in philosophy and literary studies over the past twenty-five years, the word *emotion* tends to be used in approaches informed by cognitive science, and *affect* in those drawing on poststructuralist philosophy. I am using the terms interchangeably in this book.

vironmentalists often mourn openly for nonhuman beings, for species, for places, and even for processes (certain kinds of weather, seasonal changes, animal migrations) that might not usually be considered appropriate objects of grief, to the point where melancholy can be considered an integral part of the environmentalist worldview. Mortimer-Sandilands worries that the power of environmentalist melancholy is all too often deflected and culturally reincorporated through what she calls "nature-nostalgia": "ecotourist pilgrimages to endangered wildernesses, documentaries of dying peoples and places, even environmentalist campaigns to 'save' particular habitats or species against the onslaught of development" (333). She is undoubtedly right that environmentalist mourning has been thoroughly commodified in many ways, along with many other kinds of ecologically oriented desire, longing, and nostalgia. But considering how many people are motivated to support conservation through these commodified encounters with ecological crisis, this may matter less, in the end, than the fact that melancholy over the state of nature does act as a powerful emotional catalyst in environmentalist thought and writing.[18]

Stories about species that have already gone extinct or may soon disappear frequently rely on the politically mobilizing power of mourning and melancholy. More indirectly, they also rely on some aspects of tragedy, in that not just any species can become the object of such nostalgia. This explains in part the focus on charismatic megafauna: the sheer size and the perceived majesty and fierceness of major predators makes it easy to cast them in narratives of tragic falls from grace. The aesthetic beauty of tropical birds and certain kinds of butterflies also allows their disappearances to be perceived as tragic. By contrast, animals that are less distinctive in appearance as well as most plants fit less easily into this narrative template, not to mention microorganisms that cannot even be perceived with the bare eye. Disease-bearing insects such as the *Anopheles* mosquito or pathogenic viruses and bacteria—the smallpox and Ebola viruses, for example—are usually excluded from extinction stories because they belong on the opposite end of the spectrum, among those species whose disappearance becomes a cause for rejoicing rather than mourning even among environmentalists. Certain species, in other words, lack the cultural standing that might make them tragic or elegiac figures.

One of the stories from Kolbert's *The Sixth Extinction*, a minutely researched and lucidly presented history of past and present concerns over

---

18. See also van Dooren (2014, chap. 5) for a consideration of mourning across the human-animal boundary.

extinction, illustrates the difference between the species we care about and those we do not. Kolbert begins her account with a visit to Panama to explore the extinction of the golden frog, which has run parallel to the endangerment of hundreds of other frog species around the globe (see chapter 5). The cause of the extinctions was mysterious until a veterinary pathologist at the National Zoo in Washington, DC, discovered the fungus that caused the zoo's blue poison-dart frogs to die. But whereas Kolbert's chapter abounds in expressions of alarm and regret about the fate of the frogs, the fact that the chytrid fungus that kills them was previously unknown to science and "so unusual that an entire genus had to be created to accommodate it" (2014, 13) elicits no wonder or celebration from her, indeed no comment at all. And yet it is remarkable that at the moment of investigating extinction, a new species and genus was discovered, so that the reduction and expansion of biodiversity in human knowledge go hand in hand. Surely, if the species constellation had been the reverse—a new frog species discovered as the disappearance of certain fungi was being investigated—the news would have been celebrated across the scientific and public spheres. But the logic of species preferences has it that we care about beautiful or strange frogs (somewhat), whereas fungi leave us indifferent. They do not fit into our narratives except as villains we are glad to rid ourselves of.

Stories of flagship species, those that are able to occupy the hero's role, often function synecdochically by pointing to broader crises in humans' interactions with nature, especially during periods of modernization and colonization. The first species extinction, historically speaking, that came to be seen in connection with modernization was that of the dodo, a large, flightless pigeon that inhabited the island of Mauritius and died out in the seventeenth century. Dutch sailors, who discovered this bird on Mauritius and neighboring islands, described it as unattractive in appearance and taste. Nevertheless, hunting, the introduction of nonnative species, and peculiarities of the dodo's anatomy and behavior led to its extinction only a few decades after its discovery, with the last dodo sighting reported in 1662. The dodo looms large in many books on extinction because it was the first species whose end came to be clearly attributed to human intervention: it signals a historical turning point where the deadly ecological consequences of exploration and colonization became visible (Quammen 1996, 277). The dodo formed part of the astonishingly rich flora and fauna that colonization brought to the awareness of Europeans during the sixteenth and seventeenth centuries, a natural abundance that itself became one of the lures of the imperialist enterprise. Species extinction soon came to form part of this panorama, and

European travelers and explorers sometimes expressed regret at the destruction of nature that their own arrival brought about. It was a case of "imperialist nostalgia" in Renato Rosaldo's sense—in this instance, not a nostalgia for the cultures destroyed by colonization, but for a vanished natural world (Rosaldo 1993, chap. 3). The dodo's extinction, therefore, has turned into a recurrent symbol of the destruction of nature wrought by the imperialist expansion of European modernity, a destruction that also triggered the first initiatives for conservation.

The story of the dodo lies at the heart of one of the best-known popular-science books on species extinction, Quammen's *The Song of the Dodo*. Quammen's account alternates between lists of extinct species and detailed analyses of individual cases (cf. Garrard 2004, 156; and chapter 2). His case study of the dodo aims above all to show that the demise of the last individual of a species, which can be due to quite contingent circumstances, is ecologically less significant than the factors that lead a species to become so rare that mere contingencies can push it over the edge. But in a telling non sequitur, he then proceeds to narrate precisely the death of the fictional last dodo:

> Imagine a single survivor, a lonely fugitive at large on mainland Mauritius at the end of the seventeenth century. Imagine this fugitive as a female. She would have been bulky and flightless and befuddled—but resourceful enough to have escaped and endured when the other birds didn't. Or else she was lucky.
> . . . Imagine that her last hatchling had been snarfed by a feral pig. That her last fertile egg had been eaten by a monkey. That her mate was dead, clubbed by a hungry Dutch sailor, and that she had no hope of finding another. During the past half-dozen years, longer than a bird could remember, she had not even set eyes on a member of her own species.
> *Raphus cucullatus* had become rare unto death. But this one flesh-and-blood individual still lived. Imagine that she was thirty years old, or thirty-five, an ancient age for most sorts of bird but not impossible for a member of such a large-bodied species. She no longer ran, she waddled. Lately she was going blind. Her digestive system was balky. In the dark of an early morning in 1667, say, during a rainstorm, she took cover beneath a cold stone ledge at the base of one of the Black River cliffs. She drew her head down against her body, fluffed her feathers for warmth, squinted in patient misery. She waited. She didn't know it, nor did anyone else, but she was the only dodo on Earth. When

the storm passed, she never opened her eyes. This is extinction. (1996, 275)

Quammen here translates extinction into narrative by focusing on the paradigmatic "last of the species," whom he invites his readers to envision as female. This gender fiction allows him to portray her in the well-worn elegiac tropes of the bereaved mother and wife, as well as that of the elderly lady with health problems. At the same time, he conveys a sense of affection and bemusement for this helpless senior citizen through pathetic fallacy, by making grim weather and ill health symbols of the species' fate as a whole. Quammen's last dodo is both real and completely imaginary: real in that the extinction of the species and its anthropogenic causes cannot be wished away; imaginary in that she is entirely made up as an icon of regret for those dimensions of nature that are destroyed by modernization and colonization.

That extinction stories often express a deep-felt unease over the consequences of modernization is even more obvious in the case of species that have died out much more recently. In the nineteenth century, for example, two endemic wolf species inhabited Japan: the Hokkaido wolf (*Canis lupus hattai*) on Japan's northernmost island, which died out in the last decades of the nineteenth century; and *Canis lupus hodophilax* (in Japanese, 狼 or オオカミ [ōkami]), which inhabited the central islands of Honshu, Shikoku, and Kyushu. The Honshu wolf was smaller than the Hokkaido wolf and wolves on other continents. The last known individual died in 1905, and since only five museum specimens and eight pelts exist worldwide, it is not easy for the Japanese public to preserve an exact memory of this species. Yet in the decades after its disappearance, people again and again claimed to have sighted one of the wolves in what one might want to call the "ghost species" phenomenon—sightings that could never be scientifically confirmed.

Aside from a general unwillingness to accept the demise of a culturally significant species, two factors seem to contribute to these ghost sightings. Historian Brett Walker has pointed out that wolves were referred to by two different terms before the introduction of Linnaean taxonomy to Japan: the already mentioned オオカミ [ōkami] as well as やまいぬ [yama inu], "wild dog" or "mountain dog." It is not clear whether these were in fact the designations for two different species that were amalgamated during the introduction of Linnaean taxonomy, or simply two different ways of referring to the same species. Japanese biologists have in addition suggested the possibility that some Honshu wolves may have mated with domestic dogs, which would not only make the retrospective

differentiation of species more difficult but also result in similarities between Honshu wolves and twentieth-century domestic dogs that would
account for the alleged sightings (Walker 2005, chap. 1).

A different explanation emerges from the work of the anthropologist John Knight. The wolf is an important species in Japanese folklore
and mythology; in some regions, it is associated with mountain-based
Shinto shrines as a local manifestation of the transcendental or the divine. During Knight's research, Japanese informants frequently indicated that they believed the wolf had died out in the 1940s and 1950s.
The reason for this historical misprision is, according to Knight, rather
obvious. Contemporary unease about the modernization of Japanese
society tends to crystallize around the transformations triggered in the
aftermath of World War II by Western (mainly American) power. The
sustained wave of modernization that transformed Japan at the turn of
the twentieth century is a good deal paler in cultural memory. The Honshu wolf is therefore a clear example of how the extinction of a charismatic species is integrated into cultural history and becomes a symbol of
crisis, to the point where the biological facts themselves are reinterpreted
(Knight 1997).[19]

The case of the North American ivory-billed woodpecker (*Campephilus principalis*) follows a similar pattern. This large woodpecker species used to inhabit swampy old-growth cypress forests in the southern
United States. Never a very abundant species, it fell prey to widespread
deforestation in the South in the first few decades of the twentieth century. Some photographs and a tape recording of its calls survive from
the 1930s, and the ornithologist James Tanner published his classic
book on the bird in 1942. The last confirmed sighting took place in
1944. Over the following decades, numerous "ghost sightings" without
definitive evidence were reported, as in the case of the Honshu wolf. In
1999 a graduate student claimed to have spotted a pair in the Louisiana
swamps, but the ensuing intensive search yielded no results. Then, in the
spring of 2005, a team of seventeen scientists and experts at the Cornell
Lab of Ornithology published an article in the journal *Science* claiming
that an ivory-bill had indeed been located in a remote part of Arkansas
in early 2004 and had been seen and identified on seven occasions by experienced ornithologists and birdwatchers. A blurry four-second video
showing the bird in flight and briefly sitting on a tree stump was discussed and analyzed in minute detail (Fitzpatrick et al. 2005).

---

19. Walker (2005) also explores the cultural meanings of the Honshu wolf
extensively.

This rediscovery caused a sensation in the birding world. The ivory-bill had long been something like the holy grail of birdwatching; some birdwatchers had refused to believe in its disappearance and stubbornly kept searching for it. Many of them claimed to be attracted by the ivory-bill's striking appearance—its unusual size, its starkly contrasting black-and-white plumage complemented by a red crest in males, its light-colored bill and yellow eyes. Yet a different, slightly smaller woodpecker species that otherwise closely resembles the ivory-bill, the pileated wood-pecker (*Dryocopus pileatus*), is widespread in the United States. While the two species are easy to distinguish for experienced birdwatchers, un-trained observers can easily confuse them. Undoubtedly, many of the alleged sightings of ivory-bills in the late twentieth century were really glimpses of pileated woodpeckers.

This possibility has come to seem increasingly likely even in the case of the Arkansas ivory-bill. Extensive searches after 2004 yielded no fur-ther sightings of the bird, and in 2006, the well-known ornithologist Da-vid Sibley and three other experts published a refutation of the original video interpretation in *Science*, arguing that it in fact showed a pileated woodpecker (Sibley et al. 2006). In 2009 the filmmaker Scott Crocker completed his documentary *Ghost Bird*, which is sharply critical of what he considers the ivory-bill hype, according to him a symptom of a society that had already lost any firm grip on the distinction between fact and fiction during the Bush administration's war in Iraq. Organizations such as the Cornell Lab of Ornithology and the Nature Conservancy, which had widely publicized the rediscovery as a conservation success, refused to be interviewed for Crocker's film and fell silent on the subject.

Yet the cultural resonance of the ivory-bill's fate remains nothing short of astonishing. Innumerable newspaper and magazine articles, six books—Phillip Hoose's *The Race to Save the Lord God Bird* (2004), Tim Gallagher's *The Grail Bird* (2005), Jerome A. Jackson's *In Search of the Ivory-Billed Woodpecker* (2006), Geoffrey E. Hill's *Ivorybill Hunt-ers: The Search for Proof in a Flooded Wilderness* (2007), Michael Stein-berg's *Stalking the Ghost Bird: The Elusive Ivory-Billed Woodpecker in Louisiana* (2008), and Noel F. R. Snyder, David E. Brown, and Kevin B. Clark's *The Travails of Two Woodpeckers: Ivory-Bills and Imperials* (2009)—and a contemporary classical composition demonstrate a pub-lic fascination with this species that can hardly be explained by a gen-eral interest in biodiversity. Lee Hyla's composition "Wilson's Ivory-Bill," completed in 2000, well before the ivory-bill's alleged rediscovery, evokes in particularly striking manner the elegiac mood of loss, mourning, and longing for reconnection with a vanished natural world that this particular bird species triggers (Hyla 2006).

The lyrics of this twelve-minute piece consist of an excerpt from the nineteenth-century naturalist Alexander Wilson's multivolume work *American Ornithology* (1808–14). In this passage, Wilson describes how he captured an ivory-bill and took him to a hotel room, from which the bird desperately tried to escape. Since the wild creature would accept no food from a human hand, Wilson finally witnessed his death amid professions of regret and admiration for his indomitable spirit. This text is sung by a baritone, accompanied by a piano and tape recordings of ivory-bill calls and knocks from the 1930s. The human and bird voices struggle with each other and drown each other out throughout the composition, whereas the fragmented contemporary piano score alternates with the bird's voice, seeks to imitate it, and joins it in genuine duets during the climactic moments. Hyla skillfully juxtaposes different historical moments—the beginning of the nineteenth century as a moment of biological abundance, the 1930s as the moment just before extinction, and the contemporary era with its memories of the past—and combines the varied media of book, tape, and musical instrument so as to transcend the rupture between human and environment, to reestablish the connection with the past, and at least acoustically to reach beyond extinction. In "Wilson's Ivory-Bill," the human and the ivory-bill voices can be heard together in a way that has become impossible in the real world. While Quammen laments the lack of any record of the dodo's song (1996, 262), Hyla uses the medium of contemporary classical music with its blend of sound devices to resuscitate the extinct ivory-bill's voice.

Books about the ivory-bill similarly foreground feelings of loss and mourning even on the part of individuals who have never laid eyes on the bird themselves. Occasionally, they even express regret not only at losing this particular woodpecker species, but also, with the passage of time, losing the eyewitnesses who had in fact seen one of the ivory-bills. In an interview with author Tim Gallagher, for example, James Van Remsen, curator of birds at Louisiana State University's Museum of Natural Science, observes that "the number of people who have actually seen an ivory-billed woodpecker is down to two or three. . . . We are about to lose that contact. Pretty sad" (Gallagher 2005, 126). This comment rather strikingly echoes parallel concerns about the loss of connection to the twentieth-century past that were voiced during the 1990s in the context of World War II and the Holocaust, the fear that the passing of the last eyewitnesses would make memories of these events fade.

The analogy highlights that the ivory-billed woodpecker also points to a traumatic past, the history of large-scale ecological exploitation and deforestation of the American South in the first decades of the twentieth century—a history that William Faulkner famously fictionalized in short stories such as "Delta Autumn" and "The Bear" ([1942] 1991).[20] More broadly understood, evocations of the vast southern forests and their wildlife call up memories of a wilder and more beautiful America associated with the nineteenth century. In this respect, the loss of southern cypress forests and of the ivory-billed woodpecker signals the end of the nationalist myth of the United States as "nature's nation."

The New Zealand–based sound artist Sally McIntyre experiments with the call of an extinct bird in a more explicitly postcolonial context. Two works from 2012, *Collected Silences for Lord Rothschild* and *Huia Transcriptions,* recreate the lost calls of two New Zealand birds that went extinct in the early 1900s, the huia (*Heteralocha acutirostris*) and the laughing owl or whekau (*Sceloglaux albifacies*). McIntyre points out that both of these birds died out after the invention of recording technology, but unlike the ivory-billed woodpecker, neither of them was ever recorded. For *Collected Silences for Lord Rothschild,* McIntyre visited museums that house taxidermied specimens of the extinct species, placed her recording equipment next to them, recorded the silences, and then broadcast them in the Kapiti forest, the birds' original habitat. She explains: "This inaudible transmission is a double silence, narrowcasting the silences . . . of the extinct birds without receivers. It places an inaudible trace of the melancholy remnants of Victorian museological economics and colonial attitudes to the environment into the soundscape of Kapiti, making material the still recent silence in the biospheric fabric, a hole in the air, a placeholder where these birds were projected to be" (McIntyre 2012a). This sound experiment relies on an odd redeployment of John Cage's poetics of silence. McIntyre's recording and broadcasting of animal silences reminds one of John Cage's 4'33", in which a pianist walks on the stage, opens a piano, does not play it for four minutes and thirty-three seconds, closes it, and walks off the stage. But whereas for Cage silence held a value and meaning in and of itself— among other things because it makes audible sounds we usually dismiss as noise—McIntyre's silences are clearly marked as absences, as what is missing from the contemporary ecosystem and from our inventory of animal sounds (McKinnon 2013).

---

20. Both stories form part of Faulkner's *Go Down, Moses* (Faulkner [1942] 1991).

In *Huia Transcriptions*, McIntyre used the written account of a man named H. T. Carver, who observed and took notes on the huia in the late 1800s, including an approximate musical score of its call. McIntyre gleaned this information from a 1963 book that collected various observations and annotations of the huia call. She used a sound technology from the time just before the huia went extinct, the music box, to record the score Carver had written down. She then placed the music-box recordings, like the recorded silences before, in the huia's original habitat on Kapiti Island, on the trunks of trees that the huia might have perched on, and played them back in the midst of the early-morning chorus of bird voices. Needless to say, the music box sounds nothing like a real bird, but metallic, mechanical, and repetitive instead. The musicologist Dugal McKinnon has commented, "What this allows us to hear, negatively magnified through the audible presence of living birds, is the silence of the extinct Huia, as the simple transcriptions and music box realization of these fail, poetically and affectingly, to do anything more than gracelessly approximate a call known only through musical and textual descriptions" (2013, 73).

McIntyre takes Hyla's musical approach to extinct voices one step further. Like the piano in Hyla's piece, the music box in *Huia Transcriptions* seeks to imitate a vanished bird's call. But since, unlike Hyla, she does not have recordings of the bird call to use in her composition, the inadequacy of the music box in producing a realistic bird call itself calls attention to our collective lack of any precise memory of the huia's vocalizations. By placing this (badly) recreated bird voice not alongside a human one, as Hyla does, but back into its natural environment, and by recording its interplay with the voices of still existing birds, she foregrounds the huia's absence from the landscape and ecosystem it once inhabited. This twist also allows McIntyre to draw attention to the larger sonic landscape generated collectively by the members of an ecosystem, and to its transformation on account of the colonial impact.

A related but somewhat different set of meanings surrounds the extinction of the passenger pigeon, the species most often mentioned in discussions about extinction in the United States—especially as I write these lines in the year 2014, one hundred years after the death of the last passenger pigeon, the captive-bred Martha, at the Cincinnati Zoo in 1914. Scientific information about the passenger pigeon, the details of its demise, and current efforts at "de-extincting" the species have been rehearsed in so many books of fiction and nonfiction, from A. W. Schorger's *The Passenger Pigeon: Its Natural History and Extinction* (1955) to Joel Greenberg's *A*

Feathered River across the Sky, that I will not dwell at length on the species here, except to point out that it, too, stands in for the passing of a certain kind of wild America in the cultural imagination. But as Greenberg's title indicates, the passenger pigeon, unlike the ivory-billed woodpecker or the Carolina parakeet, another U.S. bird species that went extinct in the twentieth century, is associated with visions of biological abundance. As all the stories surrounding the passenger pigeon emphasize, the species numbered in the billions, its flocks darkened the skies overhead, and they took hours to pass. Given this sheer abundance, initial warnings regarding its survival were not heeded because many Americans in the late nineteenth century found it inconceivable that the pigeons could ever disappear.

Descriptions of this past abundance by twentieth-century commentators typically go along with expressions of horrified awe that it was even possible for people to exterminate so numerous a species and anxious questions about the greed and disregard it took to accomplish the deed. The historian Jennifer Price has traced in detail the stories and meanings that the American Indian nation of the Senecas, rural white Americans, and urban Americans in the late nineteenth century variously attached to the pigeon. By the time monuments were erected to the species in the 1940s and 1950s, Americans "made the extinction a modern parable, with a moral that cautions against destructive ways of thinking about nature" (Price 1999, 49). But in the contemporary period, she argues, even this moral has waned as urbanites' ecological ties to nature have become harder to see:

> To recognize one's own involvement in resource-intensive markets, and to make nature meaningful in ways that tell us about these connections, can be difficult—especially when we so thoroughly enjoy the fruits of these markets. . . . And this, as much as the avarice of man, is the moral of the pigeon's story: the specific, modern constellation of intensive overuses of nature, urban long-distance connections and strangely unmoored meanings. In the late nineteenth century, once upon a time—if you cut through a convenient haze of memory—well-off Americans, particularly, continued to use nature to tell meaningful stories, but began to lose track of nature in the process, and of their daily connections to it. (54)

For Price, the narrative of the passenger pigeon is, in the end, about what got lost in America's modernization, urbanization, and technological advancements over the course of the twentieth century. But what is lost, in her analysis, is not just particular ties to nature but also particular stories about these ties, so that thinking about extinction becomes a story about the loss of stories, in what is perhaps a distinctively postmodernist and metafictional twist.

Questions of historical transition, of modernization, and of national and ethnic identity are also at stake in many other controversies over endangered or extinct species and their cultural representations. In Australia, current struggles over conservation issues often invoke the historical precedent of the Tasmanian tiger (*Thylacinus cynocephalus*), a doglike marsupial with a striped body that died out around the middle of the twentieth century. Exactly when the species went extinct in the wild is unknown, and this uncertainty, as in the case of the Honshu wolf and the ivory-bill, has given rise to innumerable claims of thylacine sightings without supporting evidence.[21] The last captive specimen, Benjamin, died in the Tasmanian Beaumaris Zoo in 1936, and without any further confirmed sightings in the wild, the species was officially declared extinct in 1986. Yet the thylacine's historical trajectory differs from the Honshu wolf's and the ivory-billed woodpecker's in that this species did not vanish as an unintended consequence of human activities. Rather, the thylacine was deliberately hunted to extinction beginning in the late nineteenth century, since it was perceived, probably wrongly, as a threat to Tasmania's sheep agriculture. The infamous 1886 decree by which the Tasmanian state parliament awarded a one-pound bounty for each dead thylacine resonates as a cautionary precedent in contemporary debates over conservation. It is a history of colonization and modernization whose repetition many Tasmanian and Australian environmentalists seek to forestall.[22]

Julia Leigh's sparse and incisive novel *The Hunter* (1999) rehearses a fictional repetition of this deliberate species extermination by imagining that a surviving thylacine has been spotted in a remote part of Tasmania. In spite of the secrecy that surrounds the rediscovery—those who

21. For a detailed discussion of these sightings and their implications, see De Vos (2007).

22. The most detailed treatments of the thylacine are Robert Paddle's *The Last Tasmanian Tiger: The History and Extinction of the Thylacine* (2000) and David Owen's *Tasmanian Tiger: The Tragic Tale of How the World Lost Its Most Mysterious Predator* (2004). Numerous other books and artifacts revolve around the thylacine and its extinction, and Owen alludes to many of them in his chapter on the cultural marketing of the species. Other popular-scientific and fictional approaches to the thylacine include Beresford and Bailey (1981), Guiler (1985), Hartnett ([1999] 2007), Bailey (2001), Domico (2005), and Mittelbach and Crewdson ([2005] 2006).

are truly concerned about the thylacine do not divulge its existence—a biotech company learns about it and sends a professional hunter to harvest its blood and organs for research. Over the months of his search, the hunter, simply called "M," befriends a Tasmanian family and identifies with the animal he is hunting, to the point where he lives for a while in the thylacine's cave. But if this temporary merging of hunter and hunted leads readers to believe that the hunter will not in the end carry out his mission, they find themselves disappointed. M finds the thylacine, kills her (the last of the species is here, too, a female) and with surgical precision harvests her organs, draws her blood, and burns the rest. Even if a survivor of an extinct species were found, Leigh implies, what would keep contemporary societies from exterminating it yet again? In her novel as well as the numerous other texts and artifacts revolving around the thylacine, the elegy for a species becomes a fulcrum for rethinking development and modernization.[23]

The critique of modern society through the elegiac mode also shapes poems that directly apostrophize an endangered species, such as the North American poet W. S. Merwin's "For a Coming Extinction" and Mexican poet Homero Aridjis's "Ballena gris" (Gray whale). Merwin's poem, published in 1967, asks the gray whale on its way to extinction to deliver two messages to

> The End
> That great god.

As acerbic indictments of the society that has sent the whale to its death, these messages frame the poem in its first and last stanzas. The message in the first stanza,

> Tell him
> That we who follow you invented forgiveness
> And forgive nothing,

casts humans as merciless killers who delude themselves with moral concepts that are proved to be nothing more than sentimental hypocrisies by humans' impact on other species. The equally bitter send-up at the end of the last stanza,

---

23. Leigh's novel was turned into a feature film with the same title in 2012, directed by Daniel Nettheim and featuring Willem Dafoe as M.

> Tell him
> That it is we who are important,

indicts the anthropocentric disregard for nonhumans,

> The sea cows the Great Auks the gorillas
> The irreplaceable hosts,

that the stanza earlier mentions as already having been sacrificed for humans (Merwin [1967] 2006, 81). By assigning to the dying whale the task to carry these two messages to "The End," Merwin stands the elegiac poem on its head. Even as "For a Coming Extinction" calls upon a being who will soon vanish, the poem is not meant to portray whales so much as humans, not the dead so much as those who killed them. If an elegiac poem usually seeks to attribute some meaning to a person's passing, the whale's death here turns out not to mean anything other than humans' grim and deadly self-affirmation. And if the apostrophe to a nonhuman agent usually presupposes that this agent is at least in principle capable of responding, the poem itself cuts off any possibility of response in this case (cf. Culler 1981; Johnson 1987).

Aridjis's much less strident and more indirect poem, "Ballena gris" (1990), is one segment of a longer poem entitled "Nueva expulsión del paraíso" (Another expulsion from paradise), which also addresses other species whose demise the poet anticipates. "Ballena gris" may well be meant to echo Merwin's poem, but it seems at first sight to use the elegiac mode in a far more standard manner: the poet expresses his wish to inscribe an epitaph on the whale's grave after it has gone extinct. The first four lines evoke a time when the whale will be gone, but a visual memory of it will be left, albeit a vague one of "a dark body that passed through the waters" (un cuerpo oscuro que iba por las aguas; 119).[24] But the next three lines register a more radical erasure, a moment

> when there is neither memory of your passage
> nor legend that records your life
> because there is no ocean that can hold your death.

> [cuando no haya memoria de tu paso
> ni leyenda que registre tu vida
> porque no hay mar donde quepa tu muerte.] (119)

24. Translations from "Ballena gris" are mine.

In these lines, even the shadowy memory of the poem's beginning vanishes, along with stories and perhaps the ocean itself, although the syntax
of the sentence leaves it open whether it is material oceans that have disappeared or just, more symbolically, the ocean as a space for which the
whale served as a synecdoche, and without which it cannot be imagined.[25]
Yet in the poem's concluding lines, the poet declares that the epitaph he
would like to write on the whale's watery grave (tumba de agua) is:

> Gray whale,
> point us toward another fate.

> [Ballena gris,
> danos la dirección de otro destino.] (120)

Writing on a grave, as an act of memorialization, seems to reestablish the
memory that the speaker had anticipated disappearing just a few lines
earlier. The poem tacks back and forth through memory and its erasure,
between the elegy for a species and an elegy for memory itself. The concluding phrase, "otro destino," is itself equally ambiguous. Another destiny than the whale itself has suffered? Or another destiny than that of a
world without gray whales—a society that does not exterminate its fellow species? How can the whale point the way to such an alternative fate
if its memory has been erased? Poetry may be the only remaining vehicle
for retaining such memory, but even this possibility seems tenuous when
the poetic epitaph is to be written on water. "Ballena gris," in the end,
holds out the dual challenge of how we might retain the memory of vanished species and how we might transform this memory into a vision of
an alternative future. This alternative future includes the recovery of the
gray whale since Merwin's and Aridjis's poems were written: the species
is no longer endangered, according to the IUCN Red List, and its population is stable.

As all of the works I have discussed show, elegiac stories about declining species often index histories of modernization and colonization and more or less subtly articulate skepticism regarding their consequences. Extinction narratives allow their readers or viewers to reflect
on turning points of cultural history as the loss of a particular species
comes to stand in for the broader perception that human relationships
to the natural world have changed for the worse. As such stories unfold,

25. On the crucial role of the whale as a way of imagining marine environments, see
Buell (2001, 196–223).

part of national identity and culture itself seems to be lost along with the disappearance of a nonhuman species. In literary, visual, and musical representations of extinction, biological crisis typically becomes a proxy for cultural concerns: worries about the future of nature, on one hand, and on the other hand, hopes that a part of one's national identity and culture might be preserved, revived, or changed for the better if an endangered species could be allowed to survive or an extinct one could be rediscovered.

The entanglement of stories about endangered species with tribal, national, or regional identity can also, interestingly, take a different turn away from the elegiac critique of modernity and instead become a community's way of marking its place in a modern and transnational network. The anthropologist and science-studies scholar Celia Lowe has shown in a fascinating study how the Togean macaque in Indonesia was successively classified as a subpopulation of the Tonkean macaque, a species of its own, a "dubious" population hybridized from Tonkean macaques and Balantak monkeys, and an "endemic species" over the course of the 1990s and the first decade of the 2000s. This taxonomic oscillation, in her analysis, emerged from the perspectives of different groups involved in its study: indigenous people, Indonesian scientists, and Euro-American scientists and conservationists. The species status of this particular macaque population became a way for Indonesian scientists to secure a place for their science in the transnational networks of field biology and primatology, and for the Indonesian state to legitimate a conservation project in the Togean Islands that would help to protect a national patrimony and to attract international conservation funds, even as local Togeans' own approaches to nature were overwritten in the process. Lowe comments:

> If biodiversity is a new problematization of the relationship between nature and the human, we will want to know who is this "human" that appears to trouble nature so. The figure that Indonesian scientists produced through their Togean Island work was inevitably a different human than that developed by EuroAmerican biologists in thinking through the problem of tropical biodiversity. This is because Togean Island people were necessarily more than just "threatening humanity" to Indonesian biologists. They were also Indonesian subjects and citizens who fit into recognizably Indonesian ideas of national development, belonging, and alienation. The particularity of Indonesians' biodiversity was dependent on this understanding. (2006, 18–19)

If endangered species often register the losses and regrets in the transition to modernity, Lowe here highlights the obverse possibility: a new species as a way of integrating indigenous places into national space through the intermediary of conservation, and of integrating national with international science. "Indonesian biologists became subjects of a universalizing project of scientific inquiry while simultaneously participating in the making of an Indonesian modernity that was historically and geographically distinct," Lowe says in summing up the endpoint of taxonomic reclassifications and conservation efforts around the Togean macaque (51–52). Both the vanishing of species and the emergence of new ones, then, are entangled in the making and unmaking of community identities, in modernization and the resistance to it.

3. Comedies of Extinction and Survival

Important as the genre of the species elegy has been for mobilizing public support, conservationists have also had to face its limits. The elegiac mode tends to leave out species that cannot easily be associated with particular cultural histories, and its nostalgic and pessimistic tone puts off many potential supporters. Environmentalists currently face the challenge of reenvisioning conservation in terms that enable the imagination not so much of the end of species as of their future. It may be interesting to remember, in this context, that one of the first critical works to engage questions of ecology and literary form, Joseph Meeker's *The Comedy of Survival* ([1974] 1997), argued that tragedy, with its focus on the irreversible fall of a human being, has an inherently anthropocentric bias. Meanwhile, comedy, with its emphasis on regeneration, the passage from one generation to the next, and more generally on playful behavior that Meeker considers part of humans' evolutionary heritage, relies on a more ecological architecture: "Comedy is a celebration, a ritual renewal of biological welfare. . . . Literary comedy depends on the loss of equilibrium and its recovery. Wherever the normal processes of life are obstructed unnecessarily, the comic way seeks to return to normal" (16). The idea that a particular literary form has ecological implications independently of its content or its cultural uses seems too essentialist from the viewpoint of ecocriticism today, especially since it leaves unanswered the question why tragedy has played so much larger a role in environmentalist discourse than comedy. But taken as a suggestion that might shed light on certain cultural contexts rather than as a general principle, Meeker's claim helps to explain the persuasive force of extinction stories in which the charismatic animal, in a loose sense, comes to replace the human of high social standing who undergoes a tragic fall. It thereby also raises the question whether a comic narrative about species extinction might be possible.

Models of such alternative forms of storytelling are quite rare, but at least one book on extinction manages to convey its conservationist substance in a comic rather than an elegiac mode: Douglas Adams and Mark Carwardine's *Last Chance to See* (1990), a collaboration between the author of the science fiction comedy *The Hitchhiker's Guide to the Galaxy* and a zoologist. Based on a BBC radio series the two aired in the late 1980s, it describes a series of journeys around the world to visit endangered species of various kinds.[26] Adams, as the first-person narrator, humorously recounts the adversities of air, land, and sea travel; encounters with other tourists; and confrontations with local bureaucracies. Seen through his eyes, much of the human world is unpredictable, hard to understand, even harder to control, and completely irrational. So is the natural world, which presents itself to him as persistently surprising, bizarre, dangerous, beautiful, alien, and difficult to account for in rational terms. Instead of asking how a once abundant species becomes rare and then extinct, as Quammen does, Adams comes to wonder how certain species managed to survive in the first place.

In this vein, he muses on the habits of the megapode, a nonendangered bird species he encounters in Indonesia. Rather than simply sitting on its eggs as other birds do, the megapode stashes them in a painstakingly assembled mound of rotting vegetation whose internal temperature it carefully monitors by adding or removing bits and pieces of detritus. The overwhelming inefficiency of the procedure delights Adams because it reminds him of his own pointless but ingenious uses of modern technology. "I have a well-deserved reputation for being something of a gadget freak, and am rarely happier than when spending an entire day programming my computer to perform automatically a task that it would otherwise take me a good ten seconds to do by hand. . . . The . . . megapode has a similar outlook on life," he notes with satisfaction (Adams and Carwardine 1990, 38). Adams here preempts any post-hoc explanations of animal behavior by way of evolutionary adaptation mechanisms and foregrounds instead shortfalls and failures of adaptation in human and nonhuman behavior.

26. In 2009 the BBC produced a TV series under the title *Last Chance to See: Animals on the Verge of Extinction,* in which Carwardine revisits some of the locations and species earlier explored in the radio show and book (Green, Southwell, and Davidson 2009). Adams, who died in 2001, is replaced by Stephen Fry in this series. Carwardine also published an accompanying follow-up book, *Last Chance to See: In the Footsteps of Douglas Adams* (2009).

It is precisely this inefficient, irrational unadaptedness of the natural world that makes it attractive and worth preserving for the narrator—the sheer unlikelihood of its ever having made it to the present day. This is nowhere clearer than in his account of the kakapo, a highly endangered and flightless New Zealand parrot:

> The booming noise [of the males' mating call] is deep, very deep, just on the threshold of what you can actually hear and what you can feel. This means that it carries for very great distances, but that you can't tell where it's coming from. . . .
>
> The female kakapo can't tell where the booming is coming from either, which is something of a shortcoming in a mating call. . . . Females in breeding condition have been known to turn up at completely unoccupied bowls, wait around for a while, and then go away again.
>
> It's not that they're not willing. When they are in breeding condition, their sex drive is extremely strong. One female kakapo is known to have walked twenty miles in one night to visit a mate, and then walked home again in the morning. Unfortunately, however, the period during which the female is prepared to behave like this is rather short. As if things aren't difficult enough already, the female can only come into breeding condition when a particular plant, the podocarp for instance, is bearing fruit. This happens only every two years. . . .
>
> The males therefore get extremely overwrought sitting in their bowls making noises for months on end, waiting for their mates, who are waiting for a particular type of tree to fruit. . . . The net result of all these months of excavating and booming and walking and scrarking and being fussy about fruit is that once every three or four years the female kakapo lays one single egg which promptly gets eaten by a stoat. (Adams and Carwardine 1990, 117–119)

At this point, Adams most explicitly articulates his approach to evolution and extinction: "So the big question is: How on earth has the kakapo managed to last *this* long?" (Adams and Carwardine 1990, 119). Like his account of the megapode, his description of the kakapo is studded with references to contemporary technology—the males' mating call resembles a subwoofer, their mating behavior the eccentric customs of the British motorbike industry—suggesting that the idiosyncrasies of the sociocultural realm mirror and extend the contingencies of ecology and evolution.

This use of analogies does not imply that Adams's account is politically uncritical or always lighthearted. He peppers his account of a visit to Zaire, for example, with cuttingly satirical comments on the arcane bureaucracies and brutal dictatorships that colonial rule left behind. And his seemingly easy, anthropomorphic identifications with animals turn up startling differences of perception and cognition as often as humorous similarities. The description of the kakapo, especially in comparison with Quammen's account of the last dodo, highlights that what undergirds the conservationist message in *Last Chance to See* is neither scientific reasoning, nor a sense of moral obligation, nor the elegiac investment in the last individual of a species, though of all of these do occasionally appear in the book. Instead, Adams relies on an essentially comic awareness of the contingent events, habits, and bodies it took to produce both humans and nonhumans in their present forms.

The strength of Adams's humor lies not just in its breakaway from gloom-and-doom scenarios whose rhetorical power is by now seriously undercut by their utter predictability—when the news is always bad, it isn't really news anymore. Humor in *Last Chance to See* also mobilizes a set of emotions and identifications that differs from the more typical tragic and elegiac perspectives. Rather than casting the animal at risk as a precious treasure of biological information or beauty that humans are on the verge of destroying, it portrays animals as average citizens finding unusual ways to make a living and not always succeeding, or as experimenters who do not always hit the mark. The frequent implicit and explicit comparisons between animal practices and human technologies, on one hand, and between the animal experimenters and the hapless traveler Adams himself, on the other, question human exceptionality even when the comparison turns up difference rather than similarity. The human and nonhuman protagonists in *Last Chance to See* fail in different but comparable ways, and the idiosyncrasy of their shortfalls invites readers' fondness and sympathy rather than their admiration and mourning. All of us, Adams suggests, whether we are humans or nonhumans, struggle to make it in a complex and often inhospitable world, and solidarity with each other would make the struggle easier.

Adams's comedic approach to species endangerment and extinction ultimately also suggests a different understanding of the relationship between modernization and nature from the one found in accounts that rely on elegiac or tragic templates. *Last Chance to See* suggests not a well-functioning natural realm disrupted by the advent of modern society, but a view of nature and culture as parallel and intersecting histories of experiments that continually succeed or fail. Extinction is the signal of a failure that should be prevented whenever possible, yet the failure of one experiment also becomes the point of departure for new ones. The urgency of biological conservation remains, in other words, but it is grounded in a different narrative about the evolution of life forms and modern humans' place in it. Adams and Carwardine's account highlights that in the last instance, the imperative to conserve biodiversity does not derive from science but from a human commitment to value biological otherness and shared vulnerability to contingency. In this way, *Last Chance to See* points to an understanding of extinction not only as a narrative endpoint, but as a possibility of new beginnings—not the end of nature so much as its continually changing futures.

2 From Arks to ARKive.org: Database, Epic, and Biodiversity

1. From Elegy to Enumeration

Much as the elegiac mode dominates verbal and visual representations of endangered species, it is often accompanied by a sense that the mourning for individual species cannot adequately capture the magnitude of a crisis that affects thousands of species and the entire globe. To convey a more panoramic view of mass extinction, artists and writers often resort to lists or catalogs. The structure of the travelogue, common in nonfiction books and films on endangered species, sometimes gives such enumerations a narrative progression by juxtaposing different species and locations in successive chapters, and photography collections often consist of dozens or even hundreds of photos of different species. In other cases, lists alternate with more focused accounts of individual species. David Quammen, for example, who makes up an elaborately sentimentalized death scene for the imaginary last dodo hen on Mauritius in 1667 (1996, 275; cf. chapter 1), simply ticks off lists of species at other moments: "The Laysan honeycreeper is extinct. The lesser koa-finch is extinct. So are the greater koa-finch and the Kona grosbeak and the Hawaiian rail. The greater *amakihi* is extinct, as are the Oahu *nukupuu* and the *amaui* and the *kioea* and the Oahu *oo* . . . and at least three out of four subspecies of *akialoa*" (321). And again, just a few pages later: "Then the Guam flycatcher went extinct. Blip. The bridled white-eye disappeared. Blip. The rufous fantail, the white-throated ground-dove, the Mariana fruit-dove, the Micronesian honeyeater: blip blip blip blip. Of the eleven forest-dwelling species, these six all vanished from Guam during the mid-1980s" (323). This impulse to catalog species as a means of valuing biodiversity, which alternates with other strategies in Quammen's book, informs other books of popular science as a basic organizational tool, for example Michael Gleich et al.'s *Life Counts: Cataloging Life on Earth* (2002).

Elegiac impulses also combine with this enumerative drive in fictional texts about endangered species. William Burroughs's novella *Ghost of Chance* ([1991] 2002), for example, features a "Museum of Lost Species" that one of the characters encounters on the island of Madagascar. This discovery leads to a lengthy if narratively fractured meditation on the extinct species that humans long to revive and those they rejoice in having eliminated, such as viruses causing dangerous disease. In Puerto Rican novelist Mayra Montero's *Tú, la oscuridad* (In the palm of darkness; 1995), the main plot about an American herpetologist searching for a rare Caribbean frog species with his Haitian guide is interspersed with brief vignettes enumerating amphibian extinctions around the world. In texts such as these, the catalogs that accompany and complement the narrative evoke a numerical sublime of sorts, numbers too large to be contained by conventional storytelling procedures that focus on a discrete set of events, scenes, and characters.

Canadian novelist Margaret Atwood's trilogy of speculative fiction, *Oryx and Crake* (2003), *The Year of the Flood* ([2009] 2010), and *Madd-Addam* (2013) also features extinctions on such a large scale that only databases can adequately reflect their magnitude. In *Oryx and Crake*, the two young male protagonists, Jimmy and Crake, often play a computer game, Extinctathon,

> an interactive biofreak masterlore game [Crake]'d found on the Web. *EXTINCTATHON, Monitored by MaddAddam. Adam named the living animals, MaddAddam names the dead ones. Do you want to play?* . . . Then some challenger would come on-line, using his own codename—Komodo, Rhino, Manatee, Hippocampus Ramulosus—and propose a contest. *Begins with, number of legs, what is it?* The *it* would be some bioform that had kakked out within the past fifty years—no T-Rex, no roc, no dodo, and points off for getting the time frame wrong. Then

> you'd narrow it down, Phylum Class Order Family Genus Spe-
> cies, then the habitat and when last seen, and what had snuffed
> it. (Pollution, habitat destruction, credulous morons who
> thought that eating its horn would give them a boner). . . . It
> helped to have the MaddAddam printout of every extinct spe-
> cies, but that gave you only the Latin names, and anyway it was
> a couple of hundred pages of fine print and filled with obscure
> bugs, weeds, and frogs nobody had ever heard of. Nobody ex-
> cept, it seemed, the Extinctathon Grandmasters, who had brains
> like search engines. (Atwood 2003, 80–81)

The deliberately vulgar language, meant to reflect male teenagers' dis-
missive attitude, both evokes and overwrites the mourning that a catalog
of extinction would otherwise elicit. But in spite of the reduction of extinction to a game, it is crucial to the novel. Both of the title characters,
Oryx and Crake, derive their pseudonyms from extinct species (from
Oryx beisa, an East African antelope, and the red-necked crake, an Australian bird). The game itself functions as an inverted genesis: Adam
named the living animals, MaddAddam names the dead ones, with the
doubled "dd" punning on addition in ironic contrast to the subtractions
extinction implies. As plants and animals go extinct at a rate that only
digital search engines can keep track of, Crake, who becomes an accomplished bioengineer, creates a virus that exterminates most of humankind so as to halt the ecological crisis. At the same time, he designs a new
species of posthumans, named "Crakers" after himself, whose genome
incorporates human, animal, and plant genes. In this vision of the future,
the database of extinct species functions as the master trope and framing device.

   Lydia Millet's trilogy of novels *How the Dead Dream* (2008), *Ghost
Lights* (2011) and *Magnificence* (2012) focuses, especially in its first and
third volumes, on characters who are not biologists or bioengineers like
Crake, but who are drawn into reflections on species extinctions quite
against their own intentions. *How the Dead Dream* revolves structurally
around the dialectic of singular and local experiences, on one hand, and
the global cataloging of endangered species, on the other. The protagonist of this meditative novel, Thomas Stern, called T for short, proves
adept at business ventures even while he is still at school and becomes
a highly successful real estate developer later on. Unencumbered by any
environmentalist awareness, T experiences several human tragedies: his
father leaves the family, his mother lapses into senile dementia, and his
partner, Beth, dies prematurely. These traumatic separations from loved

ones gradually attract his attention—perhaps triggered by an incident in which he runs over a coyote in his car and watches her die—to the animal species that his construction projects displace and endanger. He begins to research species extinction and visits zoos with the explicit purpose of seeing endangered animals. After Beth's untimely death, this interest evolves into a peculiar obsession: T serially breaks into zoos to spend time with animals who are the last of their kind, "terminal animals," as the novel calls them. He spends a night in the enclosure of a Mexican gray wolf, for example, tries to imagine the thoughts of a female Sumatran rhino, and meditates on the spatial experience of a swarm of pupfish in a concrete tank. All of these attempts to connect to beings who are isolated from their habitats and social ties rely quite transparently—if rather originally—on the genre template of the elegy, since it is his mourning of Beth that leads T to endangered species.

T himself is conscious of this connection, which surfaces, for instance, in a meditation on whether the killing of a rat by a fox would turn into anything other than a routine act of predation if the rat were the last of its kind:

> Was it different then? Did the world feel the loss?
>   The field stayed a field, the sky remained blue. . . . And yet a particular way of existence was gone, a whole volume in the library of being. . . . It was time that would show the loss, only time that would show how the world had been stripped of its mysteries, stripped by the hundreds and thousands and millions. But it was not the domino effect he considered most often, simply the state of being last. Loss was common, a loss like his own; he couldn't pretend to the animals' isolation, although he flattered himself that he could imagine it. He was aware that in his search a certain predictable need was being answered. Still he thought he had a glimpse of something in losing Beth. If a being could be so singular to another, there was no doubt that there was singularity elsewhere, that the irreplaceable nature of being was not limited to his own small circle. (Millet 2008, 166)

Mourning leads T from the human to the nonhuman and from singular experiences of loss to the reflection on serial biological disappearances. Even if the horizon of experience the novel portrays remains resolutely individual, the multiplication of T's objects of mourning and sympathy takes the reader relentlessly to a global panorama of loss and disaster.

The enumerative logic that emerges from T's serial zoo break-ins resonates even more forcefully in the somewhat peculiar acknowledgments
that follow the novel's ending. Millet thanks friends, family, and supporters in the usual fashion, but then she proceeds to dedicate the book
to an alphabetical list of endangered species:

> To the memory of the West African black rhinoceros, which dis-
> appeared from the world in the time it took to write this book.
> And in honor of the rarest species in the United States, any of
> which may vanish in the blink of an eye: the Alabama beach-
> mouse, Alabama lampmussel, Alabama sturgeon, Attwater's
> greater prairie chicken, Berkeley kangaroo rat, Buena Vista lake
> ornate shrew, Cahaba pebblesnail, Carolina elktoe, Catspaw,
> Devils Hole pupfish, Florida panther, Florida salt marsh vole,
> Fosberg's love grass, Franciscan manzanita, giant Palouse earth-
> worm, Guam Micronesian kingfisher, Hawaiian crow, Hawai-
> ian monk seal, interrupted rocksnail, Key Largo woodrat, Lange's
> metalmark butterfly, and Miami blue butterfly. (Millet 2008,
> 245–246)

With these concluding words, the novel has fully transitioned from the
genre of the elegy to that of the Red List of endangered species, with an
emergent database aesthetic gradually reshaping the novel's prevalent
tropes of loss and mourning. That the list stops mid-alphabet at M may
indicate that it could potentially go on ad infinitum. Or it might be an
underhanded pointer to Millet's own name, which could be next in this
list, raising the question of humans' own endangered future. Whatever
the reason for this endpoint, the dedication of the novel to a Red List
of endangered species links *How the Dead Dream* to Millet's work as a
writer for the Tucson-based Center for Biological Diversity, a nonprofit
organization that advocates for endangered species and has often initiated the legal procedures to have them protected under the Endangered
Species Act.

Magnificence, the third novel in Millet's trilogy, follows one of T's
employees, after she, too, has suffered a devastating personal loss. Susan
Lindley, a former school teacher who does clerical work for the charita-
ble foundation T starts, loses her husband, who is killed in a street mug-
ging during a trip to Central America. She feels partly responsible for his
death, since it was her marital infidelity that made him go on the trip that
ends his life. In the midst of her mourning, she inherits an old mansion

in Pasadena from an uncle she knew very little. The house, she finds, is
chock-full of taxidermied animals, hunting trophies that she finds repellent at first and simply wants to get rid of. But as she learns more about
them, she discovers that some of them are rare artifacts, and she gradually begins to like and restore them. She visits museums to learn how to
curate her involuntary collection and decides to display the animals by
geographical region, so that the house becomes a microcosmos of the
globe:

> The main part of the ground floor would be given over to North
> American mammals, each order with its own section. . . . Ro-
> dents would live in the music room, rabbits and hares in the ball-
> room. . . . The wide hallway . . . [on the second floor] turned
> into Africa. . . . The birds seemed to demonstrate a lack of inter-
> est in her personal business, so she put her bed in Birds of the
> World, which once had been Russia. . . . When the project was
> finished the house had a globe-like aspect in its sectioning off,
> its variety of scenes, its separation by palette. It was multicol-
> ored like a globe, and also like a globe it represented reality only
> partly, with the failure of all maps but also the same neatness,
> the same quiet satisfaction . . . the happy captivity of precious
> things. (Millet 2012, 148–150)

She also discovers her uncle's long devotion to hunting and to something
that an old friend of his mysteriously calls "The Legacy," without ex-
plaining what it refers to.

Eventually, Susan discovers a vast basement storage area underneath
the house that contains specimens of rare and extinct species: the coat
of a quagga, the skeleton of a dodo, taxidermied auks, and Newfoundland wolves. The house is in fact an ark of the extinct, the dark legacy
of humans' impact on other species. And white humans' impact on non-
whites: Susan's amazement at her uncle's vast collection of extinct animals turns to revulsion when she discovers, in a remote basement room,
human remains that belong to members of vanished indigenous tribes—
labeled carefully, just as the animals are, by their place of origin and
the cause and approximate date of their extinction. Overwhelmed and
horrified, Susan nevertheless decides in the novel's last scene to keep the
collection and care for it: it becomes her way of accepting responsibility
for a legacy of violence that has targeted both humans and nonhumans.
Her belief that she is at least indirectly responsible for her husband's
death here widens into the acceptance of a much broader accountability

for extinction on a global scale. Elegy gives way to database in the transition from individual mourning to the confrontation with global loss: the database here is, on one hand, associated with genocide and the trauma of pervasive violence and, on the other, linked with the possibility of taking full stock of and responsibility for this traumatic past.

Fiction and nonfiction are not the only media in which catalogs of endangered or extinct species have surfaced as a recurrent strategy in recent years. Travis Threlkel and the filmmaker Louie Psihoyos projected serial images of endangered species onto the facade of the Empire State Building in New York City in the summer of 2015 as a way of drawing attention to mass extinction (Roston 2015). In Brazil, where murals and visual art have long played an important role for environmentalist art, those media have also addressed the biodiversity crisis through the form of the catalog. A mural at the Humanidade 2012 exhibit that accompanied the Rio+20 summit in 2012 showed human accomplishments on one side of the gallery and on the other side a panoramic drawing of biodiversity, which a machine smudged and blurred to highlight the losses (McNee 2014, 151–153). The artist Siron Franco contributed to the Rio+20 convention a video presentation called *Brasil-Cerrado*, which highlighted biodiversity loss through fires and agriculture in Brazil's savannah region. Franco also exhibited a video-installation of a wall with cut-out silhouettes of animals displaced from Brazil's savannah biome, again using the enumerative power of the catalog, this time through serial cut-outs, to highlight the disappearance of species.

The Internet offers artists and writers additional means of combining narrative and catalog. The installation artist Maya Lin, best known for her Vietnam War Memorial in Washington, DC, an artwork whose central challenge arguably was to combine a sense of large-scale loss of human lives with the memorialization of individuals, has turned her attention to species loss over the past decade. Her website, What Is Missing? (2010), which Lin refers to as her last memorial (Toomey 2012), features on its home page a world map that is populated by a multitude of clickable dots. Each one leads the web user to images and stories of endangered or extinct species, as well as to Lin's own biodiversity-related installation artworks around the globe. In its attempt to zoom in to the local and back out to the global, to move the user back and forth between highly particular circumstances and a global panorama of endangerment, What Is Missing? diverts the aesthetic and functionality of Google Maps and Google Earth to the purposes of conservation.

Even more explicitly, the list as a way of expressing environmental concern has translated into digital biodiversity databases and Red Lists of endangered species. These tools of scientific classification and record-keeping, insofar as they serve as the basis for laws and treaties protecting endangered species, also possess palpable legal and political power beyond the indirect one that might be associated with the affect of melancholy. While such databases seem at first sight far removed from the narratives of film documentaries or popular-scientific books about biodiversity loss, I will seek to show in what follows how narrative—and, in fact, in some cases even the genre of the elegy—continues to inflect the encyclopedic project of databases and Red Lists, while conversely, the database aesthetic pushes environmental art and writing beyond melancholy and mourning.

2. *The Red List and the Narrative Imagination*

The rapid pace of species loss has been one of the impulses in the creation of global biodiversity databases over the past two decades, an effort originally spearheaded by E. O. Wilson in 1992 (Wilson 1992): the All Species Foundation, ARKive.org, the Catalogue of Life, the Consortium for the Barcode of Life, the Encyclopedia of Life (EoL), the Global Biodiversity Information Facility, and the International Nucleotide Sequence Database Collaboration, among others. These digital databases typically seek to inventory the totality of biological life on Earth, at least in terms of the 1.8 million species that have been scientifically named and classified. Accessible on the Internet, they aim to make information available to scientists and conservationists worldwide as a basis for structuring and coordinating their efforts. Other biodiversity databases that are global in scope focus on particular taxa or groups of species: BirdLife International focuses exclusively on the approximately ten thousand species of known birds, and the recently completed Census of Marine Life sought to document all marine species. Species+ makes available information on species listed in the appendices to CITES (the Convention on International Trade in Endangered Species of Wild Flora and Fauna), CMS (the Convention on the Conservation of Migratory Species of Wild Animals), and other multilateral environmental treaties. Yet other databases focus on invasive species for particular regions.

Putting together global biodiversity databases by assembling information from tens of thousands of sources and formats is arduous, time-consuming, labor-intensive, and expensive. It sometimes involves compiling information from two-hundred-year-old journal issues or obtaining information from countries that do not archive scientific data in digital form or are unwilling to share it across borders. Not all of the database projects have the funding they require to complete their task (Thomas 2009, 1632), and inevitably the documentation of some forms of biodiversity continues to open up new questions and areas for research. "The age of discovery is still with us," Ian Poiner, the marine ecologist who chaired the Census of Marine Life's scientific steering committee, commented in an interview (Normile 2010, 25), highlighting the open-endedness of database projects—but also, perhaps unwittingly, their historical connection to the colonial and encyclopedic strands of eighteenth-century thought. The construction of biodiversity databases, as this comment hints, is a scientific but also a cultural venture defined by the tension between the attempt to create a total knowledge base and the awareness that this task is not likely ever to reach its goal.

Global biodiversity databases typically derive a great deal of their information from other databases, thereby layering different database systems and creating networks of information whose structure is sometimes more and sometimes less obvious to the user. These databases also differ in terms of their institutional anchoring, their internal structure, their emphasis on different media, their mode of access, and their intended audience. The International Nucleotide Sequence Database Collaboration, for example, draws on three national and regional databases in Europe, Japan, and the United States, focuses on identifying species by their gene sequences, and is clearly intended for the use of scientists. The IUCN's Red List of Threatened Species, which has increasingly included non-endangered plants and animals over the past two decades and thereby has transmuted into a biodiversity database, combines textual information with spatial data for use by scientists and conservationists. Its endangerment classifications are widely used and quoted in scientific literature as well as in public media. ARKive.org, now under the auspices of the nonprofit organization Wildscreen, aims at an even more general audience of "educators, schools, communities, conservation organizations and anyone with a passion for nature" (www.arkive.org/about /story-so-far). Its goal is to "use the power of wildlife imagery to inspire the global community to discover, value and protect the natural world" (www.arkive.org/about/). Biodiversity databases, then, range from specialized and expert to broad public uses.

The Encyclopedia of Life (EoL) pursues "the bold idea to provide 'a webpage for every species'" (http://eol.org/info/the_history_of_eol) so as to enable "global access to knowledge about life on Earth" (http://eol .org/about). Unlike the IUCN Red List, which synthesizes information from a variety of sources, the EoL simply aggregates information about each species from numerous sources and provides digital links without any attempt at synthesis or reconciliation. Even though it was initiated in 2007 by E. O. Wilson, the most prominent biologist in public advocacy on behalf of biodiversity, the EoL in fact does not focus on endangered species in the way ARKive and the IUCN Red List do. Instead, it foregrounds above all "organisms [that] have an immediate impact on humans . . . commercially valuable species, invasive pests and disease organisms, charismatic and familiar animals, popular ornamental plants, newly discovered species, and plants, animals and fungi on which we rely for food." Species that feature in the news or whose pages are most often visited on the EoL website are given higher priority than those that command less public attention (http://eol.org/info/priority_taxa_on_eol), so that the EoL in fact molds itself after structures of human attention rather than patterns of biological life or ecological crisis alone. The EoL invites participation from average users in a way that is not possible with more scientifically oriented databases, where all information is carefully vetted by specialists before it is allowed to appear on the website. It also includes comment and ratings mechanisms for each information unit, such as those now common on Amazon.com and other commercial websites. No doubt the most democratic of the global biodiversity databases, EoL is also the one that to date has the least marked profile of its own, as each entry dissolves into a cloud of textual, numerical, and visual information bits gleaned from other databases and websites.

With the exception of the purely genetic inventories, digital biodiversity databases bring together text, statistics, spatial data, maps, photography, video, and hyperlinks. Global biodiversity databases differ considerably in the degree to which they integrate these varied types of information. The IUCN's explicit goal of classifying species according to their risk of endangerment provides a framework for combining data and media—text and spatial data, above all—in such a way that they deliver evidence for each classification. But projects such as EoL or the Map of Life (mol.org) function in practice less as structures for organizing data of their own than as portals that dynamically collage data from other publicly accessible sources through Application Programming Interfaces, following a more general trend in database design toward architectures for organizing "Big Linked Data."[1] A few decades in the past, an older style of literary criticism sought to describe the transfer and linkage of themes, tropes, idioms, plots, and characters between texts of different periods and genres by means of the notion of "intertextual-

1. I am grateful to Elijah Meeks for pointing out this trend to me.

ity," a concept that proved particularly fertile in the description of seemingly fractured modernist works of art and literature. At a vastly larger scale and with the involvement of different media, some contemporary databases similarly function on the basis of what one may want to call "interdata" or "convergence data," the collation and rearrangement of data drawn from a wide range of different sources and connected via the Internet.

Global digital biodiversity databases, then, can be understood to emerge from the conjunction of two tendencies: an encyclopedic, centripetal impulse that reaches back to the Enlightenment and seeks to inventory the entire known world, and the hyperlinked, centrifugal architecture of the Internet, which seeks to approximate a representation of this world through the constant movement between data sites. Umberto Eco, in his exploration of lists and catalogs across the ages, has pointed out that certain kinds of lists foreground their own incompletion as a way of pointing toward those things that exceed them, that cannot be listed or enumerated (2009, 15–17). Digital databases, to which new items can always be added, have this incompletion hardwired into their basic structure. The specific project of biodiversity databases, inventorying all life forms on Earth, can be understood in analogy to what Franco Moretti has called "modern epic" (1996). Ancient epics, from Homer's *Odyssey* and Virgil's *Aeneid* to the Finnish *Kalevala* and the Mayan *Popol Vuh*, all attempted to grasp the entirety of the world as it was then known to the community that produced the epic—not infrequently by means of long lists whose apparently antinarrative nature tends to stymie modern readers. Modern epic as Moretti analyzes it has sought to encompass the modern capitalist world system for the past two centuries, but unlike its ancient predecessors, such "world texts" proceed with the awareness that this system can in fact not be captured in the way the premodern world could be. A certain shortfall of the epic project, "a discrepancy between the totalizing will of the epic and the subdivided reality of the modern world," according to this analysis, is built into the modern version of the genre (5).[2] Biodiversity databases and Red Lists of endangered species can be understood as a new variant of the modern epic or world text and as a new form of nature writing: the forever

2. In tracing a continuing epic tradition in the modern novel, Moretti takes a position that contradicts earlier theories that had cast the epic as the antithesis of the novel, for example those of Lukács ([1920] 1971), Auerbach ([1953] 2003), and Bakhtin ([1975] 1981). This also implies a different view of the connection between epic and empire from the one outlined by David Quint, for example (1993).

incomplete attempt to map the entirety of biological life and classify it according to its risk of extinction, as part and parcel of a battle of heroic scientists and conservationists against ignorant authorities and indifferent masses. In this battle, the future of planet Earth itself is at stake, as biologists and conservationists regularly claim—an epic view of contemporary environmentalism if ever there was one!

This approach to biodiversity databases resonates with media theorists' claims that the database is in fact an emergent cultural genre of its own, "a new symbolic form of the computer age . . . a new way to structure our experience of ourselves and of the world," as Lev Manovich has argued in his seminal book *The Language of New Media* (2001, 219). "As a cultural form, the database represents the world as a list of items, and it refuses to order this list. In contrast, a narrative creates a cause-and-effect trajectory of seemingly unordered items (events). Therefore, database and narrative are natural enemies," Manovich continues (225). Casting database and narrative as "enemies" has drawn fire from literary scholars such as Jerome McGann, who has accused Manovich of using his central terms far too loosely (2007, 1589), and Katherine Hayles, who has argued that, so far from excluding each other, database and narrative condition each other: "Because database can construct relational juxtapositions but is helpless to interpret or explain them, it needs narrative to make its results meaningful. Narrative, for its part, needs database in the computationally intensive culture of the new millennium to enhance its cultural authority and test the generality of its insights. If narrative often dissolves into database . . . database catalyzes and indeed demands narrative's reappearance as soon as meaning and interpretation are required" (2007, 1603). Manovich himself, in an argument that is far more nuanced than his most quoted claim suggests, has proposed a structuralist analogy whereby narrative derives its meaning syntagmatically, by ordering data in a sequence, whereas the database is in its fundamental structure paradigmatic, an inventory of all possible data in a particular field. Narrative, in this view, becomes a particular way of drawing on or "traversing" a database. The distinctiveness of contemporary culture in this respect would be that "database (the paradigm) is given material existence, while narrative (the syntagm) is dematerialised. . . . Paradigm is real; syntagm, virtual" (Manovich 2001, 231). Concretely, this implies that the data assembled in a database can be mobilized for a variety of cultural forms and aesthetic, administrative, or scientific genres—narrative among them.

Manovich here articulates a core principle of the database that undoubtedly distinguishes it from earlier forms of printed inventories or catalogs. But he understates the way in which the encoding of the data defines and constrains what kinds of mobilizations or traversals of the data collection are possible. Typically, items in a database are tagged with so-called metadata, classificatory tags, in such a way that they can be found and retrieved.[3] Information about biological species is no exception to this rule. Historian of science Geoffrey Bowker, an impassioned critic of many of the classification and archiving systems that characterize contemporary science, has pointed out that biodiversity databases typically include information on taxonomy, ecology, and conservation measures, but no category under which indigenous forms of knowledge about the natural world could be stored. This critique does not aim at which individual data do or do not get included in a particular database, but what is recordable as a matter of principle, and how these structural inclusions and exclusions shape the available information and cultural memory. As Bowker points out, the character of an archive "comes down to the question of what can and cannot be remembered. The archive, by remembering all and only a certain set of facts/discoveries/observations, consistently and actively engages in the forgetting of other sets" ([2005] 2008, 12). He elaborates:

> In general, what is not classified gets rendered invisible. . . . The negative telling is that things that do not get classified are not considered of economic, aesthetic, or philosophical importance—weeds, noncharismatic species, and indigenous knowledge in turn. The positive telling is that our databases provide a very good representation of our political economy broadly conceived: that which we can use through our current modes of interaction with nature and other cultures is well mirrored in our data structures. What gets excluded as the "other" is anything that does not support those modes of interaction. (153)

A more optimistic perspective on biodiversity databases has been proposed by political scientist Rafi Youatt, who argues that "a biodiversity census helps construct new ideas of a multilayered and multispecies global community" (2015, chap. 2). Youatt bases his argument on the French historian Michel Foucault's theory of "biopower," the classification and administration of human life that emerged in nineteenth-century societies with new forms of demographics, health management, insurance practices, and penal codes, among other things. Much more

3. Direct-text searches circumvent such tagging.

intrusively than the disciplinary regimes of earlier societies, biopower sought to shape modern citizens and to generate a psychologically interiorized system of self-regulation that made many of the overt demonstrations of power and punishment of earlier centuries superfluous. Foucault was most centrally concerned with the modern state's modes of exerting power over its citizens. Biodiversity databases can be understood as an extension of biopower to nonhumans, Youatt argues. But he also emphasizes that this makes central assumptions of the biopower concept problematic, since animals, plants, and microorganisms cannot be induced to think of themselves in terms of the species taxonomies that modern science and its databases privilege; the element of self-regulation, therefore, does not extend to them. And nonhuman subjects often exceed or contradict the scientific predictions made about them: Youatt mentions unexpected migrations, adaptations, and mutations, though not, oddly, hybridizations, which most obviously defy species categorizations as envisioned by biological databases. "Life itself escapes biopower," he therefore claims (chap. 2), and this resistance of the nonhuman to total human classification, which he theorizes in terms of Latour's Actor-Network-Theory, allows him to envision the role of biodiversity databases more constructively than Bowker does. Rather than functioning mostly as instruments of exclusion, in his view, they create a political space that does not correspond to any state: "A global biodiversity census might be understood as part of constructing a global biocitizenry and in forming a global ecopolitical community" (chap. 2).

These analyses of how the exclusions and inclusions of species databases are shaped by underlying cultural and political impulses have particular relevance for understanding Red Lists of endangered species as a specific subtype of biodiversity database. Red Lists, in addition to the usual biological and ecological information contained in general biodiversity databases, classify species according to their risk of extinction. As opposed to purely descriptive databases, they typically have normative and legal force in a state or country: for example, a species that is included in a Red List can be hunted or harvested only within certain limits, it cannot be traded, its habitat cannot be altered in any major way, and measures for its protection have to implemented. States, nations, and supranational organizations such as the European Union all maintain such Red Lists as the basis for endangered species laws and international treaties. Because of the economic impacts and cultural implications that listing or delisting a species can have, the process is dynamic and sometimes politically embattled, as national conflicts over the status of wolves in some western states in the United States and international conflicts over the status of particular whale species at the International Whaling Commission have vividly demonstrated in recent years. Additions to and subtractions from a Red List or changes in the status of a species register a history of such conflicts and of conservationist successes and failures.[4]

Arguably the most influential current Red List is that of the IUCN (International Union for the Conservation of Nature). As a global database that in 2015 included approximately seventy-seven thousand species, the IUCN Red List of Threatened Species is an unusual hybrid: with no legal force in and of itself, it has nevertheless become a standard reference work in conservation research and planning all over the world.[5] Through this process, it has acquired an indirect legal influence that has led its administrators to draw up meticulously detailed guidelines on how to use global information in local contexts (see Gärdenfors et al. 2001; Miller et al. 2007; Rodríguez 2008). While it focused originally only on endangered species, the IUCN Red List has over the past decade increasingly included "Least Concern" or LC species, that is, nonthreatened ones. As a consequence, it is gradually becoming a global biodiversity database, a "barometer of life," as the IUCN itself calls it (http://cmsdata.iucn.org/downloads/iucn_red_list_barometer_of_life.pdf).

But it retains from its original character as a Red List the classification of each species according to its risk of endangerment (see fig. 3). On the IUCN Red List website, the category that a particular species belongs to appears highlighted in a red drop shape at the top of the entry, as in figure 4.

As is clear from figure 3, the taxonomy includes two categories, Not Evaluated and Data Deficient, referring to species for which no data have been collected or data are insufficient to determine the species' risk status; two categories, Least Concern and Near Threatened, for species that are faring well; three categories of endangerment, Vulnerable,

4. One of the most often discussed cases of conflict over the addition of a (conspicuously uncharismatic) species to a Red List was the listing of the snail darter, a small fish, just after the creation of the Endangered Species Act. Protracted battles ensued around a major dam construction project on the part of the Tennessee Valley Authority. For detailed accounts, see Ehrlich and Ehrlich (1981, 218–222) and Murchison (2007). For a brief analysis of how Red Lists have functioned in the German context and how their changes reflect cultural values, see Reichholf (2005, 223–224).

5. See Hoffmann et al. (2008, 114) for a discussion of the rapidly increasing citation of the IUCN Red List in conservation research.

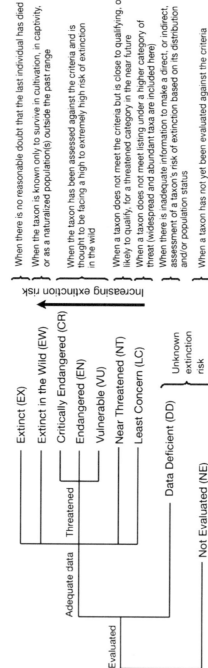

FIGURE 3 IUCN Red List classification of species according to risk. *Source:* Hoffmann et al. (2008, 115).

FIGURE 4 Risk Classification in the IUCN Red List. *Source:* Adapted from the IUCN Red List of Threatened Species, www.iucnredlist.org.

NOT EVALUATED	DATA DEFICIENT	LEAST CONCERN	NEAR THREATENED	VULNERABLE	ENDANGERED	CRITICALLY ENDANGERED	EXTINCT IN THE WILD	EXTINCT
NE	DD	LC	NT	VU	EN	CR	EW	EX

Endangered, and Critically Endangered; and two categories of extinction, Extinct and Extinct in the Wild. Obviously, a narrative of risk and of value attribution is hardwired into these very categories, where extinction and endangerment are defined positively, whereas species that thrive are tagged by means of negation or approximation: "near threatened" and "least concern"—as opposed to, say, labels such as "safe," "stable," or "increasing." In conservation biologists' jargon, a species that moves from Vulnerable to Near Threatened is "downgraded," whereas one that moves from Vulnerable to Endangered is "upgraded," in an odd reversal of the value judgments that usually come with upgrading and downgrading. Scientists have also pointed out that it is far easier to raise research funds for a species that is classified in any of the endangered categories than it is for one that is tagged "Data Deficient," although the latter may need research far more urgently. The metadata structure and the way in which it is socially used therefore imply a hierarchy of values that places the greatest investment in endangered species, with "Critically Endangered" at the top. The more endangered a species is, the more valued it becomes, in a logic that resonates both with the capitalist valuation of scarce resources and with the cultural fascination, inherited from the Romantic age, with impending death—the aura of "the last." The categorization structure of the IUCN's database, in other words, is underwritten by some of the same elegiac impulses that are also dominant in the literature and art concerning endangered species (see chapter 1).

An underlying narrative of decline shapes not only the IUCN's risk labels, but also the quantitative criteria that define them. The elaborate structure of nested risk classifications that the current IUCN Red List relies on did not, of course, come into being overnight. Red Data Books, when they were first conceived in the 1960s, listed species without much accompanying information and used simple numbered categories: Category 1, Category 2, with Category 1 being "Very rare and believed to be decreasing in numbers" (Hoffmann et al. 2008, 114; Mrosovsky 2003, 7). In 1968 the categories were changed to Endangered, Rare, and Depleted, with various modifications to the definitions of these labels and the criteria for their application following in the 1970s and 1980s. The classifications then were mostly based on experts' commonsense judgments, with no precise quantitative justifications required for placing a species into a particular category (Mrosovsky 2003, 7–8). In the 1980s, as biodiversity loss moved to the forefront of public awareness, this approximative approach increasingly came to seem unsatisfactory, and an elaborate quantitative system was developed and introduced in 1994, including a new category, Critically Endangered, which was meant to draw attention to species on the brink of extinction (Hoffmann et al. 2008, 114; Mrosovsky 2003, 8). The five core classifications of endangered species are now accompanied by precise quantitative measures that are meant to reduce speculative judgments and ensure transparency, on one hand, and to minimize inconsistency across different experts' assessments, on the other, so that species can be compared more easily (Hoffmann et al. 2008, 114).

But narrative, in some cases, has returned through the back door precisely as the consequence of this quantification. While some species entries in the IUCN Red List provide only basic bare-bones data without much explanation, especially in the case of the numerous Data Deficient species, others include elaborate textual accounts. As table 1 highlights, many of the text-intensive species are mammals. Quite a few of the narratives that profile these species explore their spatial distribution in detail. The IUCN Red List's assessment system has to address endemic species with restricted ranges as well as globally distributed species, whose multiple populations may face radically different probabilities of extinction. Some of the species narratives therefore owe their length to the different populations that need to be covered. This is the case, for example, for the two marine turtles among the top twenty-five, the hawksbill turtle (no. 4) and the leatherback turtle (no. 17). But the entry for *Eretmochelys imbricata*, the hawksbill turtle, mainly owes its length to meticulously researched details of the history of the tortoise-shell trade in the nineteenth and twentieth centuries, especially in and around Japan. Why such a foray into history to determine the current status of a species?

As it turns out, the historical narrative is meant to compensate for unavailable quantitative data. A Critically Endangered species, according to the IUCN's criteria, is one whose population has declined more than 80 percent over the last ten years or three generations (whichever is longer), with a generation defined as time to maturity plus 10 years (IUCN Species Survival Commission [2001] 2012, 16). This rule, reasonable enough for many kinds of organisms, raises considerable difficulties in the case of sea turtles, whose longevity in some species includes a 30- to 40-year run-up to sexual maturity. To document an 80 percent decline over three generations, researchers would need to have population figures from 100 or even 130 years in the past at their disposal (Mrosovsky 2003, 14–17; Godfrey and Godley 2008, 156–157; Seminoff and Shanker 2008, 57–58). Needless to say, they do not; hawksbill turtles, with many globally dispersed subpopulations, are challenging to count even in the present day, let alone in the 1880s, when there was

Table 1 The IUCN Red List's 25 most text-intensive species

Rank	Character count	Common name	Species name	Family	Order	Class	Phylum	Kingdom
1	65081	sambar	*Rusa unicolor*	Cervidae	Cetartiodactyla	Mammalia	Chordata	Animalia
2	56790	West African manatee	*Trichechus senegalensis*	Trichechidae	Sirenia	Mammalia	Chordata	Animalia
3	49983	West Indian manatee	*Trichechus manatus*	Trichechidae	Sirenia	Mammalia	Chordata	Animalia
4	47352	hawksbill turtle	*Eretmochelys imbricata*	Cheloniidae	Testudines	Reptilia	Chordata	Animalia
5	44993	markhor	*Capra falconeri*	Bovidae	Cetartiodactyla	Mammalia	Chordata	Animalia
6	43549	hog deer	*Axis porcinus*	Cervidae	Cetartiodactyla	Mammalia	Chordata	Animalia
7	42653	argali	*Ovis ammon*	Bovidae	Cetartiodactyla	Mammalia	Chordata	Animalia
8	42068	large-antlered muntjac	*Muntiacus vuquangensis*	Cervidae	Cetartiodactyla	Mammalia	Chordata	Animalia
9	39706	island fox	*Urocyon littoralis*	Canidae	Carnivora	Mammalia	Chordata	Animalia
10	38963	gaur	*Bos gaurus*	Bovidae	Cetartiodactyla	Mammalia	Chordata	Animalia
11	38915	scalloped hammerhead	*Sphyrna lewini*	Sphyrnidae	Carcharhiniformes	Chondrichthyes	Chordata	Animalia
12	38398	Ganges River dolphin	*Platanista gangetica*	Platanistidae	Cetartiodactyla	Mammalia	Chordata	Animalia
13	38022	Eld's deer	*Rucervus eldii*	Cervidae	Cetartiodactyla	Mammalia	Chordata	Animalia
14	37569	American eel	*Anguilla rostrata*	Anguillidae	Anguilliformes	Actinopterygii	Chordata	Animalia
15	36678	waterwheel	*Aldrovanda vesiculosa*	Droseraceae	Nepenthales	Magnoliopsida	Tracheophyta	Plantae
16	35071	mouflon	*Ovis orientalis*	Bovidae	Cetartiodactyla	Mammalia	Chordata	Animalia
17	34942	leatherback	*Dermochelys coriacea*	Dermochelyidae	Testudines	Reptilia	Chordata	Animalia
18	34791	shortfin mako	*Isurus oxyrinchus*	Lamnidae	Lamniformes	Chondrichthyes	Chordata	Animalia
19	34559	spurdog	*Squalus acanthias*	Squalidae	Squaliformes	Chondrichthyes	Chordata	Animalia
20	34193	European eel	*Anguilla anguilla*	Anguillidae	Anguilliformes	Actinopterygii	Chordata	Animalia
21	33433	tope	*Galeorhinus galeus*	Triakidae	Carcharhiniformes	Chondrichthyes	Chordata	Animalia
22	31207	humpback whale	*Megaptera novaeangliae*	Balaenopteridae	Cetartiodactyla	Mammalia	Chordata	Animalia
23	29546	Patagonian huemul	*Hippocamelus bisulcus*	Cervidae	Cetartiodactyla	Mammalia	Chordata	Animalia
24	28896	Nubian ibex	*Capra nubiana*	Bovidae	Cetartiodactyla	Mammalia	Chordata	Animalia
25	27505	Clanwilliam sandfish	*Labeo seeberi*	Cyprinidae	Cypriniformes	Actinopterygii	Chordata	Animalia

no compelling social interest motivating such a census. To be credible, the quantitative assessment therefore turns to narrative history for data from the tortoise-shell trade, which stand in as a proxy for actual species counts.[6]

On this basis, hawksbill turtles are classified as Critically Endangered, even though about 2 million of them are thought to exist globally. While some regional populations are under threat, none of the experts believe hawksbill turtles are at any imminent risk of extinction. Nevertheless, the Critically Endangered category lumps them together with such species as the kakapo (*Strigops habroptila*), of which 126 individuals survived in 2012, or the Baiji dolphin (*Lipotes vexillifer*), whose numbers have dropped so low that it may already have gone extinct. Some scientists have therefore advised the Marine Turtle Specialist Group, which carries out these assessments, to discontinue using IUCN criteria: "Revised criteria for assessing risk of extinction of sea turtles are needed. They should not rely on unobtainable historical data; rather they should emphasize recent, current and perceived threats in the near future" (Godfrey and Godley 2008, 157). Precisely the quantification of risk assessment, in other words, sometimes forces scientists to generate a narrative of decline that may be of dubious value in evaluating which species truly face a risk of extinction in the present and determining which conservation measures are most urgently needed.[7]

A certain kind of narrative structure, then—a focus on nature in decline, on decrease, disappearance, and the past—is hardwired into Red List categories, criteria, and the stories they make scientists tell. While Red List data do not superficially seem to be structured so as to elicit the same kind of emotion that popular-scientific elegies for vanishing species in text or image aim at, they nevertheless invoke a similar storytelling template. The focus on species decline, on last specimens and the value of biological

6. As Seminoff and Shanker point out, the availability of historical data is even more limited for marine turtles that, unlike the leatherback and the hawksbill, have no widespread economic uses (2008, 57).

7. In some of its most recent revisions, the IUCN has begun to address this problem. The entry for the leatherback turtle, revised in 2013, acknowledges the lack of historical data from a century or more ago and instead assumes that the population abundance three generations ago was similar to the first observed abundance (www.iucnredlist.org /details/6494/0, under "Assessment"). As a consequence, the overall classification of the leatherback turtle has been "downgraded" to Vulnerable, compared to its assessments as Endangered in 1996 and Critically Endangered in 2000. The profile indicates, however, that different leatherback populations are facing very divergent degrees of risk that are difficult to sum up in one global label.

rarity, links the Red List to the species elegy and highlights that they are different cultural forms expressing the same underlying perspective.

Yet it would undoubtedly be too simplistic to read Red Lists as merely another version of elegy. Species databases also offer the potential of desentimentalizing extinction, especially when they do not limit their focus to endangered species but include a broader range of taxa. However fraught with difficulty the project of mapping all of the world's species with one set of criteria may be, it redirects our attention from the fate of individual species to developments that affect tens of thousands of them. Typically, this more general perspective takes the form of statistics (table 2).

Obviously, table 2 reflects the IUCN's focus on risk and endangerment, but it also seeks to open up a view of the panoramic whole. It tells two stories. One is the story of an epic struggle for the preservation of biodiversity that results from no fewer than 38 percent of assessed species being classified as endangered, a truly frightening number. The other story is about the focus on particular kinds of species: 77,340 out of the approximately 1.8 million of species scientists have identified had been studied by 2015 (and 22,784 of them classified by the IUCN as threatened with extinction) (IUCN Red List of Threatened Species 2015). "Around 41 000 (2%) of currently described species worldwide have been evaluated using the IUCN Red List categories and criteria. Only 4% of plants have been evaluated globally against the criteria," Hoffmann et al. pointed out in 2008 (121). The selection of species that have been assessed is subject to an obvious "taxonomic bias" that privileges certain kinds of species and disfavors others. As table 2 shows, all known mammal and bird species have been assessed for their risk of extinction—several times over in the case of birds. Amphibians have also fared well, but reptiles and fishes have received far less attention. Only very small fractions of the insect, arachnid, fern, and mushroom taxa have ever been evaluated at all: 1,259 out of 950,000 insect species, 32 out of 98,000 arachnid species, just 1 out of 30,000 mushroom species (the number of mushrooms had climbed to 18 by 2014—an improvement, but still a small fraction of the total number [http://cmsdata.iucn .org/downloads/iucn_red_list_barometer_of_life.pdf]). The IUCN itself is quite aware of this problem, stating in its *Strategic Plan 2013–2020* that "assessments of plants, fungi and invertebrates need to be substantially increased to represent the diversity of life adequately" and that this will require "reaching out to groups of biologists who are studying taxa that have not previously been included on the Red List" (IUCN Red List Committee 2013, 7).

Table 2 State of the world's species. Numbers and proportions of species assessed and species assessed as threatened on the 2008 IUCN Red List by major taxonomic group.

	Estimated number of described species	Number of species evaluated	Number of threatened species	Number threatened, as % of species described	Number threatened, as % of species evaluated
Vertebrates					
Mammals	5,488	45,488	1,141	21	21
Birds	9,990	9,900	1,222	12	12
Reptiles	8,734	1,385	423	5	31
Amphibians	6,347	6,260	1,905	30	30
Fishes	30,700	3,481	1,275	4	27
Subtotal	**61,259**	**26,604**	**5,966**	**10**	**22**
Invertebrates					
Insects	950,000	1,259	626	0	50
Molluscs	81,000	2,212	978	1	44
Crustaceans	40,000	1,735	606	2	35
Corals	2,175	856	235	11	27
Arachnids	98,000	32	18	0	56
Velvet Worms	165	11	9	5	82
Horseshoe Crabs	4	4	0	0	0
Others	61,040	52	24	0	46
Subtotal	**1,232,384**	**6,161**	**2,496**	**0.20**	**41**
Plants					
Mosses	16,000	95	82	1	86
Ferns and allies	12,838	211	139	1	66
Gvmnosperms	980	910	323	33	35
Dicotyledons	199,350	9,624	7,122	4	74
Monocotyledons	59,300	1,155	782	1	68
Green Algae	3,962	2	0	0	0
Red Algae	6,076	58	9	0	16
Subtotal	**298,506**	**12,055**	**8,457**	**3**	**70**
Others					
Lichens	17,000	2	2	0	100
Mushrooms	30,000	1	1	0	100
Brown Algae	3,040	15	6	0	40
Subtotal	**50,040**	**18**	**9**	**0.02**	**50**
Total	**1,642,189**	**44,838**	**16,928**	**1**	**88**

The IUCN's 2008 overview of species that have been evaluated for their risk status shows clear taxonomic bias toward certain kinds of vertebrates. *Source*: Hilton-Taylor et al. 2008, 17.

As I pointed out in chapter 1, this means that broad claims about species decline rely on incomplete data, though that incompletion is hardly grounds for optimism. If more species were assessed, the overall picture might turn out to be worse than it seems now. A recent study that sought to assess, by means of alternative proxy procedures, extinction rates in taxa that are not well covered by the IUCN Red List suggested that "the current Red List approach grossly underestimates the extinction crisis for invertebrates" (Régnier et al. 2015, 7765). Such comments underscore the potential and the limits of the logic of proxy or synecdoche, which assumes that species can stand in for biodiversity in general and that the species that have been studied convey a broadly accurate picture of the current status of nonhuman species at large (see chapter 1). Neither of these is an unproblematic assumption, as Régnier et al.'s study and many others indicate. Some scientists have suggested if not replacing, then at least complementing Red Lists of endangered species with green lists of stable or increasing ones (Imboden 1987) or blue lists of recovered ones (Gigon et al. 2000). In recognition of such issues, the IUCN has initiated a project called IUCN Red List of Ecosystems to complement the Red List of Threatened Species. The new list focuses not only on ecosystems that are at risk, but also those that do well as a result of successful management (CEM-IUCN & Provita 2012). The IUCN has also created a Green List of Protected Areas that foregrounds conservation successes.[8] Such projects begin to shift the proxy logic of endangered species discourse and to move it away from its elegiac tenor so as to emphasize more strongly its epic and encyclopedic elements.

3. Red List Art

Global biodiversity databases and Red Lists of endangered species, then, combine elements of the elegiac narrative of nature's decline, built into the basic metadata, with an epic aspiration toward documenting a global struggle in which the future of life and the planet itself are at stake. I showed at the beginning of this chapter how a combination of elegy and enumeration also occurs in fictional and nonfictional texts, even though the elegiac mode usually dominates. In the visual arts, the enumerative mode tends to take on an even more central role. Over the past two decades, painters and photographers have frequently created visual inventories to capture the magnitude of the biodiversity crisis, often reproducing them in coffee-table-size books that portray endangered and extinct species. Tim Flannery and Peter Schouten, for example, have documented such species in meticulously realist paintings in *A Gap in Nature: Discovering the World's Extinct Animals* (2001), while Susan Middleton and David Liittschwager's *Witness: Endangered Species*

---

8. In a textual analogue to such blue or green lists, Jane Goodall, Thane Maynard, and Gail Hudson's *Hope for Animals and Their World: How Endangered Species Are Being Rescued from the Brink* (2009) focuses on recovery stories.

of North America (1994) and *Remains of a Rainbow: Rare Plants and Animals of Hawaii* ([2001] 2003) portray endangered species through photography.[9]

The work of the painter Isabella Kirkland is also clearly inspired by scientific taxonomy and cataloging. One of her series of paintings, entitled *Nova*, portrays species newly discovered over the past twenty years. Another series, called *Taxa*, consists of six paintings, with the titles *Descendant, Ascendant, Trade, Collection, Back,* and *Gone,* which represent a total of about four hundred species. "Almost every plant or animal is measured, photographed, drawn, and observed first hand, either live or from preserved materials. All are painted at life-size to ensure accuracy of scale. . . . The paintings explore how current biodiversity science can inform art-making and how art objects contribute to both political and scientific dialogues," Kirkland explains on her website, in what amounts to a manifesto for science-inspired art (http://isabellakirkland .com/paintings/taxa.html).

Kirkland sometimes works in the tradition of John James Audubon. But in the *Taxa* series, she draws on the conventions of the still life, which usually captures objects—often fruits, flowers, and edible animals—in interior spaces. In the paintings entitled *Descendant* (1999) and *Gone* (2004), which portray endangered and extinct species, respectively, the genre of the still life or *nature morte* (dead nature), as it is called in French, acquires a particularly literal meaning. *Descendant* (plate 1) shows "plants and animals . . . in decline in the mainland United States, Hawaii, or Central America" (http://isabellakirkland.com/paint ings/taxa-descendant.html). The stepped display suggests a staircase or a florist's shop window, and this impression is reinforced by the presentation of endangered plants as cut flowers in a vase. Even though the vase is barely visible among the greenery, it serves as a centering device for many other species, such as the snails crawling on it or the birds that are perched on the flowers. What looks at first glance like a fairly conventional painting of flowers in a vase in fact plays on the domestic conventions of the still life: so far from decorative garden flowers, the plants on display here are endangered wild ones, an emphasis that resonates with environmentalists' recent reflections on globally domesticated nature.

9. See also the two quite different editions of Errol Fuller's book *Extinct Birds* from 1987 and 2001, which are collections of illustrations and photographs of extinct birds species from a wide range of artists and historical moments. The photos of Mitsuaki Iwago in Bradley Trevor Greive's *Priceless: The Vanishing Beauty of a Fragile Planet* (2003) include both endangered and nonendangered species under the title's elegiac premise.

The aesthetic possibilities of the still life in the representation of extinction emerge even more clearly in *Gone* (2004; plate 2). The tabletop, the vase, the silver tray, and the glass containers all insistently foreground still-life conventions that, as in *Descendant,* bring the extinct species into the domestic realm. But within this stylistic framework, the different kinds of plants and animals—meticulously identified through a numbered species key on Kirkland's website—are presented in strikingly different fashion. Some of the birds, such as the Carolina Parakeet, the passenger pigeon, and the 'akialoa' are shown alive and perching as they would be in a natural-history painting. Other bird species are made visible through their eggs (the great auk, the pink-headed duck) or their feathers (the double-banded argus pheasant). The fish, by contrast, are dead and laid out on a tray as if they were meant to be served at dinner, with the exception of a few smaller species that swim in the vase as if it were simultaneously an aquarium, an impression that the mussels at the bottom reinforce. The Tasmanian tiger on the left is represented by a skull; dead reptiles with identifying tags on their legs float in two glass containers filled with a clear preserving liquid—both examples of what would usually be museum exhibits. But one lizard perches on the vase quite alive, along with frogs, shrews, and mice sitting on the table top. The blue buck, by contrast, is represented only by its horns.

This mixture of the living and the dead, of whole bodies and mere parts, combines realism with antirealism. In keeping with Kirkland's principle of painting to scale, species that are too large to fit on a table are symbolized by body parts. But the fact that the decorative vase doubles as aquarium gives a tinge of surrealism to the scene, as does the display of some animals in the manner of a dish and of others in the fashion of tagged museum specimens. These details allude to different social institutions and cultural habits, encouraging the viewer to reflect on the divergent taxonomies—scientific, gastronomic, historic, museal, aesthetic—that frame our perceptions of natural organisms and enable extinction to mean different things in the various contexts. In addition, the painting brings together species that would never encounter each other in any real ecosystem, through a cross-geographic collage of sorts. It combines, in other words, a reflection on the database of nature with a reflection on the database of culture and their different classifying systems of fauna and flora, and on the meanings of extinction in different cultural spheres.

Joel Sartore, whose work has often appeared in *National Geographic* and, in 2009, in a book called *Rare: Portraits of America's Endangered Species,* has taken thousands of photos and organized them in collec-

FIGURE 5 Joel Sartore, *Dusky Sea-Side Sparrow* (2009). Photograph © Joel Sartore, joelsartore.com. Reproduced by permission of the artist.

tions to document biodiversity and endangerment. Some of his photographs exhibit the power of elegy even as they point to the database as a different mode of engaging with species extinction, such as his photograph of the last dusky seaside sparrow from a series called *Last Ones: Threatened and Endangered Species*. The photograph appeared in a feature article in *National Geographic* in January 2009 (fig. 5).

The photo foregrounds how a living organism is transformed into a museum specimen, preserved in a jar and tagged for the archives; and the bird's isolation on the white background, in a jar and in fluid, visually concretizes the loss of habitat that caused its demise. At the same time, it is difficult not to feel compassion for this small, pathetic, dead bird, and Sartore's explanatory caption detailing that this male called Orange, the last dusky seaside sparrow, died in 1987, reinforces its elegiac appeal. "To see the last of any species in a glass jar of museum preservative is an absolute outrage to me. To know that it will happen again is truly heartbreaking," Sartore comments (2009, n.p.).

Most of Sartore's numerous photos of endangered or extinct species are more starkly desentimentalized. In the majority of cases, he presents the animals in crisp, beautifully detailed portraits against a stark black or white background—not, usually, in any kind of habitat. In *Rare*, he explicitly links this technique to the Endangered Species Act: "By photographing the most endangered of our plants and animals, I can make

FIGURE 6 Joel Sartore, *Delhi Sands Flower-Loving Fly* (2009). Photograph © Joel Sartore, joelsartore.com. Reproduced by permission of the artist.

the most dramatic plea to get folks to stop and take a look at the pieces and parts that we're throwing away. Putting them on black or white backgrounds gives all equal weight and consideration, from snail to sea turtle. . . . On the bright side, the United States has the Endangered Species Act (ESA). The law is designed to protect all our plants and animals, no matter how great or small" (2009, n.p.).

Sartore's zoological interests reach across taxa and include many invertebrates, sometimes also shot in a portrait style unusual for such species (fig. 6; plate 3). This technique pulls readers' emotion and attention in two different directions. Shooting an animal portrait-style, especially one that is not usually considered charismatic, generates the kind of attention that is usually reserved for humans and other primates, and it individualizes creatures that are not normally considered capable of individuality. But the equal treatment of vastly different species in Sartore's photos makes the viewer lose a sense of their size and proportion, and the empty backgrounds often isolate the subject to the point where it appears artifactual and decorative rather than biologically embedded. The photos give no sense of habitat or ecosystemic connectedness, a strategy that may seem at odds with the environmentalist emphasis on locality and rootedness. But that, I would argue, is the point: Sartore's photography seeks to deromanticize species and their disappearance by shifting the conservationist appeal to a mostly aesthetic level. Sartore's work is a visual Red List, documenting the extent of the mass-extinction crisis through the juxtaposition of dozens, in some cases hundreds, of photographs. The individual photos in his series *Rare, The Vanishing: Amphibian Extinction,* and *Fragile Nature,* among others, are joined together less by an obvious elegiac narrative than by the logic of inventory and database that conveys its meaning more through the sheer accumulation of numbers, a sort of numerical sublime, than through the expressiveness of any individual datapoint.[10]

4. ARKive.org

As Sartore's work and that of other photographers such as Susan Middleton and David Liittschwager demonstrates, the boundary between database and database art becomes porous as artists seek to articulate their sense of nonhuman life pervasively at risk. As if to confirm this close association, Sartore's photographs have actually been included in a visual biodiversity database, a project called *ARKive: Images of Life on Earth.* This database was officially launched in 2003 as the brainchild of the (by then deceased) former head of the BBC Natural History unit, Christopher Parsons, and the documentary filmmaker David Attenborough. Focusing on species defined as endangered by the IUCN Red List, ARKive seeks to compile the best photographic and film material in existence that documents a species's appearance, habitat, and behavior, with the explicit goal of fostering conservation awareness, education, and engagement.

Attenborough's video introduction of the project (www.arkive.org /about) as well as the mission statement on the website do not define ARKive primarily as a repository of information about particular species, although many of the entries are in fact detailed and well-written portraits. Rather, Attenborough emphasizes the emotional and aesthetic impact of visual representations of biodiversity. Why should we care about endangered species? Attenborough himself never answers this question explicitly in the video, but the captions interpolated between his comments do, emphasizing the sense of wonder that visual portraits of wildlife inspire. The assumption is that the visual materials will defamiliarize

---

10. This database aesthetic in contemporary art is not, of course, limited to works with an environmental orientation. For perspectives on other types of artworks, see Vesna (2007).

nature so as to highlight its beauty and strangeness and thereby create the critical distance that enables new forms of awareness. This goal is quite different from the aims of other databases that seek to convey information and thereby to encourage familiarity rather than the estrangement that ARKive's mission statement implies. Given this framework, it is no surprise that some of Joel Sartore's photographs, which rely on a similar aesthetic, have made their way into this database, among the works of the thirty-five hundred photographers and filmmakers who have been selected by ARKive's Accessions Advisory Panel.

Attenborough's introductory video uses its own filmic devices to highlight this defamiliarization strategy. Juxtaposed shots of different species—mostly animals, even though the database also includes plants, fungi, algae, and other taxa—look at first like the standard sequences that introduce nature documentaries on television. But at a certain moment, they speed up so much that the individual species are no longer recognizable, and what is left instead is a general impression of astonishing variety based on the infinite numbers suggested by high speed. Google Earth–style zooming shots are similarly disorienting; they move too fast for the viewer really to grasp what part of the world, what location or habitat the camera moves in on. Quite intentionally, ARKive here articulates its own sense of the global through the alternation of shots of the planet as a whole with precipitous "falls" forward, of a frog in one case and a man in another, into particular locations and species.

ARKive's FAQ section gives another twist to this perspective. It defines the database's mission as a "'virtual' conservation effort—gathering together films, photographs and audio recordings of the world's species":

> Continued habitat destruction and the rise in extinction rates also mean that for many species, films, photographs and audio recordings may soon be all that remains. They are, therefore, important historical and scientific records of the species they depict.
>
> This material is, however, scattered around the world, held in a variety of commercial, specialist and private collections, much of it inaccessible to the general public and unavailable for scientific and educational use. Like the wildlife they depict, the images of these rare species are themselves endangered, with no guarantee that they will survive for future generations. Many records have already been lost forever, with companies basing storage decisions on commercial, rather than scientific, cultural or historical values. (www.arkive.org/about/faqs.html#qd1)

It is not just biodiversity that emerges as endangered here, but a whole cultural history of humans' engagement with fauna and flora that ARKive also seeks to preserve. Nature appears doubly endangered through the disappearance of biological forms themselves *and* of the records that preserved the memory of these forms, in a move reminiscent of Jennifer Price's comment on the loss of the passenger pigeon and the loss of stories about that loss (cf. chapter 1). ARKive could not express more clearly that the scientific venture of saving endangered species is itself part of a larger venture of understanding and remembering cultural frameworks for understanding other species.

5. The Red List and Homo sapiens

Scientific, popular-scientific, and aesthetic genres, as this analysis has sought to show, strive to represent the current mass extinction of species by means of two quite different modes, the elegiac narrative about nature's decline and the epic cataloging of species at risk. At the same time that elements of elegy shape certain aspects of the world's most influential Red List, the database mode has made its way into the visual and verbal arts, with often striking if sometimes uneasy or contradictory results. The broader implications of the database perspective emerge most strikingly when it becomes a way of looking at humans themselves, as it does when the IUCN includes Homo sapiens in its Red List with an entry of its own. The IUCN classifies our species as Least Concern, that is, not endangered: "Listed as Least Concern as the species is very widely distributed, adaptable, currently increasing, and there are no major threats resulting in an overall population decline." Under "Major Threats," the Red List informs us that "there are currently no major threats to humans, although some subpopulations may be experiencing localized declines as a result of disease, drought, war, natural disasters, and other factors." And under the heading "Conservation Actions," the IUCN assures us that "at present, no conservation measures are required. Humans are present in numerous protected areas throughout their range," a range that includes not only all continents on Earth but also the International Space Station (www.iucnredlist.org/apps/redlist /details/136584/0).

This inclusion of Homo sapiens in a biodiversity database, however counterintuitive it may seem at first sight, is a significant gesture politically and philosophically in an age that is now increasingly referred to as the Anthropocene or "Age of Humans." When I have shown this Red List entry in presentations, the audience invariably started to laugh; the laughter seemed equal parts amusement and unease at this unexpected perspective on humans and the leveling of differences between humans and other species that it implies. As Rafi Youatt has argued at a theoretical level, "the global biodiversity census offers a way of reterritorializing the category of 'human,' grounding it relative to other species and to the wide variety of ecosystems that make up the global ecosystem" (2015, chap. 2). The IUCN's Homo sapiens entry in particular signals that the challenge confronting humans in the face of the global biodiversity crisis is to reconceive themselves posthumanistically as a species among species, a process begun with Darwin's theory of evolution but at this point requiring a new translation into multispecies ethics and politics. Millet's novels and Sartore's photographs, as well as databases such as the IUCN Red List of Threatened Species and ARKive.org, all directly or indirectly seek to articulate such a new sense of humans' relation to other species beyond the story of nature's decline. Databases may be one of the most useful tools we have in this effort, in that they make it obvious that narratives of decline are only one way of traversing or mobilizing the life data they inventory. The data themselves, these works make clear, are deeply informed by narrative through their metadata structuring, and what they mean emerges only through the stories we tell about them.

3

The Legal Lives of Endangered Species:
Biodiversity Laws and Culture

In 1984 the German satirical magazine *Titanic* featured a photo of a grove of trees, one of the trunks prominently displaying a yellow warning sign with the inscription, "Forest Dieback Prohibited—The Federal Government." "Incredible! Bonn saves the forests!" exclaims the accompanying faux-sensationalist title (fig. 7). Mocking the idea that governmental bureaucracies actually solve environmental problems rather than just wave statutes at them, *Titanic* also uses the joke to raise other questions: Who or what caused the acid rain that was then decimating forests across northern Europe? Who could be called on to remedy the problem? By what means could forests be restored? Yellow warning signs of the kind displayed on the tree trunk normally target humans, of course, whereas the prohibition here satirically seems to warn the dying trees themselves that their deaths would break federal law—as if trees could read, as if the law-abiding citizens among them could abstain from their own decay, and as if the violators could be prosecuted if caught in their flagrantly illegal demise.

Titanic's jab at the inefficiency of legal bureaucracies in tackling urgent environmental crises invites us to consider the role of environmental laws in protecting and prolonging the lives of animals, plants, and other nonhuman

FIGURE 7 *Bonn rettet den Wald!* (Bonn saves the forests). From *Titanic* 12 (1984). Reproduced by permission of Titanic Verlag, Georg-Büchner-Verlagsbuchhandlung GmbH & Co.

organisms. It also challenges us to examine how such laws form part of the stories that cultural communities tell about themselves, including stories about what is at risk and what is of enough value to deserve protection. Laws to protect biodiversity in general or endangered species in particular often go hand-in-hand with biodiversity databases and Red Lists (discussed in chapter 2), which typically list the species to which the laws apply. When and why are laws passed in particular countries or regions to protect nonhuman species from human-inflicted harm? What conflicts are these laws meant to solve, and what conflicts do they in turn give rise to? What nonhuman and human constituents do they benefit? What stories are such laws meant to tell about the society that promulgates them? What stories do their application and change over time tell?[1] Addressing these questions from the viewpoint of literary and cultural studies is particularly interesting because it is often assumed that biodiversity legislation, one of the most international areas of law, is more or less identical around the globe. International treaties and conventions loom large in the protection of endangered species, and since so many nations are signatories to CITES, the Convention on International Trade in Endangered Species of Wild Fauna and Flora (1973), and the Convention on Biological Diversity (1992), the argument goes, biodiversity laws resemble each other even though their implementations may vary.

It is true that countries and organizations that subscribe to international treaties have to make their own laws and regulations conform to these frameworks, and a good deal of legislative work over the past half century has gone into adapting national and state laws to international agreements. But when one compares actual legal texts and their backgrounds, biodiversity laws turn out to differ from one another in surprising ways, and they are passed and adjusted at particular historical moments for quite divergent reasons. At the same time, comparative studies of these laws by legal scholars are relatively rare. While an enormous amount of scholarship and commentary has focused on the U.S. Endangered Species Act as well as on the biodiversity directives of the European Union and the national laws of some other countries, comparative approaches have remained few in number. Undertaking such a comparison not as a legal but as a cultural scholar, I have found many of the comments and insights of legal experts enormously helpful as I have focused my analysis on the narratives implicit in laws about biodiversity. How do the stories these laws tell about endangered species relate to those that are told in popular-scientific books, novels, photographs, poems, and documentary films (see chapter 1)? How do they interact with those that underlie biodiversity databases and Red Lists of threatened species (see chapter 2)? In other words, I approach biodiversity laws as one of several rhetorical genres through which social collectives express their concern

---

1. The classical treatment of how natural objects function in the legal discourse of the United States is Christopher D. Stone's *Should Trees Have Standing? Law, Morality, and the Environment* ([1972] 2010).

about nonhuman species. Legal texts allow us to trace why and how these communities see the fate of nonhuman species as part of their own identity and history, and—given the institutional power of legal texts to shape and enforce social practices, which distinguishes them from the texts and databases discussed in earlier chapters—how they envision the best possible relation between humans and nonhumans now and in the future.

With these concerns in mind, this chapter compares four different laws for biodiversity protection. I begin (in section 1) with the Endangered Species Act of the United States, not because it is the oldest, the most important, the most effective, or the most typical law of its kind— it may be none of these—but simply because some of its basic assumptions are most likely to be familiar to American readers and to environmentalists in other countries. Section 2 contrasts the ESA with the German Bundesnaturschutzgesetz (Federal Nature Protection Act) to show how even in what is often lumped together as "the West" or the "global north," histories and assumptions about biodiversity conservation vary considerably. The first comprehensive national law for the protection of nature was passed in 1935 by the National Socialist regime and was maintained, essentially unchanged, by the Federal Republic of Germany until 1976. It changed substantially afterward in ways that I will briefly outline so as to emphasize that today, the German law protects biodiversity rather than endangered species, and it protects endangered species for the sake of conserving culturally defined landscapes rather than habitats for the sake of species. Section 3 segues to the biodiversity conservation directives of the European Union, which have reshaped the laws of Germany as well as those of all other EU nations, even as some of their language and assumptions veer away from the German emphasis on landscape in favor of a more scientific vocabulary as they seek to create a sense of shared transnational patrimony. Section 4 moves the focus to Bolivia, an extremely multiethnic country that has recently redefined itself as an explicitly "plurinational" state and has passed, in 2009, a new constitution that extends significant new rights not only to indigenous communities, but also to the Earth itself. Over the past few years, the legal lives of nonhuman species in Bolivia have unfolded in the tension between the new rights, participation, and autonomy of indigenous communities, on one hand, and, on the other hand, a leftist government that, in seeking to reappropriate control of the nation's resources from foreign corporations, has itself come into conflict with the communities it originally empowered. While a good deal of this conflict is playing itself out around the extraction of oil, gas, and other raw materials, bio-diversity has become an additional arena of contention in the struggle over resources, indigenous traditions, and the search for a new national self-definition.

As this brief preview already indicates, several axes of comparison emerge from these four legal stories. One of these concerns the agent of biodiversity conservation: who is in charge of designing and implement-ing conservation? In many cases, it is the national government that car-ries this responsibility, but it can be a national government that has com-mitted itself to implementing international treaties, or an international organization such as the European Union to begin with. In other cases, it is subnational units—states, cantons, *Länder,* sovereign indigenous territories—that are legally assigned this task, with consequent changes in the way in which the community's relation to the natural world is conceived.

A second axis of comparison concerns the object of conservation: while the U.S. legislation concerns species that have already been found to be at risk, many other countries rely on laws that aim to protect bio-diversity at large rather than endangered species, and yet others have moved from one to the other. Australia, for example, switched from an endangered species law to a biodiversity conservation law in the 1990s, although the listing of species remains important at both state and fed-eral levels. The third comparative perspective examines the legal ob-ject of conservation in a somewhat different fashion by focusing on the relation between species and habitats. Some laws define species as the valuable asset to be conserved, whereas others put particular places or landscapes first and cast the conservation of species as a means toward preserving places. Finally, the reasons why species or spaces are to be pro-tected vary along a fourth axis of comparison: the laws of different coun-tries and regions variously refer to nature's intrinsic value; to its value as a source of raw materials, food, and medicine; to the value of traditional human uses and ways of life (including but not limited to indigenous tra-ditions); or to specific contemporary uses such as tourism as reasons for conservation.

Once the variations along these four axes are taken into account, it be-comes clear that defining an "effective" or "successful" biodiversity con-servation law is not only or even mainly a matter of counting how many species have been preserved or have died out under the law—an account-ing that is, at any rate, quite difficult in practice—but also determining to what extent the law fulfills the political, social, and cultural purposes to which it links the conservation of biodiversity (section 5). Here again, biodiversity conservation turns out to be a matter of culture, history, and politics more than of biological science.

1. Species and Habitat in the American Endangered Species Act

The legal engagement with threatened species in the United States forms part of a history of evolving risk perceptions that I outlined in the introduction and chapter 1. From the first perceptions of nature as threatened by humans (rather than the other way around) in the early nineteenth century to the establishment of Yellowstone as the first National Park in 1872, the writings of John Muir, and the founding of the Sierra Club in 1892, environmental historians have traced in detail the development of the American concern over a wild nature increasingly perceived as endangered.[2] The extinction of species began to play an explicit and central role in these perceptions in the late nineteenth century with the disappearance of the passenger pigeon and the near-extinction of the American bison.

The new urgency in conservation that resulted from the idea that extinctions were not just a fact of natural history but also of America's lived present led to the passage of the Lacey Act in 1900 and to several treaties and acts to protect migratory birds in the 1910s and 1920s. In 1942, the U.S. Fish and Wildlife Service published *Fading Trails: The Story of Endangered American Wildlife,* and with widespread publicity and annual counts surrounding an alarming decrease in whooping cranes, the Department of the Interior established the Committee on Rare and Endangered Wildlife Species in 1964. This committee published the first "Redbook" of sixty-two endangered species in 1966, and the federal government passed the Endangered Species Preservation Act in the same year. The ESPA, as well as its successor, the Endangered Species Conservation Act, passed in 1969, focused mainly on habitat protection, and the ESCA also began to regulate commerce that might endanger wildlife. The Endangered Species Act, part of a broader environmental program undertaken by President Richard Nixon, resulted from the perception that none of these legislative tools had yet done enough to halt the disappearance of species.

In his 1972 message to Congress regarding his environmental initiative, Nixon noted, "Even the most recent act to protect endangered

2. For more detailed histories of American nineteenth-century conservationism, see Cohen (1988), Worster (2008), and Black (2012).

species, which dates only from 1969, simply does not provide the kind of management tools needed to act early enough to save a vanishing species. In particular, existing laws do not generally allow the Federal Government to control shooting, trapping, or other taking of endangered species. I propose legislation to provide for early identification and protection of endangered species. My new proposal would make the taking of endangered species a Federal offense for the first time" (Nixon 1972). The Endangered Species Act passed with unanimity in the Senate and an overwhelming majority in the House of Representatives.[3]

Nixon's message to Congress starts with an evocation of the "American spirit of self-reliance and confident action" and segues into the "new recognition that to a significant extent man commands as well the very destiny of this planet where he lives, and the destiny of all life upon it." He added, "We have even begun to see that these destinies are not many and separate at all—that in fact they are indivisibly one" (1972). But this expanded sense of the collective human mastery of nature comes into question just a few sentences later, when Nixon invokes a new American spirit, where the "commitment to responsible partnership with nature replaces cavalier assumptions that we can play God with our surroundings and survive" (1972). This sense of crisis and transformation also appears in the opening sentences of the ESA, which presents itself as a law that seeks to remedy errors of the past:

> The Congress finds and declares that—
>
> (1) various species of fish, wildlife, and plants in the United States have been rendered extinct as a consequence of economic growth and development untempered by adequate concern and conservation;
>
> (2) other species of fish, wildlife, and plants have been so depleted in numbers that they are in danger of or threatened with extinction;
>
> (3) these species of fish, wildlife, and plants are of esthetic, ecological, educational, historical, recreational, and scientific value to the Nation and its people. (*Endangered Species Act* 1973, sec. 2, paras. 1–3)

3. My brief survey here is informed by Yaffee (1982) and Scott, Goble, and Davis (2006, 4–7).

The assertion of value and the prospect of its loss, in this opening sentence, is clearly linked to excessive, "untempered" economic growth and a perceived lack of ethical concern for other, noneconomic values that the nation relies on (clause 3, interestingly, does not mention the economic value endangered species might have, perhaps because clause 1 identifies economic growth as a central problem).

As the ESA goes on to enumerate the international conservation treaties that the United States has signed on to, international law emerges as one standard to which the country must hold itself accountable. The opening section concludes with the collective intent "to develop and maintain conservation programs which meet national and international standards [a]s a key to meeting the Nation's international commitments and to better safeguarding, for the benefit of all citizens, the Nation's heritage in fish, wildlife, and plants" (*Endangered Species Act* 1973, sec. 2(a), para. 5). This perception of nature, and nonhuman species in particular, as part of an inherited collective property, as we will see, is shared by conservation laws in other countries even when their conceptual framework differs in other respects. What distinguishes the ESA's language is that international treaties and programs frame and ensure the individual nation's patrimony.

Another crucial characteristic of the ESA is its focus on species as that which is to be protected, whereas conservation laws in other countries and regions often focus on biodiversity rather than endangered species. The term *biodiversity* was coined by Raymond Dasmann in 1968, but it was not commonly used until the 1980s and was therefore not readily available for legislation in the early 1970s, which may partially explain why the ESA foregrounds species. But the idea of *natural diversity*, which preceded *biodiversity*, does not appear in the ESA either (and neither is it mentioned in Nixon's message, whereas the idea of *wildness* is). It may be worth recalling, in this context, that the 1966 Endangered Species Preservation Act, which the laws of 1969 and 1973 modify and elaborate, was limited to endangered "native species of fish and wildlife" and "native wild animals" (*Endangered Species Preservation Act* 1966, sec. 1 [a]). This limitation to native species disappears in the 1969 and 1973 versions, but the original formulation may serve as a reminder that diversity as such figured less prominently in the discourse about endangered species at the time than the particular set of species that is associated with national character. Nixon, in his message to Congress, highlights that the expanded list of more than one hundred endangered species starts with "our national symbol, the bald eagle" (1972), further evidence of the sense of a crisis in national identity that framed environmental discourse.

The original ESA of 1973 was substantially modified several times over the following decades. Significant amendments in 1978 and 1979 made the procedures for listing a species as endangered considerably more complex and altered the ESA's initial categorical prohibitions on taking or killing endangered species. One of the most important amendments specified that "critical habitat," that is, habitat considered necessary for the survival of a species, be designated as part of the species listing: "the specific areas within the geographical area occupied by the species, at the time it is listed in accordance with the provisions of section 4 of this Act, on which are found those physical or biological features (I) essential to the conservation of the species and (II) which may require special management considerations or protection" (*Endangered Species Act* 1973, sec. 3, para. 5 [A] [i]). Additional amendments in 1982 and during the 1990s redefined how these prohibitions were to be implemented on private land and sought to provide incentives for private landowners to obey the law (Scott, Goble, and Davis 2006, 8–11).

The inclusion of the "critical habitat" amendment widens the ESA's focus from species to the places and ecosystems they form part of, even though the efficacy of this amendment is much debated.[4] And in practical implementations of the ESA, conservationists often focus on the protection of a listed "umbrella species" so as to achieve broader conservation goals that include other species and the surrounding ecosystem. But the primary purpose of the act remains the protection of those species that have already been identified as imperiled: "The purposes of this Act are to provide a means whereby the ecosystems upon which endangered species and threatened species depend may be conserved, to provide a program for the conservation of such endangered species and threatened species" (*Endangered Species Act* 1973, sec. 2 [b]). Legal scholars have explored at great length the strengths and weaknesses that follow from this focus—a precise focus that allows for effective legal action, on one hand, and limitations in addressing conservation at the ecosystem level, on the other (see Kuhlmann 1996; Patlis 1996, 45–57; Doremus 2010). Other controversies have revolved around the procedures and temporal delays that precede the official listing of a species, to the

4. For an analysis of how the categorization of animals as being *in situ* or *ex situ* (in their natural habitats or away from them) affects their protection through the ESA, see Braverman (2015, chap. 5).

point where some species have gone extinct by the time they finally come up for listing as endangered. A review of the statistics led Scott et al., in "By the Numbers," to conclude in the early 2000s that "listing and recovery planning are implemented when extinction risks have already reached critical levels. ... Our biggest challenge may lie not in the recovery of endangered species but in preventing imperiled species from becoming endangered" (2006, 34). The focus of the ESA on species, in this sense, remains formative for the handling of biodiversity conservation in the United States.

Other countries have not followed this path. Instead of focusing on species at the moment that they are already endangered, conservation laws in many parts of the world target the preservation of biodiversity in general, and endangered species conservation forms part of this broader goal. In this respect, the Endangered Species Act is less paradigmatic than American environmentalists tend to think, though it has undoubtedly been influential as a precursor to conservation laws in other regions. Countries and regions that have passed biodiversity protection laws tend to link the law's intent to the conservation of national heritage and national patrimony, just as the ESA does. Yet the stories that biodiversity conservation laws tell do differ significantly from that of the ESA, as the following three examples show.

2. Biodiversity and Landscape in the German Federal Nature Protection Law

In Germany, as in the United States, the concern about human threats to nature crystallized institutionally in the late nineteenth century. Rapid population growth, industrialization, and the explosive growth of cities between 1890 and 1910 triggered a turn to nature and against modernization, urbanization, and the mass society. The founding of utopian colonies outside cities and a wide variety of movements revolving around organic food, alternative medicine, vegetarianism, teetotalism, nudism, sexual reform, gardening, and hiking sought to reorient Germans toward various dimensions of nature. In 1897 the composer Ernst Rudorff, who had witnessed the transformation of rural landscapes around his parents' estate in Lower Saxony, used the term *Heimatschutz* (protection of the homeland), which had previously had military connotations, to refer to conservation, and he coined the term *Naturschutz* (protection of nature) as a watchword for the return to nature. He participated in the founding of the Deutscher Bund Heimatschutz (German association for the protection of nature) in 1904. In 1898 Wilhelm Wetekamp asked for the creation of "state parks" on the model of American national parks such as Yellowstone in the Prussian House of Representatives, though his request remained unsuccessful; a Naturschutzpark (Nature protection park) was established for the Lüneburg Heath in 1905, however. The wealthy and charismatic Lina Hähnle founded the Bund für Vogelschutz (Association for the protection of birds) in 1899 and presided over it for the following four decades, earning the title "Deutsche Vogelmutter" (German bird mother). Hugo Conwentz, a Danzig-based museum director who had researched and published on Germany's forests for a quarter of a century, published his treatise *Die Gefährdung der Naturdenkmäler und Vorschläge zu ihrer Erhaltung* (The endangerment of natural monuments and proposals for their conservation), in 1904, which led to the creation of the Staatliche Stelle für Naturdenkmalpflege (State office for the care of natural monuments) as part of the Prussian Ministry of Culture in 1906. Robert Mielke proposed the term *Landespflege* (care for the land or, in a more contemporary idiom, landscape management) at the general assembly of the Deutsche Gesellschaft for Gartenkunst (German society for the art of gardening) in 1907, and 1909 saw the establishment of the Verein Naturschutzpark (Association for nature protection parks) (Linse 1986, 19–20; Wöbse 2003; Zwanzig 1989, 16, 21–22). Many more local and regional clubs, associations, and societies for the protection of nature sprang up during the same time period.

But wilderness or a preference for landscapes untouched by humans did not shape these movements as much as it did their North American counterparts. The notion of *Naturdenkmal* (natural monument), which Alexander von Humboldt had first used in 1799 to refer to an almost six-hundred-foot-tall mimosa he saw during one of his trips to Venezuela (Zwanzig 1989, 18), combines natural objects with human-built structures, and natural monuments were considered worthy of protection in the same way as cultural monuments (*Kulturdenkmäler*) were. *Naturschutzgebiete* (protected natural areas) and endangered species and animals became objects of protection alongside particular architectural styles and art forms, local and regional customs, and the *Eigenart* (peculiarity) of landscapes (Linse 1986, 20; Körner 2000, 19–23). Indeed, if there is a core concept that shapes Germany's early conservationist thinking, it is precisely that of landscape (*Landschaft*) as it had been historically shaped by regional customs and communities in distinctive ways.

Beyond the civic engagement that these central ideas catalyzed in the face of modernization and urbanization, they also led to a variety of often quite divergent legislative initiatives for the protection of various types of "monuments" in Germany's multiple regions and duchies. The 1919 constitution of the Weimar Republic included an article stipulating the protection of art monuments, natural monuments, and landscapes (Zwanzig 1989, 20–21). But comprehensive national environmental legislation was not passed until the National Socialists came to power. This may come as a surprise to the mostly left-oriented environmentalists of the late twentieth and early twenty-first centuries in Europe and North America, who tend to think of the Nazis as so violent and disdainful of life that it is hard to envision them as conservationists. Yet it was one of Hitler's most notorious associates, Hermann Göring, who helped to pass the Reichstierschutzgesetz (Animal protection act) in November 1933, the Reichsjagdgesetz (Hunting act) in July 1934, and the Reichsnaturschutzgesetz (Nature protection act) in June 1935; these constituted the first unified, nationwide legislation of its kind in German history. The animal protection law, which outlawed vivisection and severely punished cruelty to animals, would probably be called "progressive" if the historical context were different (see fig. 8).[5]

One might be tempted to dismiss the Nazis' passing of comprehensive environmental legislation as no more than a shrewd appropriation of the rhetoric and cultural capital that the conservationist movement had accumulated since the late nineteenth century. It is true that the protection of nature, the homeland, and historical patrimony all became yoked to Nazi patriotism, militarism, and imperialist expansion, as Walther Darré's propaganda for the German connection to "blood and soil" vividly demonstrated. The protection and restoration of "typically German" landscapes was used to legitimate Germany's eastward expansion, even as Göring created game reserves and sought to bring the extinct aurochs back to the forests of Lithuania and Poland, and Hitler proposed reforesting the Ukraine in the process (Hermand 1992, 281; Daskiewicz and Aikhenbaum 1999). At the same time, the Nazis' sustained efforts at modernization (for example, through the construction of a national highway system) and the focus on the war effort starting in the late 1930s often overrode environmentalist concerns and entailed brutal transformation of landscapes and exploitation of natural resources.[6]

But precisely because of this context, the question is not why the Nazis exploited the natural world, but why they bothered to pass laws that at least in theory constrained this exploitation. Moreover, some

---

5. Boria Sax notes that "the Animal Protection Law of 1933 was probably the strictest in the world" (2009, 112).

6. For a more detailed discussion, see Imort (2005).

FIGURE 8 Caricature of Hermann Göring as a champion for animal rights in the satirical magazine *Kladderadatsch!*, September 3, 1933. The title of the image, *Eine Kulturtat* (A cultural accomplishment), is undoubtedly intended ironically in the context of this magazine. Photograph by Digitalisierungszentrum, Universitätsbibliothek Heidelberg.

National Socialist officials and scientists had a genuine commitment to and deep knowledge of the natural world, and not all the conservationists whose organizations were taken over by the Nazis committed themselves to the new ideological regime.[7] The nature protection law itself was so sound in its basic assumptions and so untainted by National Socialist rhetoric that the newly established Federal Republic of Germany took it over after World War II as its own legislation. It was challenged in 1957 not because of its ideology or detectable errors in the way in which it addressed environmental problems, but because it attributed powers to the German government that were no longer constitutional in the framework of postwar federalism, which shifted a good deal of the responsibility for environmental protection to the *Länder* (states).

7. By way of example, see Wöbse's nuanced analysis of Lina Hähnle's manipulation of and by Nazi officials after the Bund für Vogelschutz was taken over (2003).

Over the next two decades, individual German states passed a variety of nature protection laws of their own. But this fragmentation of responsibility also led to a call for an improved and unifying legal framework, as did the rise of initially quite varied environmentalist movements. In 1961 Count Lennart Bernadotte presented his Grüne Charta von der Mainau (Green charter of the Mainau) as part of a movement with roots in the early twentieth century, Landespflege, which culminated in the founding of the Deutscher Rat für Landespflege (German council for the care of the land) in 1962. The green charter called for the creation and maintenance of a "balance between technology, economy, and nature" (Ausgleich zwischen Technik, Wirtschaft und Natur) and for "improved measures for the conservation and regeneration of a healthy economy of nature, especially through protection of soil, climate, and water" (verstärkte Maßnahmen zur Erhaltung und Wiederherstellung eines gesunden Naturhaushaltes, insbesondere durch Bodenschutz, Klima- und Wasserschutz) (Deutscher Rat für Landespflege 1961; translation mine).

In the 1970s, both left-wing and right-wing movements began to push for an environmentalist agenda, culminating in the founding of the Green Party in 1980. The left wing derived a good deal of its energies from the disappointment that communist and socialist aspirations had suffered after the student uprisings of the 1960s, a context in which environmentalism promised a new framework for social reform. The right wing was for a time led by Herbert Gruhl, a conservative politician who first alerted West Germany to the dangers of "forest dieback" (*Waldsterben*) in 1971 and published a bestseller called *Ein Planet wird geplündert: Die Schreckensbilanz unserer Politik* (A planet is plundered: The horrific outcomes of our politics) in 1975. He participated in the founding of the Green Party but lost a leadership vote to a more leftist candidate in 1979 and exited from the party in 1981. In his view, it no longer left enough room for conservative approaches to environmental issues. It was the leftist wing of the environmentalist movement under Petra Kelly's leadership that rose to prominence in German politics, whereas conservative environmentalism, which had initially commanded one-third of the Green Party's membership, gradually atrophied. Against the background of vigorous debates about nuclear power, nuclear weapons, pollution, and the role of nature in a nation mostly oriented toward economic growth after the destruction of World War II, the parliament passed a new Federal Law for the Protection of Nature in 1976 (effective 1977) that created a general framework for environmental protection, to which state laws had to adapt. This new framing law took into account international treaties for the protection of species such as CITES, to which Germany had become a signatory in 1973.

Over the following decades, international treaties led to further modifications of the law, as did the reunification of the Federal Republic of Germany with the German Democratic Republic in 1989.[8] The FRG's Federal Nature Protection Act was updated in 2002, during the Green Party's stint as part of the federal government, so as to implement in national law the European Community's Council Directive on the Conservation of Birds, or Birds Directive (Council of the European Communities 1979), and the Council Directive on the Conservation of Habitats and of Wild Fauna and Flora, or Habitats Directive (Council of the European Communities 1992). One of the most important tools for implementing these directives has been the Natura 2000 project, which was initiated in 1998 and gradually created a network of protected areas for the conservation of endangered plants, animals, and their habitats across the territory of the European Union. In 2010 the Federal Nature Protection Act was modified yet again, shifting far more responsibility for detailed legislation from the states to the federal government as the end result of a reform in Germany's federal structure that had been passed in 2006. From 2010 on, the federal government no longer provided only a general legislative framework that the individual states had to translate into concrete laws and regulations; instead, federal laws are directly effective and binding. The states' responsibility, as a consequence, is now reduced to complementing the federal laws with state-specific regulations.

The German Federal Nature Protection Act does not focus primarily on species at risk, as the ESA does. One of its three broadest goals, as articulated in §1, is the protection of nature and landscape—a phrase to which I will return below—in such a way that "biological diversity . . . is ensured over the long term" (die biologische Vielfalt . . . auf Dauer gesichert ist) (Lütkes 2010, 3). The laws concerning "Protection of wild animal and plant species, their habitats and biotopes" are spelled out in §§37–55 of the act. The tasks of species conservation are defined in §37 (1) as

> 1. protecting wild species of animals and plants and their life communities from damage by humans and safeguarding their other essential living conditions,
> 2. protecting the habitats and biotopes of wild species of animals and plants as well as

8. In the aftermath of the reunification, the FRG's Federal Nature Protection Act replaced the GDR's Landeskulturgesetz (National culture act), which I do not have the space to discuss in detail here.

3. restoring displaced wild species of animals and plants in suitable biotopes within their natural ranges.[9]

[Der Artenschutz umfasst

1. den Schutz der Tiere und Pflanzen wild lebender Arten und ihrer Lebensgemeinschaften vor Beeinträchtigungen durch den Menschen und die Gewährleistung ihrer sonstigen Lebensbedingungen,
2. den Schutz der Lebensstätten und Biotope der wild lebenden Tier- und Pflanzenarten sowie
3. die Wiederansiedlung von Tieren und Pflanzen verdrängter wild lebender Arten in geeigneten Biotopen innerhalb ihres natürlichen Verbreitungsgebiets.]

It is immediately obvious that the German law understands conservation in a much broader sense than the American ESA does, in that it aims to protect biodiversity at large and, in principle, all wild animals and plants regardless of their endangerment status. Only the third goal refers to species that can no longer be found in their original habitats, but even then the language alludes to space rather than risk by calling such species "displaced" rather than "endangered." As a consequence, the articles under the subheading "General Species Conservation" include regulations that relate not only to nonnative species but also to zoos, whereas endangered species, which the German law refers to as "especially protected species" (besonders geschützte Arten), appear only in §44, in the section "Special Species Conservation."

One might summarize this difference by saying that the German law is far more holistic in its conception of conservation than the American one (see Gassner and Heugel 2010, 15). This is true, but only up to a point. The ESA, as I discussed earlier, does aim to conserve ecosystems so as to rescue species from extinction, and the addition of the requirement to designate a "critical habitat" concurrently with a species to be listed extends the focus of the law from individual species to the ecological spaces and networks of which they form part.[10] The German law, on the other hand, is not as inclusive as it seems at first. If the clauses

9. Translations from the Federal Nature Protection Act are mine.
10. It is also worth remembering, in this context, that the U.S. government had already passed the Wilderness Act in 1964, which set 9.1 million acres of federal land aside as protected areas.

I have quoted seem to suggest that no flower could be picked and no deer hunted without a special permit in Germany, the law in fact allows such actions, and it generally exempts agriculture, forestry, hunting, and fisheries from its provisions so long as their activities do not overtly contravene the goals of the Federal Nature Protection Act and obey the rules of "best practice" (gute fachliche Praxis) that are also held up as the standard in the specific laws governing them, such as the agriculture law, the forestry law, the hunting law, and the fishery law. Since agriculture and fisheries are two of the principal contributors to species loss, this exemption significantly limits the power the nature protection law would otherwise command.

But even granting that the American and German laws for the protection of endangered species may be shaped by practical implementations more than is apparent in their original formulations, their conceptual approach to the problem remains strikingly different. The cultural and historical reasons for this difference emerge more clearly when we consider that the German law not only concerns itself with biodiversity more than with endangered species, but also does not in fact mention either biodiversity or endangered species in its title. The law is called Bundesnaturschutzgesetz for short (Federal nature protection act), but its full title is Gesetz über Naturschutz und Landschaftspflege (Act on nature protection and landscape management).

The law's three goals, according to §1, are quite broad: to ensure biological diversity; to ensure the performance and functioning of ecosystems, including the sustainable use of natural resources; and to ensure the diversity, particularity, beauty, and recreational value of landscapes.[11] The second goal, ensuring ecosystem functioning, seems particularly general, given that this law is not centrally concerned with clean air or water, with mining, fishery, or agriculture, all areas that are covered by other laws. At its core, as the third goal reveals, the act aims at the protection of spaces (including oceans) and of species. The formulaic phrase "Natur und Landschaft" (nature and landscape), repeated obsessively in this and other legal texts, as well as its companion "Naturschutz und Landschaftspflege" (nature conservation and landscape management) convey this combined concern with species and spaces.

---

11. I have translated the German term *Naturhaushalt,* literally "nature household," simply by the adjective *ecological.* But the text of the law avoids the technical term *Ökologie* (originally a German term coined by Ernst Haeckel before it was translated into English) or *Ökosystem* here in favor of a less scientific and more domestic term that implies balanced and orderly functioning as well as economic account-keeping.

The concept of *"Landschaft"* might at first sight appear to function as the equivalent of the "critical habitat" that the American Endangered Species Act includes as part of the conservation of plants and
animals. But even a cursory look at the Federal Nature Protection Act
reveals that it dedicates as much space to the protection of landscapes
as to that of species, including a long list of specific conservation designations: "Naturschutzgebiete," "Naturdenkmäler," "Nationale Natur-
monumente," "Biosphärenreservate," and "Landschaftsschutzgebiete"
(nature conservation areas, natural monuments, national nature monuments, biosphere reserves, landscape protection areas), to name a few.
Neither simply critical habitat for endangered species nor merely natural
space seen in its pictorial or aesthetic dimension, as the English cognate
landscape might suggest, *Landschaft* lies at the very core of what the
Federal Nature Protection Act aims to preserve.

   This concept has been central for German conservation movements
since the nineteenth century, as the historian Stefan Körner has pointed
out: "In traditional nature conservation (at least in the strand that derives
from the tradition of homeland protection, which, unlike in the United
States, is widespread in Germany), the pristineness of the environment
and thereby the role of non-native species is measured by the logic of
the *cultural identity* of humanly altered landscapes, even if the rhetoric
is about ecosystem functions" (Körner 2000, 15–16; translation mine).
Indeed, Körner criticizes contemporary environmentalist rhetoric in Germany because it tends to equate traditional landscapes altered by humans
with the scientific concept of the ecosystem (2000, 15).[12] This superimpo-
sition of the traditional cultural meanings of *Landschaft* on the scientific
implications of biodiversity and ecosystem functionality is also visible in
the Federal Nature Protection Act. Indeed, one might argue that if the
German law establishes a hierarchy between the protection of species and
the protection of landscapes, it reverses the one implied by Endangered
Species Act, which puts "critical habitat" at the service of species conservation. In the German Federal Nature Protection Act, one of the major

---

12. Körner argues elsewhere that indeed the scientific rhetoric of ecology was deliberately used in Germany to overwrite the cultural meanings of nature conservation after
World War II and thereby to dissociate it from particular sets of values (particularly, of
course, those of the Nazi period), with a view toward establishing democratic consensus.
Körner considers this attempt to elide the cultural meanings of ecology ultimately unsuccessful; for environmentalism to regain broad public acceptance, he argues, it has to embrace the cultural meanings of nature and to develop a politically progressive framework
for concerns about "Heimat" (Körner 2003, 406, 423–434).

functions of species conservation is to preserve intact or to restore the *Eigenart*, the particular character, of landscapes.

The prominence of the concept of *Landschaft* in German environmental law distinguishes it from corresponding U.S. laws as well as from European Union legislation, in which scientific terms such as *habitat* or *ecosystem* are far more frequently used. *Landschaft* has a long philosophical and cultural tradition that associates the character of a people with the place it inhabits and that can be traced back to Johann Gottfried Herder's late-eighteenth-century philosophy of cultural difference. Quite often, this idea that the characteristics of a community derive from the way in which it engages with the particularities of its natural environment was put to politically conservative uses as a means of criticizing modernity, industry, capitalism, and democracy (Körner 2003, 410–413). As I mentioned earlier, the idea of *Naturschutz* at the turn of the twentieth century emerged in close conjunction with the older notion of *Heimatschutz* (homeland protection), and many nature conservation associations and strategies were modeled on earlier cultural conservation projects. Nature conservation, in this context, was not perceived as fundamentally different from the conservation of historical buildings or monuments: both served to document and sustain the particular characteristics of a cultural community. And even though the notion of a primal landscape before human intervention occasionally appears in the history of German conservationism (for example, in the writings of the biologist Walther Schoenichen, who most centrally linked nature conservation to National Socialist ideology, or in the more general admiration of supposedly pristine alpine landscapes), far more prominent are landscapes that have acquired their characteristic profile through human intervention, *Kulturlandschaften* or humanly altered landscapes.[13]

The historical prominence and cultural resonance of the landscape concept in German conservationism explains why the terms *Natur* and *Landschaft* co-occur so frequently in legal texts, why one of the primary goals of the law is to maintain the "Eigenart" of nature and landscape, and also why the Federal Nature Protection Act combines the imperative to conserve nature with the mandate to plan and shape landscapes. In some of the general clauses that frame more specific dispensations,

13. Ludwig Fischer delivers a sharp-eyed analysis of the paradoxes and inconsistencies in Schoenichen's evocation of an *Urlandschaft*, a primal landscape that is at the same time distinctively German. Schoenichen himself outlines the relentless human exploitation and decimation of German forests since the early Middle Ages, but he squares the argumentative circle by attributing to the *Urlandschaft* warlike and heroic qualities that he identifies as quintessentially German (Fischer 2003, 183–190).

the Federal Nature Protection Act stipulates that if the performance and function of an ecological system or the appearance of a landscape (Landschaftsbild) have been compromised, the damage is reversed "when and as soon as the compromised functions of the ecological system have been restored in equivalent fashion and the appearance of the landscape has been restored or newly designed in a manner appropriate to the landscape" (Ausgeglichen ist eine Beeinträchtigung, wenn und sobald die beeinträchtigten Funktionen des Naturhaushalts in gleichartiger Weise wiederhergestellt sind und das Landschaftsbild landschaftsgerecht wiederhergestellt oder neu gestaltet ist; §15, para. 2, sentence 2). Restoring a landscape appropriately, "landschaftsgerecht," presupposes precisely an understanding of the landscape's "Eigenart." Far more insistently than the Endangered Species Act in the United States, then, the German Federal Nature Protection Act subordinates the protection of animal and plant species to the protection of natural landscapes that are conceived in resonance with long-standing philosophical, cultural, and conservationist traditions.[14]

To a large extent, the protection of nature and the conservation of endangered species as conceived by the Federal Nature Protection Act are thoroughly human-centered (Gassner and Heugel 2010, 25). Even where the law focuses on uses of nature that may not appear at first sight purely instrumental, it aims at "recreation" (*Erholung*, lit. recuperation) for humans. But in one instance right at the beginning, the law clearly goes beyond the human-centered instrumentalization of nature. Under the heading "Goals of Nature Protection and Landscape Management," §1 spells out the following principle: "(1) Nature and landscape, because of their intrinsic value and as foundation for human life and health, also in view of responsibility for future generations, are to be protected in inhabited as well as non-inhabited areas in such a way" as to ensure the three goals I discussed earlier: biological diversity, ecosystem performance, and the continued diversity, particularity, beauty, and recreational value of landscapes (Ziele des Naturschutzes und der Landschaftspflege. (1) Natur und Landschaft sind auf Grund ihres eigenen Wertes und als Grundlage für Leben und Gesundheit des Menschen auch in Verantwortung für die künftigen Generationen im besiedelten und unbesiedelten Bereich nach Massgabe der nachfolgenden Absätze . . . zu schützen [*Naturschutz-*

14. In clear confirmation of this interest in the cultural uses of nature, the Federal Nature Protection Act includes regulations for zoos and animal displays (§§42–43) as well as an entire chapter titled "Recreation in Nature and Landscape" (chap. 7, §§59–62).

recht 3]). This foundational sentence spells out an ecocentric as well as an anthropocentric rationale for nature conservation: nature's value on its own *and* as the basis for human existence. The act specifies in §2 (3) that "The goals of nature protection and landscape management are to be realized in individual cases insofar as they are possible, necessary, and appropriate when all the requirements deriving from § 1 (1) are weighed against each other and against the public's other requirements of nature and landscape" ([3] Die Ziele des Naturschutzes und der Landschaftspflege sind zu verwirklichen, soweit es im Einzelfall möglich, erforderlich und unter Abwägung aller sich aus § 1 Absatz 1 ergebenden Anforderungen untereinander und gegen die sonstigen Anforderungen der Allgemeinheit an Natur und Landschaft angemessen ist [*Naturschutzrecht* 5]). Abstract as this language may be, it spells out the task of balancing nature's intrinsic value against its uses for humans.

What this amounts to in practice, however, is unclear. As legal scholars Gassner and Heugel point out in their comment on the law, the concept of "intrinsic value" does not have any specific weight that could be assessed in the balancing act §2 (3) asks for, and they highlight that the attribution of intrinsic value is itself an anthropocentric act. But, as the philosopher Martin Gorke has pointed out, the fact that the subject is human in any attribution of value does not automatically erase distinctions between the objects to which value is attributed, any more than egocentrism is equivalent to narcissism just because they both describe individual attitudes (Gorke 1999, 203–211). Even if its practical value in legal proceedings cannot be precisely determined, then, the acknowledgment of nature's intrinsic value in the Federal Nature Protection Act remains a significant philosophical gesture beyond its otherwise anthropocentric and humanist approach.

3. Species across Borders: Biodiversity Conservation Law in the European Union

If the German Federal Nature Protection Act as it was passed in 2010 must be understood in terms of national culture in that it builds on histories and ideas about nature that have emerged from distinctively German traditions of thought and politics, it is at the same time a product of international legal frameworks. As a signatory to CITES (1973), the Bern Convention (Convention on the Conservation of European Wildlife and Natural Habitats, 1979), the Bonn Convention on Migratory Species (1979), the Birds Directive (Council Directive 79/409/EEC, passed in

1979 and amended in 2009), and the Habitats Directive (Council Directive 92/43/EEC on the Conservation of Natural Habitats and of Wild Fauna and Flora, passed in 1992 and amended last in 2007), Germany has adjusted its legislation to conform to the demands of international species conservation treaties and laws.

The Federal Nature Protection Act was reformulated in the early 2000s in part so as to make it conform to European Union legislation (Gassner and Heugel 2010, 1). The Birds and Habitats directives are binding for European Union member states, in that they have to be translated into national legislation within a limited time period, which is identified in each directive (Verschuuren 2004, 41). If a member state delays transposing a directive into the national context or commits errors in doing so, its provisions may take "direct effect" regardless of existing national legislation. Where the obligations arising from the directive are transparent, national courts and authorities must implement them over existing national legislation (42). During the past fifteen years, the European Commission has demonstrated that it is serious about these provisions by bringing numerous infringement cases against member states before the European Court of Justice.

The Birds and Habitats directives both consist of two sets of provisions, one for habitat protection and the other for species protection. Conservation areas called Special Protection Areas (SPAs) under the Birds Directive and Special Areas of Conservation (SACs) under the Habitat Directive were initially nominated by individual member states. Some of these were selected by the European Commission as Sites of Community Importance (SCIs), that is, areas at the borders of different member states or areas that contain "priority habitat types" or "priority species"—habitats or species, that is, which are especially endangered. Such areas then had to be designated as Special Areas of Conservation by the national legislation. Endangered habitats and species are identified in the various annexes to the Habitat Directive as "Natural Habitat Types of Community Interest Whose Conservation Requires the Designation of Special Areas of Conservation" and "Animal and Plant Species of Community Interest Whose Conservation Requires the Designation of Special Areas of Conservation" (Council of the European Communities 1992, Annexes I and II). The main tool for the protection of species at risk, then, is the designation of an area as a Special Area of Conservation, and the ultimate goal of establishing SPAs and SACs is to create a continental ecological protection network called Natura 2000 (Council of the European Communities 1992, art. 3; Verschuuren 2004, 43–44). The Natura 2000 network, which currently includes approximately

THE LEGAL LIVES OF ENDANGERED SPECIES

18 percent of European Union territory, is meant to preserve both habitats and species and to protect species primarily through a focus on habitat conservation.[15]

The areas that form part of Natura 2000 are by no means wilderness areas; they can include significant human use. The preamble to the Habitat Directive already states that its main aim is "to promote the maintenance of biodiversity, taking account of economic, social, cultural and regional requirements. . . . The maintenance of such biodiversity may in certain cases require the maintenance, or indeed the encouragement, of human activities" (Council of the European Communities 1992, 2). But construction or modification of projects in protected areas have to undergo an environmental-impact assessment, and infringements on the safety of habitat or species are allowed only under certain exceptions. The Birds Directive allowed them only for reasons of public health and safety, air safety, or to prevent significant damage to crops or livestock. The Habitats Directive, somewhat more leniently, also allows exceptions "for imperative reasons of overriding public interest," including social or economic interest, but only if no alternative ways of serving those interests are available, and with the condition that any damage to protected areas or species is compensated for by other measures (Council of the European Communities 1992, art. 6, para. 4; Verschuuren 2004, 45–46).

The European Court of Justice has been strict in enforcing a precise translation and implementation of the directives in national law. It ruled, for example, against Greece in 2002 for failing to protect the endangered loggerhead sea turtle (*Caretta caretta*), one of whose main breeding grounds is on the Greek island of Zakynthos; against the Netherlands for issuing mechanical fishing licenses for a Special Protected Area; and against Germany in 2006 for insufficiently translating the Habitats Directive into the Federal Nature Protection Act: the specific aspect the commission was concerned about was that the 2002 German law did not include consideration of impacts on SACs of projects undertaken outside their boundaries (Commission of the European Communities v. Federal Republic of Germany 2006; García Ureta 2007, 90–91). Some of the 2010 revisions to the German law were designed to address the flaws that the European Court of Justice had ruled to be noncompliant with the Habitats Directive.

15. Verschuuren notes that the presence of various listed habitat types and species in a Special Area of Conservation can give rise to conflicting conservation goals and incompatible conservation measures (2004, 58).

The current Federal Nature Protection Act in Germany conforms to the Habitats Directive, yet, as one might expect, the language of the two legal documents differs quite substantially. Both of them emphasize biodiversity as well as, to a lesser extent, sustainability. But the Habitats Directive uses none of the language referring to the care, appearance, and particularity of landscapes in the way the German law does. The German rhetoric of landscape here gives way to the scientific rhetoric of "natural habitats" and "habitat types," a language that no doubt appeared more culturally neutral and unifying to European legislators than terms with particular histories and cultural traditions that might resonate differently in the European Union's twenty-eight nations. Yet the Habitats Directive shares with the Federal Nature Protection Act an emphasis on the conservation of particular types of places as the principal conservation tool, and this emphasis distinguishes it from the Endangered Species Act, which does not list particular habitats in their own right as worthy of protection. "Habitat conservation in the US [Endangered Species Act] is always aimed at the conservation of a certain species, while in the EU, habitat conservation can be aimed at a certain type of habitat as well. The latter approach seems to be more function oriented and, thus, more precautionary, because it aims at protecting habitat, regardless of whether a certain species on that site is endangered," the Dutch legal scholar Jonathan Verschuuren comments (2004, 59).

In the language of the Habitats Directive, the conservation of natural spaces does not so much grow out of a particular cultural tradition as it seeks to create one—a by-product, so to speak, of conservation. "The threatened habitats and species form part of the Community's natural heritage," the preamble to the Habitats Directive states, and since "the threats to them are often of a transboundary nature, it is necessary to take measures at Community level in order to conserve them" (Council of the European Communities 1992, 2). Similarly, the European Court of Justice, especially in cases involving conservation, has often emphasized that "the management of the common heritage is entrusted to the Member States in their respective territories" (quoted in Verschuuren 2004, 41). The idea that the biodiversity of ecosystems and species constitutes a kind of national patrimony is common in the environmental rhetoric of various countries. The U.S. Endangered Species Act, as I mentioned earlier, uses similar language as it aims to "safeguard . . . the Nation's heritage in fish, wildlife, and plants" (Endangered Species Act 1973, sec. 2 [5]).

But the idea of biodiversity as patrimony is somewhat more adventurous in the case of a sprawling multinational conglomerate such as the

European Union: in this expanded context, it is meant to create the idea of a shared ancestry and tradition more than it attests to an already existing one. The 2007 amendment of the Habitats Directive seeks to give this shared heritage a somewhat more concrete shape when it defines "natural habitats," which even in earlier versions could always be "natural" or "semi-natural" (i.e., humanly altered or cultural): it includes among "habitat types of Community interest" not only those that are reduced to a small range or in danger of disappearing, but also those that "present outstanding examples of typical characteristics of one or more of the nine following biogeographical regions: Alpine, Atlantic, Black Sea, Boreal, Continental, Macaronesian, Mediterranean, Pannonian and Steppic" (Council of the European Communities 1992, art. 1 [c] [iii]). Unlike the habitat types listed in Annex I, these nine designations combine ecological with old cultural distinctions and might be understood as one of the Habitat Directive's attempts to give flesh to the skeleton of the "Community's natural heritage."

4. Biodiversity and the Rights of Mother Earth in the Bolivian Biodiversity Law

Like the legislation of Germany and the European Union, Bolivia's current environmental law targets biodiversity at large, rather than endangered species in the way the American Endangered Species Act does. But in other ways Bolivia's legal biodiversity culture differs radically from the cases I have considered so far. Not only is Bolivia one of the world's most biodiverse countries (Mérida 2004, 193, 196)—its ecosystems vary dramatically, from the Andean *altiplano* to rainforests and the dry forests of the Chaco—but it has also recently passed some of the most radical laws regarding the environment and conservation, in close parallel with its neighbor Ecuador. After the election of Evo Morales Ayma as president in 2006, Bolivia put in place a new constitution in 2009 that grants considerably expanded rights and political participation venues to the country's multiple indigenous communities, closely following a similar new constitution of 2008 in Ecuador. Since then, it has passed laws that, like the Ecuadorian Constitution, attribute legal rights to nature itself, thereby creating a new kind of legal and political subject.

As in many other countries, indigenous traditions in Bolivia spelled out modes of interaction with the natural world before the advent of Europeans, and codified legal concern for specific aspects of nature can be traced back to the colonial period. Simón Bolívar passed a decree regulating the hunt and domestication of vicuñas so as to increase their

population (Heinrich and Eguivar 1991, 29–30), but their numbers were
so reduced by the 1960s that they were believed to be in danger of extinction across the four countries they inhabit (Argentina, Bolivia, Chile,
and Peru), and Bolivian president René Barrientos Ortuño prohibited
their commercial exploitation and export in 1965 (24). Wagner Terrazas
Urquidi exposed Bolivia's environmental degradation, mostly caused by
extractive industries, but also by slash-and-burn agriculture, in his book
Bolivia: País saqueado (Bolivia: Pillaged land) in 1973, and several environmental laws were passed during the 1970s. General Hugo Banzer,
who had become president after a coup d'état in 1971, established the
Committees for the Defense of Flora and Fauna in 1972, prohibited the
capture of and commercial hunt for various kinds of Amazonian bird
species, and passed the General Forestry Law (Ley forestal general de
Bolivia, 1974), which regulated the exploitation of Bolivia's forests to
protect them as a material and commercial resource. The Law concerning Wildlife, National Parks, Hunting, and Fishing (Ley de vida silvestre,
parques nacionales, caza y pesca), passed in 1975, regulated the use and
commercialization of wildlife, including protection for some endangered
species, habitat conservation for plants and animals, and the creation of
national parks, biological reserves, and other wildlife sanctuaries (Heinrich and Eguivar 1991, 25). Banzer's successor, General David Padilla,
created the Cross-Institutional Committee for the Environment (Co-
mité interinstitucional del medio ambiente, 1979) to analyze Bolivia's
environmental condition, as well as a committee specifically to address
desertification (Heinrich and Eguivar 1991, 25–26).

   In 1987, Bolivia became the first country to negotiate a debt-for-
nature swap with Conservation International, a U.S.-based nonprofit
organization, which purchased $650,000 of Bolivian debt in return for
Bolivia's setting aside 1.5 million hectares (3.7 million acres) of tropical
lowlands in three conservation areas (Steinberg 2001, 110–111). None
of these initiatives, however, succeeded in halting Bolivia's deepening
ecological crisis, and in 1990, President Jaime Paz Zamora initiated a
five-year Pausa Ecológica (Ecological moratorium), a ban on the hunting
or harvesting of wild animals and plants, essentially to give the government time to pass appropriate legislation before the situation deterio-
rated further (118–119). At the same time, he created the Fondo Nacional para el Medio Ambiente or FONAMA (National environmental
endowment) as an umbrella financial account for directing money toward environmental projects (Heinrich and Eguivar 1991, 26–27). The
first comprehensive environmental law in Bolivia was passed in 1992

following efforts by a small group of longtime environmental activists who succeeded in pushing the law through both of Bolivia's legislative chambers. It led to the creation of the new Ministry of Sustainable Development and the Environment in 1993, under Gonzalo Sánchez de Lozada's presidency, and the establishment of a far-reaching legal framework for subsequent laws on forestry and biodiversity (Steinberg 2001, 120–21).

As Heinrich and Eguivar note, most of Bolivia's environmental legislation in the twentieth century revolved around wildlife conservation and the regulation of land, water, and forest resource usage (1991, 27). Issues such as air and water pollution, waste, industrial accidents, and ownership of basic resources, while they certainly manifested themselves politically, did not become objects of legislation to the same extent. Yet political and legal attention shifted to these issues in the late 1990s and early 2000s. The collapse of a tailings dam at a mine in 1996 and the ensuing toxic spill of 235,000 tons of mine tailings, affecting more than twenty thousand mostly indigenous people, led to a protest march (Hindery 2013, 34). Battles over privatization of water and gas after 2000, together with sustained political mobilization on the part of indigenous communities, culminated in the March for Popular Sovereignty, Territory, and Natural Resources in 2002 and became the first impulse for negotiation regarding a new constituent assembly. It also helped pave the way for the eventual electoral victory of the MAS party (Movimiento al Socialismo [Movement toward socialism]). Evo Morales Ayma, who had made the call for a new constitution part of his electoral campaign, became Bolivia's first indigenous president in 2006 (Hindery 2013, 105–106).

The constitution that went into effect in 2009, after several years of negotiation, is known above all for its emphasis on Bolivia as a "plurinational" state including thirty-six different indigenous nations as well as an Afro-Bolivian population. The constitution grants extensive rights of autonomy and national political participation to the indigenous communities. At the same time, in explicit resistance to neoliberalism and the influence of foreign corporations in the country, it transfers power over Bolivia's crucial hydrocarbon resources to the state. "We leave behind the colonial, republican, and neoliberal state. . . . We found Bolivia anew" (Dejamos en el pasado el Estado colonial, republicano y neoliberal. . . . Refundamos Bolivia), the preamble of the Bolivian Constitution ambitiously asserts (*Constitución política del Estado* 2009).[16] Article 8

16. Translations from Spanish are mine unless otherwise indicated.

combines, as goals of the new constitution, indigenous moral ideals that translate into Spanish as "vivir bien" (live well or good life) with Enlightenment ideals:

Article 8.

I. The State assumes and promotes as ethical and moral principles of the pluralist society: *ama qhilla, ama llulla, ama suwa* (do not be lax, be neither liar nor bandit), *suma qamaña* (live well), *ñandereko* (harmonious life), *teko kavi* (good life), *ivi maraei* (Earth without evil), and *qhapaj ñan* (noble way of life).

II. The State rests on the values of unity, equality, inclusion, dignity, liberty, solidarity, reciprocity, respect, complementarity, harmony, transparency, balance, equal opportunity, social and gender equality in participation, shared well-being, responsibility, social justice, distribution and redistribution of products and social assets so as to live well.

[Artículo 8.

I. El Estado asume y promueve como principios ético-morales de la sociedad plural: ama qhilla, ama llulla, ama suwa (no seas flojo, no seas mentiroso ni seas ladrón), suma qamaña (vivir bien), ñandereko (vida armoniosa), teko kavi (vida buena), ivi maraei (tierra sin mal) y qhapaj ñan (camino o vida noble).

II. El Estado se sustenta en los valores de unidad, igualdad, inclusión, dignidad, libertad, solidaridad, reciprocidad, respeto, complementariedad, armonía, transparencia, equilibrio, igualdad de oportunidades, equidad social y de género en la participación, bienestar común, responsabilidad, justicia social, distribución y redistribución de los productos y bienes sociales, para vivir bien.]

Besides detailed bills of rights and the basic architecture of government and judiciary, the constitution also includes a section titled "Economic Structure and Organization of the State" that addresses, among many other issues, "The Environment, Natural Resources, Soil, and Land" (Medio ambiente, recursos naturales, tierra y territorio). Article 342 states that in general terms, "it is the duty of the State and of the population to conserve, protect, and use natural resources and biodiversity sustainably and to preserve environmental balance" (Es deber del Estado y de la población conservar, proteger y aprovechar de manera sustentable los recursos naturales y la biodiversidad, así como mantener el equilibrio del medio ambiente). Article 348 names biodiversity among the natural resources that are of strategic value and public interest for the country's development, and Article 381 specifies that "native animal and plant species are a natural patrimony. The State will establish the necessary measures for their conservation, use, and development" (Son patrimonio natural las especies nativas de origen animal y vegetal. El Estado establecerá las medidas necesarias para su conservación, aprovechamiento y desarrollo). Article 383 specifically refers to endangered species:

> The State will establish partial or total, temporary or permanent restrictions on the extractive uses of biodiversity resources. These measures will target the needs of preservation, conservation, recovery, and restoration of biodiversity that is at risk of extinction. Illegal keeping, handling, and trafficking of species will be penalized.
>
> [El Estado establecerá medidas de restricción parcial o total, temporal o permanente, sobre los usos extractivos de los recursos de la biodiversidad. Las medidas estarán orientadas a las necesidades de preservación, conservación, recuperación y restauración de la biodiversidad en riesgo de extinción. Se sancionará penalmente la tenencia, manejo y tráfico ilegal de especies de la biodiversidad.]

While decrees such as these may seem overly general and abstract, it is worth remembering that they are not part of a biodiversity or endangered species law of the kind that I have considered in previous sections, but part of a nation's *constitution*. That the conservation of biodiversity and endangered species is mentioned at all in Bolivia's constitution, much less highlighted as an explicit part of the state's tasks and duties, is astonishing in comparison with the constitutions of most nations in North America or Europe, which one would scour in vain for any reference to such issues. Biodiversity is explicitly envisioned not just as part of the national patrimony, as it is in many other countries, but also as a strategic resource; and beyond this modern legal and economic language, it becomes part of an ambitious attempt to reconceptualize the state by combining indigenous and Western Enlightenment traditions of thought.

The new constitution of 2009 was followed in 2010 by the passage of the Law of the Rights of Mother Earth (Ley de derechos de la Madre Tierra), which has attracted a good deal of attention from environmentalists worldwide. The law defines its understanding of "Mother Earth," establishes it as a legal subject, and outlines the state's and society's obligations toward it. Mother Earth is, the law specifies in article 3, "the dynamic, living system made up of the indivisible community of all life systems and living beings, interrelated, interdependent, and complementary, which share a common destiny. Mother Earth is considered sacred from the perspective of the cosmologies of original indigenous peasant nations and peoples" (el sistema viviente dinámico conformado por la comunidad indivisible de todos los sistemas de vida y los seres vivos, interrelacionados, interdependientes y complementarios, que comparten un destino común. La Madre Tierra es considerada sagrada, desde las cosmovisiones de las naciones y pueblos indígena originario campesinos; *Ley 71* 2010, art. 3). Article 5 declares: "For purposes of protection and custody of her rights, Mother Earth becomes a collective subject of public interest. Mother Earth and all her components, including human communities, are holders of all the inherent rights established in this Law" (Para efectos de la protección y tutela de sus derechos, la Madre Tierra adopta el carácter de sujeto colectivo de interés público. La Madre Tierra y todos sus componentes incluyendo las comunidades humanas son titulares de todos los derechos inherentes reconocidos en esta Ley). The second of the seven basic rights that the law attributes to Mother Earth is the right to "diversity of life" (la diversidad de la vida), defined as "the right to the preservation of the differentiation and variety of the beings that make up Mother Earth, without such genetic alteration or artificial modification of their structure as would endanger their existence, function, and future potential" (el derecho a la preservación de la diferenciación y la variedad de los seres que componen la Madre Tierra, sin ser alterados genéticamente ni modificados en su estructura de manera artificial, de tal forma que se amenace su existencia, funcionamiento y potencial futuro). The enshrinement of nature as sacred in national law, noteworthy in and of itself, is less surprising here than the way in which a thoroughly modern language of legal subjects and rights is applied to an entity that cannot in any way be construed as an individual or a group of individuals (even in the way in which a "legal person" in the laws of other countries can be a human individual, an organization, or a corporation). If the Irish climate scientist James Lovelock's "Gaia" concept sought to make global ecosystems comprehensible as a living superorganism via a detour through mythology, Bolivia's law turns global ecosystems into a legal superperson via a detour through indigenous cosmology, effectively creating what one might want to call a "bill of rights of Nature."

One could also approach the "Law of the Rights of Mother Nature" as a first step toward the realization of the "Parliament of Things" that French anthropologist Bruno Latour has called for in the context of Actor-Network-Theory (Latour [1991] 1993, 142–145). Latour envisions a political sphere in which not only human agents have a voice, but also nonhuman ones, though humans may serve as the nonhumans' representatives (Latour sees natural scientists, for example, as representatives of the nonhuman in society). The designation of nature as a legal entity with rights not only allows but in fact obligates all Bolivian citizens to respect, promote, and defend these rights (*Ley 71* 2010, art. 9). In addition, the law creates the "Defense Council for Mother Earth" (Defensoría de la Madre Tierra), whose "task is to attend to the validity, promotion, diffusion, and fulfillment of the rights of Mother Earth established by this law" (cuya misión es velar por la vigencia, promoción, difusión y cumplimiento de los derechos de la Madre Tierra, establecidos en la presente Ley [art. 10]).

The constitution and the Law of the Rights of Mother Earth, along with other legislation, seemed to turn Evo Morales into the champion of both indigenous communities and the natural environment against the power of the World Bank, the International Monetary Fund, and the foreign oil and gas corporations that were partly expropriated after his election. Nevertheless, conflicts erupted between Morales and some of the indigenous constituencies who had supported him during the campaign for a new constitution over, precisely, environmental matters. In part, as scholars such as Derrick Hindery and Jason Tockman have pointed out, these conflicts derived from tensions or even contradictions in the constitution itself. Seeking to reestablish Bolivia's political sovereignty and economic control of the country's natural resources—particularly in oil and gas—against European and North American corporations and financial institutions, the constitution attributes expanded power to the Bolivian state as well as to its indigenous communities. But these two spheres of power are, of course, not necessarily aligned with each other, and while the constitution grants indigenous communities the right to be consulted on matters of resource exploitation in their territories, it does not grant them rights of refusal should the state decide to use these resources in a manner they do not agree with (Hindery 2013, 164–184; Tockman 2012, 141–144).

Such a conflict erupted in 2011 when the Morales government sought to construct a highway through TIPNIS, Territorio Indígena y Parque Nacional Isiboro-Sécure, an area in Bolivia's Cochabamba and Beni Departments that was declared a National Park in 1965 and Indigenous Territory in 1990. TIPNIS is a major biodiversity hotspot, but it had already experienced substantial agricultural modification and deforestation. The one-hundred-mile highway segment in question, part of the larger Villa Tunari–San Ignacio de Moxos Highway, would have provided the first link of its kind between the Cochabamba and Beni departments and had been planned for decades. But it was only when the Morales government approved a major loan from the Brazilian National Bank for Economic and Social Development that the construction became financially possible. However, the project ran into fierce resistance from some of the indigenous communities in the territory, who pointed to the deforestation and damage to biodiversity it would cause. Three indigenous organizations, TIPNIS Subcentral, CIDOB (Confederation of Indigenous Peoples of Bolivia), and CONAMAQ (Consejo Nacional de Ayllus y Markas del Qullasuyu), organized a march from Villa Tunari to La Paz in protest of the highway. Hundreds of marchers were arrested and then released, other organizations mobilized their members to advocate for the construction project, and the marchers were greeted enthusiastically by masses of people at their arrival in La Paz in October 2011. The Legislative Assembly approved the construction later that month against the opposition of indigenous representatives. Morales gave in to the pressure from indigenous constituencies by announcing that he would veto the Legislative Assembly's bill, and an alternative bill proposed by the indigenous representatives that prohibits highway construction in TIPNIS was voted into law in late October 2011.

This conflict put a spotlight on the potential conflicts between state power and the power of indigenous communities when it comes to defining how the goals of "vivir bien" and "holistic development" (desarrollo integral) in the Bolivian Constitution should be translated into practice. As Hindery and Tockman argue, it also pinpointed some of the tensions between Morales's use of income from the export of gas, oil, and other natural resources to lift Bolivians out of poverty, on one hand, and his resistance to capitalism, neoliberalism, and more generally the commodification of nature, on the other (Hindery 2013, 148–163; Tockman 2012, 130, 144–146). While he was able to reduce the percentage of Bolivians living in extreme poverty from 38 percent in 2005 to 24 percent in 2011 (Neuman 2014), in other words, this increased prosperity was achieved through continued extraction of natural resources and with the help of international capitalist markets.[17]

In spite of these conflicts and tensions, Morales and the Legislative Assembly reaffirmed their commitment to the goals spelled out in the constitution and the 2010 Law of the Rights of Mother Earth when they passed the Framework Law of Mother Earth and Holistic Development for Living Well (Ley marco de la Madre Tierra y desarrollo integral para vivir bien) in 2012 (*Ley 300* 2012). This law reasserts some of the central principles that had already been spelled out in the Law on the Rights of Mother Earth: "Madre Tierra" is defined as the totality of living systems, as sacred (art. 5) and as a juridical person (art. 9), and the state is committed to the "complementarity of living beings in Mother Earth for Living Well" (la complementariedad de los seres vivos en la Madre Tierra para vivir bien). But this law spells out the political and economic implications of these basic assumptions in far greater detail:

> Living Well (*Sumaj Kamaña, Sumaj Kausay, Yaiko Kavi Päve*) is an alternative civilizational and cultural horizon to capitalism and modernity. It springs from the cosmologies of the original indigenous peasant nations and peoples and from intercultural and Afrobolivian communities, and it is conceived in the context of interculturality.

> [El Vivir Bien (Sumaj Kamaña, Sumaj Kausay, Yaiko Kavi Päve). Es el horizonte civilizatorio y cultural alternativo al capitalismo y a la modernidad que nace en las cosmovisiones de las naciones y pueblos indígena originario campesinos, y las comunidades interculturales y afrobolivianas, y es concebido en el contexto de la interculturalidad.] (art. 5, para. 2)

In this explicit critique of modernity and capitalism, development is not an end in itself but a stage on the way to achieving the "Living Well"

---

17. Jorge Marcone provides an excellent survey and critique of documentaries that have focused on these conflicts in a variety of Latin American countries in his essay "Filming the Emergence of Popular Environmentalism in Latin America: Postcolonialism and Buen Vivir" (2015). While these films portray the political conflict between indigenous communities and the state, Marcone argues, they tend to underemphasize or omit the different relation to the nonhuman world that indigenous cosmologies introduce into the political sphere (208–209).

ideal as a new sociocultural horizon (No es un fin, sino una fase interme-
dia para alcanzar el Vivir Bien como un nuevo horizonte civilizatorio y
cultural; art. 5, para. 3). "Living Well" is explicitly linked to social justice and to climate justice (art. 4, paras. 13, 14), and Morales opposed it
in an interview to the idea of "vivir mejor," living better than another in
constant competition (Morales 2011, 9). "Vivir Bien" implies actively resisting the commodification of nature: "The environmental functions and
natural processes of the components and life systems of Mother Earth are
not considered commodities, but gifts of the sacred Mother Earth" (Las
funciones ambientales y procesos naturales de los componentes y sistemas
de vida de la Madre Tierra, no son considerados como mercancías sino
como dones de la sagrada Madre Tierra [*Ley 300* 2012, art. 4, para. 2]).

Practically, affirming such principles has not implied that Bolivia has
attempted any wholesale exit from capitalism or international markets;
the country continues to export gas to Argentina and Brazil in large quan-
tities, for example, as well as lithium (which is used for electric car batte-
ries). But the 2012 Framework Law provides language that could potentially be used to challenge uses of natural resources that not all Bolivians
agree upon, and it does spell out some more specific policies. In article 13,
which is mainly concerned with nutrition, the state commits to "actions
to prevent the commodification of genetic resources, the privatization of
water, biopiracy, and the illegal transfer of genetic resources as well as
the participation of monopolies and/or oligopolies in the production and
commercial distribution of seeds and foods" (Acciones para evitar la mer-
cantilización de los recursos genéticos, la privatización del agua, la biopi-
ratería y el traslado ilegal de material genético, así como la participación
de monopolios y/o oligopolios en la producción y comercialización de
semillas y alimentos [*Ley 300* 2012, art. 13, para. 5]).

The commitment to fostering biodiversity also reappears in this law
outside of the issue of biopiracy. Biodiversity, the Framework Law indicates, pertains at a variety of levels, from variation within and across
species to ecosystems (art. 5), and the state is committed to precaution as
an environmental principle:

> Precaution. The Plurinational State of Bolivia and each individ-
> ual or collective person are obligated to prevent and/or avoid
> effectively and efficiently any harm to the components of Mother
> Earth, including the environment, biodiversity, human health,
> and intangible cultural values, without any possibility of void-
> ing or postponing this commitment by claiming lack of scientific
> certainty and/or lack of means.

[Precautorio. El Estado Plurinacional de Bolivia y cualquier persona individual o colectiva se obliga a prevenir y/o evitar de manera oportuna eficaz y eficiente los daños a los componentes de la Madre Tierra incluyendo el medio ambiente, la biodiversidad, a la salud humana y a los valores culturales intangibles, sin que se pueda omitir o postergar el cumplimiento de esta obligación alegando la falta de certeza científica y/o falta de recursos.] (*Ley 300* 2012, art. 4, para. 4)

Biodiversity conservation, in this law, is even more explicitly associated with a commitment to cultural diversity and to social justice than in the previous legal documents. Article 13, paragraph 10, spells out the principle of

enhancement and strengthening of the life systems of small producers, of the original indigenous peasant nations and peoples, intercultural and Afrobolivian communities, cooperatives and other types of associations, through the sustainable management of their biodiversity and through the respect, enhancement, and reaffirmation of their forms of knowledge in the framework of cultural diversity.

[Revalorización y fortalecimiento de los sistemas de vida de los pequeños productores, de las naciones y pueblos indígena originario campesinos, comunidades interculturales y afrobolivianas, cooperativas y otros sistemas asociativos, a través del manejo sustentable de su biodiversidad y del respeto, revalorización y reafirmación de sus saberes en el marco de la diversidad cultural.]

In the constitution as well as in the Framework Law, biodiversity conservation goes together with the use of and respect for different knowledge systems that Bolivia's varied cultural communities bring to bear on nonhuman life. Similarly, the Framework Law emphasizes equal access to nature in article 19: "*Provide equal access to the components of Mother Earth:* The Plurinational State of Bolivia will reduce differences in the Bolivian people's access to soil, water, forests, biodiversity, and other components of Mother Earth" (*facilitar el acceso equitativo a los componentes de la madre tierra*. El Estado Plurinacional de Bolivia facilitará la reducción de las diferencias con relación al acceso del pueblo boliviano a la tierra, agua, bosques, biodiversidad y otros componentes de la Madre Tierra).

For radical environmentalists in North America or in Europe, the Bolivian Constitution of 2009 and the laws concerning Mother Earth of 2010 and 2012 may be as close as they will come to utopian texts with actual legal force. To say this is not to ignore or deny the two central problems I pointed out earlier: on one hand, the tension between centralized state power (pitted in old leftist style against private corporate power) and the centrifugal powers of varied indigenous and other cultural communities, and on the other hand, the tension between the aspiration to break away from the capitalist commodification of natural resources and the necessity to participate in it so as to alleviate poverty. "Just as the extractivism of the Latin American 'New Left' is challenging popular environmentalism in terms of national interests, Buen Vivir and other popular environmentalisms are challenging the anticolonial stance of these governments," Jorge Marcone sums it up (2015, 221). But it is to say that in spite of their flaws, these recent Bolivian laws have emerged from the ambitious enterprise of envisioning a contemporary fusion of indigenous codes of knowledge and behavior toward the natural world with ecological and biological science, and a combination of indigenous forms of community with Western leftist traditions of thought regarding social and environmental justice.

The conservation of endangered species, from this perspective, becomes part of a broader social and political vision than is apparent in the American, German, and European Union laws I focused on in earlier sections. Even though the rhetoric of national and transnational patrimony appears in all the versions of biodiversity protection law analyzed here, the Bolivian law clearly goes beyond the focus on species at risk and the ties to critical habitat in the United States' Endangered Species Act, beyond the focus on the conservation of cultural landscapes in the German Bundesnaturschutzgesetz, and beyond the commitment to biodiversity conservation through species and habitat conservation in the European Union directives. It ties the conservation of biodiversity and endangered species to a far more encompassing vision of a socially just and culturally diverse society that draws on traditional forms of knowledge as well as modern science and management to develop sustainable ways of breaking out of poverty. It also explicitly recognizes the more-than-human world as a legal subject. If all laws for the protection of endangered species, habitats, or biodiversity rely on underlying ties of these natural entities to social histories and cultural visions, as I have attempted to show throughout, the Bolivian laws are far more explicit than the North American and European laws in making biodiversity conservation part of an encompassing social vision that includes the natural world.

PLATE 1 Isabella Kirkland, *Descendant* (1999). From *Taxa* series. Oil paint on polyester over wood panel, 48 × 36 in. Reproduced by permission of the artist.

PLATE 2 Isabella Kirkland, *Gone* (2004). From *Taxa* series. Oil paint and alkyd on canvas over panel, 48 × 36 in. Reproduced by permission of the artist.

PLATE 3 Joel Sartore, *Delhi Sands Flower-Loving Fly* (2009). Photograph © Joel Sartore, joelsartore.com. Reproduced by permission of the artist.

5. Comparison and Assessment

Hard-headed conservationists may argue at this point that it is all well and good to examine what social and cultural underpinnings endangered species laws rely on. But what kind of law is in practice most effective at conserving biodiversity? The answer to this question is much harder than it may at first sight appear. American scientists, legislators, and activists often tout the U.S. Endangered Species Act as an immensely powerful tool for conservation and one of the most important environmental laws in the world. The Center for Biological Diversity in Arizona, for example, one of the organizations that focuses on launching procedures for listing particular species as endangered, claims on its website that "the Endangered Species Act is the strongest law for protecting biodiversity passed by any nation" (Center for Biological Diversity 2014). But the center provides no evidence from outside the United States to support this global claim, and scientific assessments even of the Endangered Species Act on its own are complex. Some of the factors that make a quantitative assessment difficult include the interaction of biodiversity protection with other laws, the interaction of laws with other social variables in conservation, the question of what should be measured to gauge success, and the difficulty of arguing on the basis of historical counterfactuals.[18] Such complications multiply in the comparison of conservation laws from different countries. As a consequence, comparative data about conservation in countries with differently structured conservation regimes are scarce.

This chapter has focused on legislation that directly addresses endangered species or biodiversity, and the laws in each of the areas I have chosen are examples that define that country's or region's vision of conservation. But as I have already mentioned during this analysis, how effective these laws are in practice is in part determined by how they interact with a wide range of other laws. Laws regarding land use, toxic chemicals, hunting, fisheries, forestry, agriculture, and oceans, to name just a few, can significantly enhance or limit the effectiveness of biodiversity protection laws. Tracing the positive and negative feedback loops between such arrays of laws and treaties would take hundreds of pages worth of legal analysis as well as detailed studies of individual cases. Legal scholar Anke Holljesiefken, for example, toward the end of a four-hundred-page

---

18. I leave aside the fact that claims about the relative success of the Endangered Species Act are as a rule self-serving, in that they are made by individuals or organizations who advocate for its use in conservation.

analysis of invasive-species regulations in German law, diagnoses self-contradictory definitions of what is "native" and "invasive," regulations for different sectors that do not sync with each other, and the absence of a unified national strategy (2007, 321–323).

Second, how effective laws are in protecting biodiversity obviously depends on their interaction with social and economic dimensions. Depleted state coffers and underpaid public servants prone to accepting bribes can undermine any rule of law, as can limited funds for conservation and the power of social actors opposed to certain kinds of conservation. The extended conflict over the protection of the spotted owl in areas used by the timber industry in the northwestern United States serves as a vivid example of such opposition. But other cases are even more complex: Alexander N. Songorwa, director of wildlife for the Tanzanian Ministry of Natural Resources and Tourism, published a plea to the American Fish and Wildlife Service in the *New York Times* in 2013 *not* to list the African lion as endangered. In practice, he argued, this would put lion conservation in Tanzania at risk: "We are alarmed that the United States Fish and Wildlife Service is considering listing the African lion as endangered," he wrote. "Doing so would make it illegal for American hunters to bring their trophies home. Those hunters constitute 60 percent of our trophy-hunting market, and losing them would be disastrous to our conservation efforts" (Songorwa 2013). Songorwa's plea acquired a new resonance in 2015 as international debate erupted over the killing of a popular and well-known lion, Cecil, in Zimbabwe at the hands of an American game hunter. As these examples show, conservation laws passed by particular nations interact with legal dispensations as well as patterns of socioeconomic inequality across national borders.

Determining how effective particular biodiversity conservation laws are also often requires arguing from historical counterfactuals—determining what would have happened if the law had not passed. In the case of the Endangered Species Act, which singles out animal and plant species that have already been identified as at risk, this would seem easier to accomplish than in the case of laws that seek to protect species and ecosystems no matter what their original state. Scott et al., in "By the Numbers," attempted such an evaluation in 2006 and estimated that 227 species were prevented from going extinct by the ESA in the thirty years between 1973 and 2003, but these numbers are heavily dependent on initial assumptions about the rate at which species that are associated with certain categories of risk might be presumed to die out (2006, 31). A different study, published in 2005, found that the likelihood of a species being classified as "recovering" by the U.S. Fish and Wildlife Service increased with the number of years it was listed (Taylor, Suckling, and Rachlinski 2005). Wilcove and McMillan, in an analysis of how the species on the first U.S. endangered species list from 1967 have fared, describe the ESA ambiguously as having "a complicated history . . . a mixture of success and failure, hope and disappointment" (2006, 50). A 2007 study that explicitly sought to overcome the problem of counter-factuals compared listed species with unlisted ones that resembled each other in taxonomy, charisma, and endangerment status. The researchers found that listing under the ESA was effective when accompanied by substantial federal funding but actually counterproductive if the listing was not accompanied by such funding—presumably because listing a species as endangered creates incentives for landowners to hasten its demise if they are not compensated for the complications and costs that arise from owning endangered species habitat (Ferraro, McIntosh, and Ospina 2007).

Beyond the United States, the signatories of the 1992 Convention on Biological Diversity committed themselves to reducing species extinction rates significantly by the United Nations' International Year on Biodiversity, 2010. The European Union went the CBD one better by pledging to halt species loss by 2010. Neither of these goals was reached, and the European Union has now moved its goalpost to 2020. In Germany, while species such as otters, beavers, and wolves as well as some bird species have significantly benefited from protection, the overall picture is less positive. In a report issued in 2015, the German government indicated that 28 percent of vertebrates are endangered, as well as 45.8 percent of the invertebrates that have so far been assessed (Bundesamt für Naturschutz 2015, 17–18). The European Commission similarly issued a mixed report, "The State of Nature in the European Union," in 2015, claiming that some species and habitats under EU biodiversity legislation are recovering with the help of the Natura 2000 network but that "the overall status of species and habitats in the EU has not changed significantly 2007–2012, with many habitats and species showing an unfavourable status and a significant proportion of them deteriorating still farther" (European Commission 2015, 19). Conservation outcomes across a variety of countries, then, are mixed, and precise assessment is hard to come by.

Clearly, if the goal of conservation is defined not by species numbers but by other concepts such as landscape, as it is in the German Bundesnaturschutzgesetz, the quantification becomes even more complicated and tenuous. And if biodiversity protection becomes part of a more general agenda for a sustainable and socially just society, as it does in the Bolivian Ley Marco de la Tierra Madre y Desarrollo Integral para Vivir Bien, species numbers in and of themselves are of limited diagnostic value. The question of how successful a conservation law is, in other words, simply cannot be dissociated from what the law sought to achieve in the first place. For this reason, it cannot be answered in separation from the analysis that I have undertaken in this chapter, which will hopefully be complemented by similar analyses for other communities, countries, and regions. Analyzing conservation laws and their outcomes may tell us something about the state of nature, but it certainly tells us something about the state of culture.

In this context, asking how many species have gone extinct, how many have changed their listing status, and how many have recovered—the usual measure of conservation success in scientific papers on the subject—misses the point if the conservation laws under scrutiny were not formulated around endangered species in the first place. To put it a little more pointedly, it may imply imposing a U.S. yardstick on laws conceived in different legal, political, and cultural frameworks. While such measures are obviously useful as one set of data to consider, they tell no more than part of a story that needs to be put into the context of the larger story that communities tell about themselves through their conservation laws. This is not to argue that quantitative evaluation does not have a role to play. It clearly does. But conservation laws, like other narratives about endangered species, are part of the stories cultural communities tell about themselves, their pasts, and their futures. Knowing what the numbers mean, and for whom, requires a knowledge of these stories.

4 Mass Extinction and Mass Slaughter: Biodiversity, Violence, and the Dangers of Domestication

1. Where the Wild Cats Are: Protest, Animal Welfare, and Conservation

One does not usually imagine large metropolises as biodiversity hotspots, and urban conservation has only recently become a major topic of interest for environmentalists.[1] My hometown of Los Angeles, for example, is better known for its traffic jams, disaster movies, and droughts than for its green spaces, wildlife, and ecological restoration efforts. Yet questions of biodiversity, of what belongs and what does not in the urban context, keep coming up along with struggles over water use, decarbonized transportation, and gentrification. Many of the city's iconic palm trees, planted in the 1930s on the occasion of the Olympic Games, are nearing the end of their seventy- to one-hundred-year life spans (Techentin 2009, 134–135). Should these symbols of tropical ease, most of them nonnatives, be replaced by more ecologically functional and native trees such as live oaks and sycamores? Or are such considerations irrelevant

1. I am grateful to Jon Christensen, Vasile Stănescu, and Julia Adeney Thomas for their helpful comments on drafts of this chapter, as well as to the participants of the seminar on endangerment held at the Max Planck Institute for the History of Science in Berlin in July 2012.

in a city whose official tree is the Coral Tree (*Erythrina caffra*), a native of South Africa, and many of whose human residents hail from other countries and continents?

So long as such questions are framed mostly in terms of taste and aesthetics, they may seem marginal enough. But when violence becomes part of the options, debate heats up, and the underlying issues turn out to be less innocuous. In Los Angeles, a long-running battle over feral cats has pitted animal rights activists against conservationists. Just how many feral cats roam the city and county of Los Angeles is unknown, but estimates run from the hundreds of thousands to 2 million. Clusters of the cats in certain neighborhoods have made residents skittish about dirt, fleas, and possible disease transmission, while conservationists worry about the impact of a large number of free-roaming cats on urban wildlife. A study carried out by the Smithsonian Institution's Conservation Biology Institute in 2012 that used local surveys and pilot studies to compute a national number estimated that feral and stray cats, together with those that owners let run outside of their houses, kill a median of 2.4 billion birds and 12.3 billion mammals a year (Loss, Will, and Marra 2013). In Los Angeles, members of the Stray Cat Alliance and other animal welfare organizations advocate so-called TNR programs— trap, neuter, and release—that capture and sterilize cats and send some of them to the limited sanctuary spaces that exist, releasing the rest back into the urban matrix. Their goal is to make the city a no-kill zone, a place where nonhuman lives are respected and where animals that were introduced by humans in the first place are not then exterminated by humans.

Conservation organizations such as the Urban Wildlands Group point out that even in the unlikely case that all feral cats could be accounted for by such programs, the cats' impact would continue for another decade or two, and no-kill policies might in fact encourage people to release more unwanted cats into the urban ecosystem (Muller 2013; Angier 2014). "What is so difficult for people to understand is that managing and controlling unowned, free-roaming cats will require euthanasia. There are not enough shelter spaces, there is not enough sanctuary space. And we have to stand up and be honest. But the thing is something is going to die in this equation," the founder of Urban Wildlife, Travis Longcore, argues (Muller 2013). In the animal welfare view, killing feral animals continues a long tradition of disregard of lives that are considered expendable. In the conservationist view, humans are responsible for animal death even if the cats are left alive, insofar as depriving a species—or even just a local population of a particular species—of the possibility to propagate into the future implies an even more terminal kind of erasure than the trapping or shooting of individuals.[2]

Such problems, of course, are not new. Animal welfare advocates and environmentalists have had a mixed history of convergences and conflicts that have come and gone. In the 1960s and 1970s, they often worked together, for example in protests against the hunting of seal pups, against which humane societies began to protest in 1957. The confrontations between animal advocates and seal hunters received intensive media coverage at the time. "A stocky 26-year-old Newfoundlander with a blond scraggly goatee, his jacket and shirt thrown open at the throat, had just killed a whitecoat over the protest of Alice Harrington [*sic*], founder and President of Friends of Animals, Inc., of New York City. She screamed, 'That one is mine! That one is mine! Don't touch it!' The club came down several times, the knife began to work. Miss Harrington berated the hunter. He replied that he was only trying to make a living" (Cowan 1971, 43). This description in a 1971 *New York Times* article portrays a confrontation between a prominent animal welfare advocate, Alice Herrington, and a hunter of seal pups, whose distinctive white fur was a prized commodity at the time. The environmental organization Greenpeace, founded in 1971 with an initial focus on antinuclear protest, soon joined the fray. "Expedition leader Paul Watson physically carried an 80-pound baby seal out of the way of the Norwegian sealing ship, saving it from being crushed in the ice. At one point, four Greenpeacers grouped in a line and brought the Norwegian ship to a halt," Greenpeace claimed in one of its statements on the 1976 seal hunt ("Seal Hunters" 1976). Throughout the 1970s, Greenpeace, Friends of Animals, the International Fund for Animal Welfare, and other environmental and animal advocacy organizations worked side by side to bring the slaughter of baby seals to a halt, effectively closing down the seal-fur industry: from $12 million in 1982, its value had dwindled to almost nothing by 1986 (Martin 1986).

Fast-forward to 1999. After extensive preparation, a group of Makah hunters—an American Indian people inhabiting the coast of what is

---

2. This problem is not sufficiently addressed in Thom van Dooren and Deborah Bird Rose's otherwise eloquent plea for a "multispecies city" that would move beyond the anthropocentric assumption that cities are living space only for humans (2012). Van Dooren and Rose accurately pinpoint the unnecessary pressures that humans put on wildlife, but they do not engage the difficult choices that arise for humans when different nonhuman species compete for urban survival. I will return to the framework of multispecies theory, which offers important opportunities for rethinking ideas of justice in the relationship between species, in chapter 5.

today the U.S. state of Washington—set out and killed a gray whale, surrounded by the protest ships of several animal protection groups. There was nothing illegal about the hunt. The Makah had hunted seals and gray whales for at least a millennium and a half, and the Neah Bay Treaty of 1855 explicitly granted them the right to continue this tradition. But since the number of gray whales diminished steadily from the second half of the nineteenth century on, the Makah stopped hunting them in the 1920s. In 1946 the International Whaling Commission (IWC) began to regulate the international whaling industry, and by 1986, given the endangered status of many whale species, it issued a moratorium on whale hunting. Indigenous peoples were exempt, provided they had kept up a continuous tradition of hunting—a difficulty for the Makah, who had discontinued whaling sixty years earlier. By 1994 gray whale populations had recovered enough that the National Oceanic and Atmospheric Administration of the United States delisted them from its Red List and gave the Makah permission to hunt on condition that the IWC would allow it. Complicated negotiations ensued between Russia, the United States, and the IWC, since the IWC sets global hunting quotas for particular species, which are then distributed among different hunting groups: in this case, the 124 gray whales at stake were to be distributed between the Makah and the Chukotka of eastern Russia. In the end, the Chukotka were assigned 120 and the Makah 4 whales over a five-year interval. The 1999 Makah hunt was therefore legitimated by fifteen hundred years of indigenous tradition, the Neah Bay Treaty, the permission of the IWC, and the agreement between Russia and the United States.

None of this mattered much to organizations such as the Sea Shepard Conservation Society (led by Paul Watson, who had by then split off from Greenpeace), the American Humane Society, the Cetacean Society International, the West Coast Anti-Whaling Society, and In the Path of Giants, which considered the killing of highly intelligent and social animals such as whales morally unacceptable in any cultural or legal framework. They surrounded the Makah hunt with vigorous protests at sea and on the Makah Reservation, and subsequent litigation quickly ended the Makah's attempt to revive their cultural tradition. In frustration, five Makah men hunted and killed a gray whale in 2007 without any legal permit or tribal authorization, propelling the question of the legitimacy of hunting once more into the media limelight.[3]

3. For the Makah hunt, see Robert Sullivan's book-length account (2000); for a detailed discussion of the whale-hunting debates in general, see Glavin (2006, chap. 6).

Compared to the protests against seal hunting in the 1970s, the anti-whaling protests of the 1990s stand out by the absence of environmental organizations. Neither Greenpeace, so active on the issue of hunting in its first decade, nor other powerful environmentalist organizations participated in the protests against the Makah hunt. In part, this change in perspective was due to attacks on conservation organizations' disregard for the rights and traditions of indigenous peoples that took on full force in the 1980s with the emergence of the environmental justice movement. Greenpeace, after its seal-hunt activism, had been harshly criticized for contributing to the collapse of an industry that Inuit and Aleuts had pursued sustainably for millennia and now saw themselves stripped of at the hands of mostly white environmentalists. Other environmental organizations, too, had been attacked for their disregard of indigenous ways of life and their displacement of indigenous peoples from ancestral homes for the sake of wildlife conservation, in confrontations that I will discuss in greater detail in chapter 5. By the 1990s these organizations saw little point in protesting indigenous practices whose effects were limited and local; they concentrated instead on combating commercial practices with systemic and destructive consequences for habitats, species, and the globe as a whole. Greenpeace, for instance, has continued to oppose commercial whaling such as that of the Japanese and the Norwegians and to fight for the protection of whales from pollution and habitat degradation. Compared to these large-scale threats, the Makah hunting tradition entailed no real danger, in Greenpeace's view.

The comparison of anti–seal hunting protests in the 1970s and the protests against Makah whale hunting in the 1990s highlights not mere differences of policy between animal welfare advocates and environmentalists, but more fundamental differences in the risk perceptions around which the two movements have crystallized. Animal welfare and environmentalism emerged historically from somewhat different traditions of resistance to modernization, and each has radicalized since the 1960s and 1970s around its own characteristic risk culture. Environmentalists see ecosystems, habitats, species, waterways, soils, and the atmosphere as endangered. Threats to biodiversity as they have emerged since the 1980s have focused on endangered and extinct species, typically symbolized by charismatic species, for reasons that I examined in chapter 1. Animal welfare advocates, by contrast, see the greatest danger to animals in institutions such as research labs, zoos, circuses, and above all in the living and dying conditions inflicted upon them in the factory farms of industrial-scale agribusiness. Both movements, even as they resist facets of modernization and its institutions and cultural practices, also draw on Enlightenment thought to formulate their protests: ideas of citizenship, emancipation, liberation, and individual rights resonate in the thought and rhetoric of both movements at various moments of their historical development.

While animal welfare and conservationism share a deep concern about humans' relation to nonhumans, and both agree that humans' interests should not always and by default be privileged over those of other living beings, fundamental differences separate the environmentalist emphasis on the well-being of wild species and ecosystems from the animal-liberationist focus on the welfare of individual, mostly domestic animals. I will examine these differences in section 2. Eminent philosophers have sought to reconcile these two perspectives, and the interdisciplinary research area that has emerged under the label of Human-Animal Studies or Critical Animal Studies over the past two decades includes many scholars who, like myself, find a great deal of value in both perspectives. But that does not mean that the moral and political imperatives that have issued from the two movements—each of which has by now also branched into several, sometimes quite divergent, traditions of thought—are easy to combine even today. The recent debate in Los Angeles over feral cats is just one example of the continuing difficulty of integrating animal welfare and conservationist impulses.

In thinking through the differences here, my goal is not to achieve a conceptual reconciliation, which, at any rate, would likely accomplish little in solving the practical problem of which animals get to live and to die in Los Angeles. Rather, what I find instructive about animal welfare and environmental perspectives is that in their disagreements and critiques, they highlight the ways in which each of them privileges a different spectrum of diversity and of species whose specificity tends to be glossed over with appeals to the dignity of all life or the health of ecosystems. The choice of what kind of biodiversity is valued more than other kinds in each regime ultimately obeys cultural orientations that are rooted in different perspectives on modernization understood as a grand-scale process of domestication. In section 3, I will therefore return to the trope of the "end of nature" in contemporary environmentalism that I discussed in the introduction, an idea that implies not only the destruction of habitats and the loss of biodiversity, but more broadly the fact that nature has been so comprehensively reshaped by humans that it can no longer be conceived as a realm outside human society. Nature has been brought too close to us to be "wild" anymore, in the view of some conservationists. But as I will show, the conclusions that different kinds of conservationists draw from this observation diverge quite sharply.

From the perspective of animal welfare, by contrast, nature has not yet come close enough to us, in that we still collectively relegate even some of our closest biological relatives to mere objects of consumption and use. At the same time, we arbitrarily elevate some of them, pet animals, to the status of family members who enjoy better nutrition and health care than is available to many humans. If excessive and sometimes unintended domestication, then, is what puts animals and the natural world in peril from the environmentalist perspective, it is incomplete or misguided domestication that leads to the abuse of biological others in the animal welfare view.

One consequence of these divergent perceptions of endangerment is a different approach to the question of a political community that would include both humans and nonhumans. The discourse of "animal rights," one variant of animal welfare thought, aims to make at least some animals quasi-citizens within the purview of human law and society, while environmental ethics, at least in the influential variant represented by the American conservationist Aldo Leopold, seeks to make humans citizens of an ecological community beyond the bounds of society. But, as section 4 will briefly outline, the insights of animal welfare advocacy may become newly useful to environmental ethics as environmentalism shifts from its principal investment in wilderness as the ecological ideal to a view of nature as globally domesticated in the framework of the Anthropocene.

2. Animals at Risk

Scientifically and culturally, the concern over particular endangered species, as I discussed in chapters 1 and 3, gained force in the mid- to late nineteenth century and took a new turn in the 1970s and 1980s with the emphasis on the possibility that a mass extinction was under way in the contemporary age. Environmental historians and historians of science have shown that the concern over wild nature in general and wild animals in particular is closely related to the rise of a middle class whose livelihoods no longer involved daily work with animals, and the emergence of large urban spaces in which work animals were gradually marginalized and displaced by technological devices and by pets (Jasper and Nelkin 1992, 13; Philo 1998, 58–71; White 1996, 176–181).[4] The same sociological changes also led to the sentimentalization of family

---

4. On the emergence of earlier sentiments for animal protection in the Renaissance and their connection to Calvinist theology, see Watson (2014).

life, of which domestic animals increasingly came to be a part, and to the growth of animal welfare movements. The humane tradition that extends compassion from animals that live in the house to those kept on the farm, in laboratories, or in zoos, originated in nineteenth-century Britain and has persisted in Britain and the United States until the present day.[5]

The rise of the animal *rights* movement, a new variant of animal welfare that was inspired both by the new social movements of the 1960s and by the Australian philosopher Peter Singer's seminal book *Animal Liberation* ([1975] 2009), radicalized this tradition.[6] Animal abuse shifted from being perceived as an occasional aberration to being viewed as part and parcel of modern agriculture and of a techno-scientific establishment that the public no longer trusted as unconditionally as it had until World War II. The public display of animals in zoos under often deplorable conditions, their extensive use as experimental subjects in scientific labs, and their woeful treatment in increasingly industrialized factory farms caused public outrage, often triggered by animal welfare groups' highly mediatized reports and demonstrations. The language of "rights," borrowed from human rights legislation and the civil rights movement, combined with exemplary action and direct-mail strategies borrowed from the environmentalist movement (especially Greenpeace) to drive home humans' moral obligations toward animals that contemporary society was systematically violating (Jasper and Nelkin 1992, 73–75).

With shared historical roots in rights liberalism and humans' changing relationship to nature in the early nineteenth century and in the social uprisings of the 1960s, environmental ethics and animal welfare, which crystallized as forceful presences in public debate at roughly the same time, have a good deal in common in their philosophical orientation. Both movements are deeply critical of certain aspects of modernity, especially the instrumentalization and commodification of the nonhuman (I will explore this aspect in more detail in section 3). They share a deep concern over the welfare of nonhuman living beings, which in both movements have mainly come to be represented by certain charismatic animal species. Rabbits used for painful eye experiments in the development of mascara, baby seals skinned alive for their fur, whales and

5. I do not have the space here to unfold the complex relations between the animal welfare and antislavery movements in Britain and the United States over the course of the nineteenth century. I thank Jon Christensen for reminding me of these historical ties.

6. As Varner points out (1998, chap. 5), Singer has come to be associated with the animal rights perspective, although his utilitarian approach in the 1970s actually stood in tension with the attribution of inalienable individual rights.

dolphins degraded for marine park entertainment, and highly intelligent pigs confined in gestation crates have served as iconic species in the animal welfare movement. In campaigns for environmental conservation, gorillas, polar bears, pandas, tigers, rhinos, and whales, along with raptors, parrots, and smaller colorful birds usually stand in for endangered species at large in books, photographs, and documentaries concerned with biodiversity loss (see chapter 1).

Both movements put in question the assumption that humans' rights and interests should by default take precedence over the interests of other species, and both of them seek to define human identity anew in altered relations with nonhumans. This has sometimes earned them accusations of misanthropy from their opponents. Both of them seek to change cultural traditions and customs, all the way from those of indigenous cultures to those of contemporary mass consumption economies, that in their view do not duly respect nonhumans. Both the environmental movement and the animal welfare movement derive some of their sense of moral urgency—as well as, not infrequently, their self-righteousness and smug sense of moral superiority—from the conviction that what they perceive as nature has been egregiously violated.

But they differ fundamentally in how they conceive the nature that exerts such a powerful moral pressure. The animal welfare movement is concerned with individual animals at risk and makes its claims on their behalf by pointing to the many characteristic features and abilities they share with humans: the ability to suffer, to use tools, to communicate with sign systems, to experience emotions, and to live in complex social structures. This does not erase their differences from humans—animal welfare advocates readily admit that even with some of the same capabilities, animals do not necessarily have the same interests as humans, such as an interest in voting, owning property, or learning new forms of communication: "The basic principle of equality does not require equal or identical *treatment;* it requires equal consideration. Equal consideration for different beings may lead to different treatment and different rights," Singer has argued ([1975] 2009, 2). But within this framework, animals have the right not to have their interests violated by humans simply because they belong to another species, a bias that Richard Ryder named "speciesism," in analogy to sexism and racism, in 1971. While the use of the legal "rights" framework is not universally accepted by all animal welfare advocates, the commitment to the well-being of the individual animal is. By contrast, environmentalist thought is generally committed to species rather than individuals, it seeks to protect species well beyond just animals, including plants, fungi, and microorganisms, and it aims ultimately at the preservation of complex ecosystems.

In practice, these different philosophical orientations have often converged. Factory farming, for example, is not any more desirable from an environmentalist than from an animal welfare perspective, since it creates high volumes of toxic runoff and greenhouse gases that contribute to climate change. Eight to 18 percent of greenhouse gases are generated through livestock farming (Gerber et al. 2013). Wildlife poaching of elephants in Africa or tigers in India causes animal suffering and puts already ecologically stressed species at increased risk of extinction.[7] Excessive pesticide use causes suffering for birds and fish that ingest contaminated insects, and it also contaminates the food web. In militating against such practices, environmentalists and animal welfare advocates have sometimes worked hand in hand.

But in other cases, the interests of the two movements do not converge as smoothly. Animal welfare advocates tend to focus on the fate of domestic and farm animals, whereas environmentalists are most centrally concerned with wild species. Even when animal welfare activists engage with wild species, they often concentrate on their treatment in captivity, a matter that is of relative indifference to environmentalists (Jasper and Nelkin 1992, 75). Conversely, conservationists' worry over vanishing species is of little concern to animal rights advocates when it does not involve direct violence or cruelty. Hunting, which environmentalists often accept or even participate in as an ecologically functional practice with deep historical and cultural roots in many regions, is greeted with outrage and protest by animal welfare activists, whether it be the aristocratic custom of fox-hunting in England or the indigenous one of hunting seals or whales for subsistence. To environmentalists, sustainable hunting is merely the human variant of predation, one of the most basic processes in ecological food webs.[8]

Animal welfare advocates have not always found it easy to address natural predation, which is often accompanied by pain and intense suffering even without the involvement of humans. Peter Singer's and other animal welfare thinkers' ambivalence toward predation and toward

7. Wildlife poaching has been a recurrent concern in Africa and Asia from the second half of the twentieth century to the present. Elephant poaching in Africa has recently reached new heights and has attracted renewed media attention because of increased demand for ivory in China (Gettleman 2012).

8. For a detailed discussion of different types of hunting and the overlaps and conflicts between animal welfare and environmental advocates about them, see Varner (1998, chap. 5).

what human responsibility might consist of in this context (do humans have an obligation if not to eliminate, then to reduce the suffering of the prey populations, for example?) led to their fierce rejection by environmental philosophers in the 1980s. J. Baird Callicott accused the animal welfare movement of adhering to a "life-denying philosophy" because "the most fundamental fact of life in the biotic community is eating . . . *and being eaten.* . . . Whatever moral entitlements a being may have as a member of the biotic community, *not* among them is the right to life" (1989, 57).

Introduced species similarly tend to pit environmentalist and animal welfare advocates against each other. Environmentalists tend to claim a commitment to biodiversity, but this commitment often excludes nonnative species. Especially when they see introduced species as threats to biodiversity, environmentalists accept the infliction of harm on individual plants or animals as a legitimate means of ensuring the survival of other species or the ecosystem as a whole. In Italy, for example, gray squirrels were introduced into the Piedmont region on at least three different occasions between the 1940s and the 1990s. The rapid growth of their population caused concern both because of fears of bark-stripping, which is damaging to trees, and because gray squirrels had already displaced native red squirrels in most of Great Britain earlier, a prospect that seemed likely in Italy also. In 1996 the gray squirrel population of more than six thousand individuals was still inhabiting a limited enough area that it was thought possible to keep them from spreading farther, and Italy's National Wildlife Institute, after consultation with animal welfare groups and NGOs, started a trial eradication in 1997. Alternatives to eradication, such as transporting the squirrels back to their native habitat in North America or neutering them, had been discussed and ruled out for financial reasons during the consultation. But just a few months later, animal welfare groups initiated a lawsuit against the NWI. Even though the NWI's actions were eventually vindicated by the courts, the eradication measures were delayed for three years, and by then the gray squirrel population had spread far enough beyond its initial range that eradication was no longer feasible. The gray squirrel is projected to expand widely in the coming decades, and biologists fear it might eventually colonize the entire range of the red squirrel and endanger the species. "From an animal rights perspective, the preservation of a species does not outweigh the life of even a single individual animal. From an ecologist's view the preservation of a species is of the highest priority, especially when an alien that should not have been there in the first place is threatening that species" (Perry 2004).

But from the perspective of an animal welfare advocate, causing the death of even a single animal to save something as abstract as a "species" may seem like a kind of "ecological fascism," as the well-known animal rights philosopher Tom Regan once bluntly put it ([1983] 2004, 362). Philosopher Dale Jamieson attacks environmentalists' valuation of biological species even more directly: "We compound the problem when we think that it is species to which we have obligations rather than the creatures themselves. This is an instance of the general fallacy of attributing to species the properties of individual creatures. Individual creatures have hearts and lungs; species do not. Individual creatures often have welfares, but species never do. The notion of a species is an abstraction; the idea of its welfare is a human construction. While there is something that it is like to be an animal there is nothing that it is like to be a species" (2002, 186).

I will put aside Jamieson's focus on certain kinds of animals at the apparent expense of others—many animals do not have "hearts and lungs" to win the philosopher's goodwill. But it is difficult to imagine in his framework of "moral individualism," as James Rachels has called it (1999), how one could possibly determine what the "welfare" of a particular individual means without reference to species. As the philosopher Martha Nussbaum has argued, "the species norm (duly evaluated) tells us what the appropriate benchmark is for judging whether a given creature has decent opportunities for flourishing" (2004, 310). Neither can moral individualism and the rejection of species provide guidance in a case where introduced organisms threaten the survival of those already inhabiting a particular ecosystem.[9]

For the average citizen, the difference between a population of red squirrels and one of gray squirrels may seem too unimportant to justify killing animals. But other cases, especially involving animals in urban spaces, have led to heated confrontations, as I have already shown with regard to feral cats. This problem is even more obvious in cases where an introduced species is not only projected to trigger the extinction of other species in the future, but has already done so. The accidental introduction of the notorious brown tree snake, *Boiga irregularis,* to the island of Guam in the 1950s has led to the extinction of most native forest vertebrates, at least a half dozen native bird species, and several native liz-

9. Jamieson is right, however, in pointing to the difficulties inherent in the concept of "species" as a basis for conservation insofar as biodiversity applies both below the level of species (genetic variance between individuals and populations of a species) and above it (in the diversity of ecosystems); see chapter 1.

ard and gecko species (Quammen 1996, 321–337). Similarly, introduced populations of European rabbits (*Oryctolagus cuniculus*) in Australia have wreaked havoc on local ecosystems. "We already acknowledge that we need not permit human beings to lay waste to the environment. Nor should we permit rabbits and pigs to do so, especially given the fact that it was our own wrongdoing that enabled their destructiveness in the first place," the philosopher Elizabeth Anderson reasons (2004, 295).

In some cases, methods other than eradication may be feasible, and in these cases, a reconciliation between the animal welfare and environmentalist perspectives is easy to envision. But in other cases, the options are limited enough that they allow for no solution that does not involve violence to some group of animals: the concrete physical violence that consists of killing some kinds of animals, on one hand, and on the other hand, what one might, in a sociological analogy, call the "structural" or "slow violence" of making survival impossible for other species (Galtung 1969; Nixon 2011). Elephants, for example, threatened by habitat destruction and poaching in many parts of Africa, can themselves become a danger to other species when their populations grow and devastate the local vegetation. In the South African Kruger National Park, elephant culling had been practiced for this reason, but public pressure and lack of solid scientific evidence regarding the elephants' destructive impact led to the suspension of culling in 1995 (Van Aarde, Whyte, and Pimm 1999, 287). In subsequent years, however, scientific evidence began to accumulate that growing elephant populations reduce other kinds of biodiversity, as the elephant population in the park shot up from nine thousand in 1995 to twenty thousand in 2008. When the South African government therefore decided to resume culling in 2008, its decision was greeted with dismay and anger by animal welfare advocates (Timberg 2008). Similarly, a proposal by the Australian Department of the Environment in 2015 to cull 2 million of the estimated 20 million feral cats on the continent by 2020, based on the cats' devastating impact on native species such as the lesser bilby, the desert bandicoot, the crescent nailtail wallaby, and the big-eared hopping mouse, was met with outrage by such celebrity animal rights activists as Brigitte Bardot and the singer Morrissey (Ramzy 2015). Animal welfare thinking tends to focus exclusively on the first kind of violence; environmentalists, who admit that both kinds of violence are undesirable, tend to focus on the second kind and to accept physical violence as means of preventing structural violence. By referring to both processes as "violence," I do not mean to minimize the important differences between them: in many cases, denying animals the possibility of propagating (by neutering or spaying them, for example) may be a more "humane" solution than killing them. But in other cases, the difference between our hunting a population of birds to death and, alternatively, letting them be hunted to death by introduced predators such as feral cats may not be as categorical as animal welfare discourse would lead us to believe.

Philosopher Dale Jamieson's categorical claim that "animal liberation is an environmental ethic" (2002, 197) rings hollow against the background of such conflicts. His own argument in practice ends up denying most conservationist interventions any practical use or validity, which conveniently eliminates the problem of having to decide between morally justifiable but mutually exclusive options. Other philosophers, such as Mary Anne Warren, Mary Midgley, and J. Baird Callicott (at a later stage of his career), have sought more complex ways of conceptually bringing together animal and environmental ethics.[10] All of these approaches seek to make aspects other than animals' inherent capacities part of the kind of moral consideration they are owed from humans: for example, their degree of domestication (on the grounds that humans have different responsibilities toward populations that they themselves have brought into being, and whose existential horizons they control completely); their ability to coexist with humans (on the grounds that viruses, whose survival is sometimes incompatible with the well-being or survival of their human hosts, cannot claim the same consideration as domestic cats or chimpanzees); or their ecological functions (on the grounds that humans have greater obligations toward those species whose survival is necessary either for the survival of humankind itself or for a significant number of other species). But conflicts such as those over feral cats in urban spaces make clear that in practice, cultural factors play a crucial role in shaping decisions about the life and death of other species: ideas about what belongs and what does not belong in the city, what is desirable and what is undesirable in one's neighborhood, what forms of multispecies cohabitation are acceptable and which ones are not.[11]

10. The most important contributions to this debate from the 1980s and 1990s are collected in the volume *The Animal Rights/Environmental Ethics Debate*, edited by Eugene Hargrove (1994).

11. Such cultural dimensions emerge clearly in cases where environmentalists justify the rescue of charismatic animals on ecological grounds, even though the evidence that the rescue benefits populations, species, or ecosystems is scant. James Estes, a biologist in the U.S. Fish and Wildlife Service, for example, has questioned whether expensive efforts to rescue and clean individual animals after an oil spill can be justified on ecological grounds: cleaning sea otters after the 1988 Exxon Valdez spill, for example, cost $18.3 million but had no measurable effects on the otter population (Estes 1991).

Since the fierce confrontations between environmentalists and animal welfare advocates in the 1980s and 1990s, the field of animal philosophy itself has become considerably more complex through the emergence of a different strain of thinking about the animal, a view based on the work of continental philosophers such as Michel Foucault and Jacques Derrida rather than on the Anglo-Saxon analytic tradition of Peter Singer, Tom Regan, Mary Midgley, and their successors. Classical calls for animal rights, according to this alternate school of thought, leave in place speciesist assumptions about the exceptionality and unique rights of Homo sapiens: animals are attributed rights only by virtue of their similarity to humans. Theorists such as Donna Haraway, Jacques Derrida, Giorgio Agamben, Roberto Esposito, and Cary Wolfe question this approach and suggest instead that humanness is always established in relation to animality. Boundaries between humans and other species, they propose, are not fixed in nature but set up through cultural practices and therefore always retain a certain degree of arbitrariness. Derrida, in *The Animal That Therefore I Am* (*L'animal que donc je suis*), emphasizes the absurdity of lumping together vastly disparate organisms under one category: "The animal is a word, it is an appellation that men have instituted, a name they have given themselves the right and the authority to give to the living other," he points out (Derrida 2008, 42) ("C'est un mot, l'animal, c'est une appellation que des hommes ont instituée, un nom qu'ils se sont donnée le droit et l'autorité de donner à l'autre vivant" [Derrida 2006, 23]). And he elaborates:

> Confined within this catch-all concept, within this vast encampment of the animal, in this general singular, within the strict enclosure of this definite article ("the Animal" and not "animals"), as in a virgin forest, a zoo, a hunting or fishing ground, a paddock or an abattoir, a space of domestication, are *all the living things* that man does not recognize as his fellows, his neighbors, or his brothers. And that is so in spite of the infinite space that separates the lizard from the dog, the protozoon from the dolphin, the shark from the lamb, the parrot from the chimpanzee, the camel from the eagle, the squirrel from the tiger, the elephant from the cat, the ant from the silkworm, or the hedgehog from the echidna. (2008, 34)

> [Dans ce concept à tout faire, dans le vaste camp de l'animal, au singulier général, dans la stricte clôture de cet article défini ("l'Animal" et non pas "des animaux") seraient enclos, comme

dans une forêt vierge, un parc zoologique, un territoire de chasse
ou de pêche, un terrain d'élevage ou un abattoir, un espace de
domestication, *tous les vivants* que l'homme ne reconnaîtrait pas
comme ses semblables, ses prochains ou ses frères. Et cela malgré
les espaces infinis qui séparent le lézard du chien, le protozoaire
du dauphin, le requin de l'agneau, le perroquet du chimpanzé, le
chameau de l'aigle, l'écureuil du tigre ou l'éléphant du chat, les
fourmis du ver à soie ou le hérisson de l'échidné.] (2006, 56–57)

Why would a starfish and a gorilla belong in one category and humans
in another, even though humans and gorillas are from every conceiv-
able point of view far more closely related to each other than either of
them is to a starfish? From this perspective, it becomes clear not only
that the classification of certain organisms as "animals" legitimates their
treatment (or abuse) as property, experimental subject, or entertainment spectacle, but that it is also meant to define the contours of "the
human" itself. Ultimately, the engagement with the animal leads, in this
school of animal studies, to a radical questioning of the human subject
that is not part of animal rights arguments in the tradition of analytical
philosophy.

Factory farming is crucial to this strand of animal philosophy, just
as it is to the animal rights tradition. But in light of Michel Foucault's
concept of "biopolitics," the theory that modern societies increasingly
aim at the total classification, management, and control of all aspects of
plant, animal, and human life—from reproduction and birth to education, legal practices, medical practices, risk insurance, incarceration, and
death—factory farming takes on even broader implications. Even more
than in the animal rights school of thought, factory farming from the
viewpoint of continental philosophy is institutional and systemic, part
of the vast network of institutions and practices whereby modern societies regulate modes of birth and death. The mass breeding, "processing,"
and slaughter of approximately 55 billion animals worldwide per year,
from this perspective, forms part of a social system that subjects both humans and animals to total regimentation. In Giorgio Agamben's extension of Foucault's thought, this social system is characterized by a sinister "thanatopolitics" structured by the encounter between the political
sovereign and the subtly disempowered subject that would ultimately see
the same logic at work in factory farming as in the systematic genocide
of Jews in Nazi concentration camps (Agamben 1998, 199, 166–180).
Cary Wolfe, rejecting this reading of Foucault, emphasizes instead the
multiple *dispositifs* or technologies whereby biopolitics operates, which

allows for a far more dynamic understanding of power relationships in modern society (2012, 47–49). Wolfe's version of biopolitics leads not so much to the critique of a political system that hides its totalitarianism under the cover of democracy and citizen empowerment, but to a conceptualization of human and animal identities as politically, legally, and culturally fluid and subject to change. Because it radically questions the ontological foundations of human identity through the question of the animal, the thought of Haraway, Derrida, and Wolfe has come to be called "posthumanist."[12]

Animal advocates who base their claims on the idea of human rights as well as those who, posthumanistically, see human identity as culturally and legally constituted in the first place through casting the animal as the Other, tend to focus on humans' close connections to pet animals and on the horrific abuse of modern farm animals, topics that are also central to other types of animal advocacy. Vicki Hearne, in this vein, writes in detail about the human-horse relations that dressage training establishes (1986), and Donna Haraway meditates on the bacterial, viral, and perhaps even genetic transfers between humans and the dogs they live with (2008). On the obverse side, social historian Charles Patterson (2002), activist Karen Davis (2005), and novelist J. M. Coetzee (2001, [2003] 2004) have compared the industrial-scale atrocities of contemporary animal production to the Nazis' extermination of Jews, communists, and homosexuals during the Holocaust—a comparison whose moral and philosophical implications have been widely and controversially debated.

One might want to describe this style of thought and writing as "paradigmatic" in the structuralist sense, in that human and animal form part of a single set of elements that can substitute for each other in the grammar of law, ethics, or culture. This does not mean that the writers

12. When the concept of posthumanism was first widely used in the 1980s, it referred to new understandings of human identity associated with rapid advances in technology. The figure of the "cyborg," the partly cybernetic and partly organic being, came to function as a central trope for the new techno-biological fusions. While such technologically inflected redefinitions of the human continue to occupy the philosophical as well as the popular imagination, the focus of posthumanist thought has shifted from the human-machine to the human-animal boundary. Donna Haraway's sequel to her "Cyborg Manifesto" ([1984] 1991), the *Companion Species Manifesto* of 2003, is one clear manifestation of this shift. This reorientation is no doubt in part due to rapidly advancing scientific research on the cognitive abilities, emotions, communication systems, tool uses, complex social structures, and culturally transmitted forms of custom and knowledge among a variety of animal species, from ants and cephalopods to birds and primates. But it is also, more broadly, related to shifting cultural conceptions of nature, which I will discuss in greater detail in section 3.

in question claim that human and animal are actually equivalent with each other (though some do), but that their comparability, the *possibility* of their substitution, underwrites the vast majority of discourses about animal welfare, animal rights, and biopolitics. The environmentalist approach to the human-animal relation, by contrast, might be described as "syntagmatic." It seeks to explore how different kinds of organisms, human and nonhuman animals included, combine and interact in functional and dysfunctional ecosystems, how they compete or collaborate, and what challenges and opportunities they create for each other and in interaction with conditions of soil, water, topography, and climate. When environmentalists write about their close relations to animals, they tend to highlight less their connection with particular individuals than their fascination with a species or a whole taxon: Aldo Leopold's and Gary Snyder's wolves, E. O. Wilson's ants, or Scott Weidensaul's migrating birds. Even though environmentalists, like some animal advocates, sometimes invoke the metaphor of kinship and family to characterize their relationship with animals, their main focus is on humans and animals as noninterchangeable participants in ecosystemic processes. Questions of similarity and difference, in this optic, are subordinate to questions of function—"syntactic" function, one might say, expanding the linguistic metaphor—in the grammar of ecology. Consequently, one of environmentalists' main concerns regarding current species extinctions is the disruption of such ecological networks, while animal suffering plays a very marginal role.

Let me illustrate this "grammatical" difference through a brief look at two texts, one from the environmentalist tradition and the other from the strand of continental philosophy that has most radically challenged the human subject conceived as the animal's other. In one of the most famous scenes from his 1949 environmental classic *A Sand County Almanac*, the American conservationist Aldo Leopold describes his encounter with a wolf that he and his companions have just shot: "We reached the old wolf in time to watch a fierce green fire dying in her eyes. I realized then, and have known ever since, that there was something new to me in those eyes—something known only to her and to the mountain. I was young then, and full of trigger-itch; I thought that because fewer wolves meant more deer, that no wolves would mean hunters' paradise. But after seeing the green fire die, I sensed that neither the wolf nor the mountain agreed with such a view" ([1949] 2001, 129).

A conversion scene: this is the moment when the narrator's relationship to the natural world changes profoundly. As he encounters the wildness and otherness of undomesticated nature at the moment of the predator's death, his own position as hunter comes into question. Not only the animal, but inanimate nature, evoked through a mountain that is here endowed with knowledge and the ability to agree or disagree, impresses upon the human an altered consciousness of his own status within a complex web of ecological relations. The animal's gaze at the moment of her death singles Leopold out from the "we" of his group and forces him to confront a nature that is embodied in the dying wolf's eyes and yet transcends her through its fiery, highly symbolic, and distinctly supernatural intensity (green is not the color one would expect from a flame). On a par with the explicit content of the passage, the lyrical pattern of its rhymes, alliterations, and assonances—fierce/fire, fire/die/eyes, known/new/only, see/green/agree—drive home hidden connections that the human, at this moment of the narrative, intuits more than understands.

Derrida's *The Animal That Therefore I Am* has also become famous for a scene in which the speaker sees an animal looking at him:

> I often ask myself, just to see, *who I am*—and who I am (following) at the moment when, caught naked, in silence, by the gaze of an animal, for example, the eyes of a cat, I have trouble, yes, a bad time overcoming my embarrassment.
>
> Whence this malaise?
>
> I have trouble repressing a reflex of shame. Trouble keeping silent within me a protest against the indecency. Against the impropriety [*malséance*] that can come of finding oneself naked, one's sex exposed, stark naked before a cat that looks at you without moving, just to see. The impropriety of a certain animal nude before the other animal, from that point on one might call it a kind of *animalséance*: the single, incomparable and original experience of the impropriety that would come from appearing in truth naked, in front of the insistent gaze of the animal, a benevolent or pitiless gaze, surprised or cognizant. The gaze of a seer, a visionary or extra-lucid blind one. (2008, 3–4)

> [Souvent je me demande, moi, pour voir, *qui je suis*—et qui je suis au moment où, surpris nu, en silence, par le regard d'un animal, par exemple les yeux d'un chat, j'ai du mal, oui, du mal à surmonter une gêne.
>
> Pourquoi ce mal?
>
> J'ai du mal à réprimer un mouvement de pudeur. Du mal à faire taire en moi une protestation contre l'indécence. Contre la

malséance qu'il peut y avoir à se trouver nu, le sexe exposé, à
poil devant un chat qui vous regarde sans bouger, juste pour
voir. Malséance de tel animal nu devant l'autre animal, dès lors,
on dirait une sorte d'animalséance: l'expérience originale, une et
incomparable de cette malséance qu'il y aurait à paraître nu en
vérité, devant le regard insistant de l'animal, un regard bienveil-
lant ou sans pitié, étonné ou reconnaissant. Un regard de voyant,
de visionnaire ou d'aveugle extra-lucide.] (2006, 18)

In this scene, too, the human is changed irreversibly by the encounter with
the animal's gaze. Innocuous though the domestic cat's perhaps merely
curious glance may seem compared to the dying wolf's fierce green gaze, it
too ends up questioning the foundations of human identity. Who is the
human in this encounter with biologically related yet otherwise alien creatures? How are humans different from animals, and what self-definitions
and social relations does this boundary enable or proscribe? Like the
canine gaze in Leopold's text, the feline one in Derrida's redefines the
human-animal border just by crossing it.

But the differences between the two scenes are just as striking as their
similarities. Leopold faces a wild other, Derrida a domestic one. Leopold's encounter occurs in the outdoors and is staged as the encounter
between two primeval hunters, wolf and human; Derrida's is set not just
indoors, but at the threshold of the most modern as well as the most in-
timate space of the human household, the bathroom. Leopold's wolf
could be a threat to humans but is not, struck down as she is by a bullet
from his rifle—a synecdoche for humans' lethal impact on their natural
surroundings. Derrida's cat is utterly harmless and yet manages to unsettle its owner so deeply that the conditions that allow him to call himself "human" become visible and at the same time uncertain: "The gaze
called 'animal' offers to my sight the abyssal limit of the human: the inhuman or the ahuman, the ends of man, that is to say, the bordercrossing
from which vantage man dares to announce himself to himself, thereby
calling himself by the name that he believes he gives himself" (2008, 12)
("Ce regard dit 'animal' me donne à voir la limite abyssale de l'humain:
l'inhumain ou l'anhumain, les fins de l'homme, à savoir le passages des
frontières depuis lequel l'homme ose s'annonce à lui-même, s'appelant
ainsi du nom qu'il croit se donner" [2006, 30]). What is at stake for Leopold is not primarily the embedding of the human into the animal matrix
that Derrida reaches for by describing his affect with the neologism "ani-
malaise" (animalséance), but the embedding of humans into an ecologi-

cal community that Leopold refers to by the shorthand of "the land" and the idea of a "land ethic."

This difference resonates even in the stylistic texture of the two passages. Instead of Leopold's fluid syntax patterned by alliteration and assonance, Derrida's sentences are halting and fractured, interrupting themselves to probe the meaning of their own words through repetitions, puns, and substitutions: the double meaning of "je suis" as "I am" and "I follow"; the dual resonance of "à poil," which means literally "down to the hair" but is a common expression for "naked"; the play on "mal/animal/malséance," which leads to the portmanteau neologism "animalséance" to capture the human's ontological unease vis-à-vis the animal; and the play on the speaker's "pour voir" and the cat's "juste pour voir" that turn it into a "voyant" or "visionnaire." Rather than establishing webs of relation syntagmatically through alliteration, assonance, and rhyme as Leopold's syntax does, Derrida's diction isolates each central word paradigmatically, breaks it out of its normal meanings, and restacks it on top of other words it is not normally associated with, to the point of giving individual syllables unexpected new meanings: the "mal" in "animal" in this passage, or later in the text the reinterpretation of the plural "animaux" as "animot," animal-word. Leopold and Derrida, in other words, mirror even in the details of their styles the conceptual differences that separate conservationism from posthumanist animal philosophy. These different orientations, as the next section will show, derive ultimately from different conceptions of the impact of modernity on humans' relations to animals.

3. Danger and Domestication

As I highlighted in the introduction and chapter 1, environmentalists' alarm over vanishing animal and plant species and the impact that shrinking biodiversity will have on the functioning of ecosystems is usually articulated as part of the broader narrative about the decline of nature because of the impact of modern societies. The ultimate consequence of humans' displacement of other species through habitat alteration and destruction, environmentalists worry, may be the end of nature such as modern Western societies have conceived of it: as the wild outside, the nonhuman counterpart to human-shaped environments and organisms. Bill McKibben's book *The End of Nature* explicitly made this point by claiming that "we have deprived nature of its independence, and that is fatal to its meaning. Nature's independence *is* its meaning;

without it there is nothing but us" (1989, 58; see chapter 1). Many other environmentalists, following a tradition that runs from Henry David Thoreau to Gary Snyder in North American thought and writing, have also associated the essence of what environmentalism seeks to preserve with "the wild" or with "wilderness." In this line of thinking, the decline of nature ultimately leads to a completely domesticated world. Conventional environmentalism, one might say, associates risk with domestication, the gradual assimilation of the natural world to the human sphere.

Domestication is obviously also at the heart of much advocacy on behalf of animals, which tends to focus on the spaces of the factory farm, the scientific lab, the zoo, and the circus as sites of animal endangerment, rather than the island ecologies that feature prominently in the environmentalist concern about species die-off. Islands often feature endemic species found nowhere else on the planet and offer their animal inhabitants few means of escape when an ecological or technological threat to their survival emerges. This often turns them into "hot spots" of biodiversity loss. Animal welfare, by contrast, tends to be concerned with overcrowded animal shelters and the CAFOs (Concentrated Animal Feeding Operations) that house tens of thousands of cows, pigs, and chickens in the smallest possible space so as to maximize economic profitability. Images of such facilities and accounts of how industrial breeding techniques have generated disease-prone pigs and turkeys with breasts so heavy that they can neither walk nor procreate naturally (all "normal" turkey breeding in the United States proceeds by artificial insemination) might lead one to surmise that excessive domestication is the core concern of animal welfare discourse as well as of environmentalist thought.

Yet, clearly, there is no return to the wild for farm or pet animals, who would not even exist in their present forms if it were not for millennia of agricultural breeding. Neither do advocates for lab animals, abandoned pets, or abused farm animals envision a life without human interference for the objects of their concern. Rather, they call for a kind of husbandry that would grant such animals the fulfillment of basic needs such as freedom from pain, species-appropriate feed, space to move, care for injuries, and a humane death. Writers such as Michael Pollan (2006) or Jonathan Safran Foer (2009), who have eloquently indicted current farming practices, hold up as an alternative smaller-scale agricultural operations that take such basic needs into account. At the core of the animal welfare movements' vision of what endangers animals, then, is not really excessive domestication but an incomplete domestication process that reduces animals to commodities rather than making them members—however defined—of human society and subjects of human law.

Animal welfare, animal rights, and other forms of advocacy on behalf of animals, including the posthumanist variant in recent philosophy, therefore, typically seek to establish animals as members of the human social, political, and legal community. The attempt to extend something like human rights to those mammals who are most closely related to us—primates and cetaceans—demonstrates this most clearly, but so do far more limited attempts to, for example, extend laws against animal cruelty from pet to farm animals in the United States. The crux of such endeavors is to ensure that animals are not simply outside the purview of the law and, more broadly speaking, outside moral consideration. Whether it proceeds by highlighting the humanlike qualities of certain kinds of animals or by investigating how the idea of "the human" historically crystallized into its present shape and how it constantly needs to be shored up against the encroachments of its putative animal other, advocacy on behalf of animals seeks to make them quasi-citizens of the human community. Animals, especially those owned by humans, are at risk when they are denied this status.

Environmental ethics, by contrast, seeks to keep animals away from being absorbed or displaced by human communities. It endeavors to make humans themselves citizens of an ecological community that reaches beyond the bounds of human culture, politics, and legislation. This principle is articulated quite clearly in the American conservationist Aldo Leopold's idea of the "land ethic" that I alluded to earlier:

> All ethics so far evolved rest upon a single premise: that the individual is a member of a community of interdependent parts. . . . The land ethic simply enlarges the boundaries of the community to include soils, waters, plants, and animals, or collectively: the land. . . . A land ethic of course cannot prevent the alteration, management, and use of these "resources," but it does affirm their right to continued existence, and, at least in spots, their continued existence in a natural state.
>
> In short, a land ethic changes the role of *Homo sapiens* from conqueror of the land-community to plain member and citizen of it. ([1949] 2001, 203–204)

Leopold starts from a premise that sounds similar to that of animal welfare advocacy: the extension of moral consideration and perhaps rights beyond the human sphere. Yet he turns this idea around by postulating as its outcome the integration of humans into nature rather than the integration of nonhumans into the human sphere.

The practical applications of these two different orientations, as I discussed earlier, are sometimes similar. I have focused here on differences that seem to me more interesting than similarities in highlighting the cultural foundations of thinking and activism about biodiversity. Inevitably, I have had to generalize, in the process, about movements that have changed over time and have become enormously diverse and contentious within themselves. This generalization underemphasizes those branches of the animal advocacy movement that resist discourses of domestication and emphasize animals' autonomy. The legal scholar Gary Francione, for example, has proposed an "abolitionism" that militates against animals as human property; only if their legal status is changed, he argues, can the exploitation of animals genuinely end. Attempts on the part of animal welfare organizations to improve the condition of, for example, zoo or farm animals are, in his view, actually counterproductive in that they soothe the consciences of humans who benefit from those animals and thereby postpone a definitive end to exploitation (Francione 1995; 2008). Needless to say, this position has put him at odds with the many animal welfare advocates whose work aims precisely at gradual improvement of animal lives.[13]

Even more sweepingly, Carter Dillard, the litigation director of the Animal Legal Defense Fund, has argued that the main focus of animal advocacy should be ensuring animals' autonomy. Where Francione condemns mere animal welfare activism as insufficient, Dillard makes the same argument about environmentalism, which according to him focuses too much on human well-being: "Despite the fact that we have dragged many species into our human world, and concerned ourselves with their welfare, really protecting the interests of animals may mean ensuring their autonomy from human influence more generally. And if we do that, if we respect the interests of animals to live autonomously and largely free of human influence in their natural habitats, we would have to set a standard for the protection of the earth's ecology that makes the traditional environmental standards of sustainability, and health and safety, look pathetically meager by comparison" (2013).

---

13. The discussion about the ethics of meat consumption and whether a "humane" form of meat production is possible has often been a focal point of such confrontations.

Clearly, such arguments do not fit neatly into the larger divergence I have traced here between efforts to make animals part of the human moral, legal, and political sphere and efforts to make humans morally, legally, and politically part of the environmental sphere. Rather, they resonate with the deep ecology movement of the 1970s and 1980s, which also emphasized animals' autonomy and protested against their integration into the human sphere even by way of efforts to stave off their extinction—efforts that the movement denounced as precisely a form of domestication that diminished the dignity of the wild creature. Kenneth Brower, for example (son of David Brower, who was director of the Sierra Club for more than a decade), wrote in protest against the recovery program for the endangered California Condor: "What use to us is a great soarer that has been handled, marked, laparotomized, popcorned by zoo crowds, and radio-tagged? What use is such a bird to itself?"[14] In his view, the conservationists in the Audubon Society and the U.S. Fish and Wildlife Service who spearheaded the recovery had "become so concerned with the problem of the bird that they have lost sight of what a *bird* is" (Brower 1981, 35).

In certain radical variants of environmentalist thinking as well as of animal advocacy, then, the wild, autonomous animal as untouched as possible by human intervention emerges as the gold standard of what is to be valued about other species. To the extent that this construction of other species has been criticized for at least two decades in environmentalist thought and is of limited practical use in a context in which no area of nature lies truly outside of human influence anymore, I have given it shorter shrift here than the engagement with dynamics of domestication and modernity that have shaped other variants of animal welfare and environmental discourse. Such varieties of human intervention into the lives of animals and into natural spaces none of which are truly autonomous or wild, even though some humans like to think of them as such, are also the core concern of T. C. Boyle's novel *When the Killing's Done.* The question of who belongs, who does not, and which individuals and institutions are able and qualified to make and enforce this distinction

---

14. The essay from which this quote is taken, "Night of the Condor," was also published in an edited version in *Omni Magazine* in August 1979, which can be accessed online: https://archive.org/stream/omni-magazine-1979–08/OMNI_1979_08#page/n5/mode/2up/search/134. David Brower himself contributed two pieces to the anthology *The Condor Question: Captive or Free?* that echo his son's sentiments (see David R. Brower 1981a, 1981b).

structure the novel's plot, which revolves around the confrontation between conservationists and animal welfare advocates.

4. Species, Spaces, and Invasions

The novels and short stories of Thomas Coraghessan Boyle have long shown deep interest in if not always sympathy with environmentalism, and they often focus at least in part on humans' relations with natural spaces and nonhuman species. The novel *A Friend of the Earth* (2000) and the short story collection *After the Plague* (2001) feature explicitly environmentalist characters, as does *When the Killing's Done* (2011), whose plot pits an employee of the National Park Service, Alma Boyd Takesue, against David Francis LaJoy, founder of For the Protection of the Animals and a fierce defender of animal rights. Their fictional verbal and legal battle unfolds against the background of an all-too-real scenario of endangered and invasive species on two islands off the coast of southern California, Anacapa Island and Santa Cruz Island, both part of Channel Islands National Park. As the National Park Service plans and proceeds with the eradication of introduced species on each of these islands—rats on Anacapa, pigs on Santa Cruz Island—Takesue sees herself rudely confronted, again and again, with LaJoy's public and often aggressive assertions of the animals' right to live.

Dave LaJoy is by most counts a repellent character. A self-important and power-hungry bully, he is often blind to his own errors and shortfalls but loses patience in an instant when other people fail. In many scenes, his pompous and self-righteous pronouncements degrade quickly into incivility and outright hostility when he perceives other people as slighting him in any way, from a waitress in a café to his own partner, the singer Anise Reed, who grew up on Santa Cruz Island and is an equally committed if far less aggressive animal rights activist. This thoroughly unflattering behavior might make him easy to dismiss as a spokesperson for any cause Boyle wants his readers to take seriously. Not infrequently, animal rights seem to be just another arena in which LaJoy fights his lifelong battle against the individuals and powers that perpetually deny him what he sees as his own just deserts.

Yet LaJoy has experienced a genuine awakening to the horrors of factory farming through the activism of an employee in one of the stores he owns, and his rudeness often exposes the inconsistencies and hypocrisies of environmentalism. In an early shouting match during a lecture Takesue is trying to deliver on the National Park Service's plan to eradicate rats from Anacapa, he defies admonitions to be polite by yelling, "How can you talk about being civil when innocent animals are being tortured to death? Civil? I'll be civil when the killing's done and not a minute before." And as he is being escorted out of the lecture hall, he calls, "Those rats have been there for a hundred and fifty years! . . . What's your baseline? A hundred years ago? A thousand? Ten thousand? Hell . . . why not just clone your dwarf mammoth and stick him out there like in *Jurassic Park?*" (Boyle 2011, 62).

Uncivil though he may be, LaJoy has a point. Considering that ecosystems evolve dynamically over time, restoration ecology of the kind Takesue and the National Park Service are undertaking has always been plagued by the question of which past ecosystem the present one should ideally revert to. And his facts are correct: rats were most likely introduced to Anacapa Island in December 1853, when the passenger ship *Winfield Scott* ran aground on the island in dense fog. While the passengers and crew were rescued a day or so later, the rats probably swam from the wreck and then stayed on the island. What LaJoy does not mention is that they wreaked havoc on many of the native bird species, including Xantus's murrelet and the ashy storm petrel, by preying on eggs and chicks. In the novel, he makes an unsuccessful attempt to rescue the rats by surreptitiously putting out an antidote wherever the National Park Service places poison. As in the novel, the real eradication campaign the National Park Service undertook in 2001–2002 ended up being successful, and populations of several seabirds rebounded after the rats' disappearance. Still, LaJoy's question is not unfounded: What is the reason for preferring the Anacapa ecosystem pre-1853 to the one after, or for preferring that of the nineteenth century to that of earlier epochs?

Such questions become more uncomfortably complicated when the action shifts to Santa Cruz Island, whose ecology poses even more vexing questions about which species belong and which ones do not. Again, Boyle sticks meticulously to the facts of Santa Cruz Island's history in constructing his plot: its complicated human history from the sheep-ranching operations at Scorpion Ranch, among which Anise Reed grew up, to the division of the island's management between the National Park Service and The Nature Conservancy and its equally complex ecological development, "a parable of cause and effect that might have seemed like a sick cosmic joke if it weren't so catastrophic" (Boyle 2011, 203). Takesue summarizes the history to her uncomprehending mother:

> The whole thing started with Montrose Chemical dumping DDT during the war, the DDT working its way up the food chain and preventing the eggs of native bald eagles from forming

properly. The balds—aggressive, highly territorial and primarily
piscivorous—died back, and the goldens, which prey on land animals, cruised in from the coast to colonize the islands, attracted
by the bountiful food resource represented by the wild hogs, *Sus
scrofa*, that should never have been there in the first place. But
then . . . you can never foresee how a closed ecosystem is going to
react not only to introduced elements but to their elimination as
well. The sheep had overgrazed and that kept the invasive fennel
down, but once the sheep were removed the fennel sprang up in
all but impenetrable thickets ten feet high, which provided ideal
cover for the pigs. "So . . . you've got no balds to keep the goldens away and the goldens are nesting and hungry but with fewer
and fewer pigs available. In that case, what do you think they're
going to eat?" (203)

What they preyed on was native dwarf foxes, whose population began in
turn to decline. The discovery of the golden eagles' change of diet posed a
problem to the National Park Service: unlike rats, golden eagles, symbols
of the majesty of wild nature, could obviously not simply be poisoned,
so they were trapped and relocated instead. "In the interim the biologists trapped as many foxes as they could and caged them for a captive-
breeding program, which to date had produced eighty-five kits to be released once the goldens were gone and balds could be brought in from
Alaska to reestablish a viable breeding colony. The thinking was that the
balds would keep the goldens at bay and that the goldens would have
no incentive in nesting on the island once the pigs were removed." This
thinking explains Takesue's eagerness to see the pig eradication program
go forward. Unlike golden eagles, pigs, she explains, cannot be trapped
and relocated because they have inhabited Santa Cruz Island as a separate
population for 150 years, and therefore might harbor diseases that could
endanger the mainland hog industry (204).

If Takesue's reasoning provides a cogent ecological rationale for the
eradication program, it also sounds rather like another act in the "surrealist performance art" that American wildlife conservation has become
in Jon Mooallem's view (see introduction): a complex choreography of
human interventions that is meant to restore the state of nature before
human intervention. And that is no doubt Boyle's point: the National
Park Service's project sounds both perfectly rational and quite insane, a
mad patchwork of native, introduced, relocated, reintroduced, and captively bred species, all in the name of a natural balance thought to have
prevailed in an earlier historical moment, with the bald eagles attain-

ing the dubious distinction of being both native *and* introduced. At the same time, Takesue herself emerges as something of a hypocrite when she runs over a squirrel with her car. Even as she is engaged in planning the slaughter of hundreds of pigs, she cannot bring herself to administer the coup de grâce to the agonizing animal—a young boy ends up crushing its head instead to end its suffering. Shying away from the direct, graphic violence involved in killing an individual animal, she nevertheless has no hesitation in making decisions about the life and death of entire populations of animals.

If this is not enough to make readers uneasy about the environmentalist side of the conflict, the conservationists also indulge in a language of violence that slides easily from animals to humans. After expressing his irritation with Dave LaJoy's signs indicting the National Park Service and The Nature Conservancy as "animal killers" and "Nazis," Frazier, the New Zealand hunter whose crew the National Park Service has hired to exterminate the pigs, suggests jokingly that perhaps the project's first phase should be to eliminate LaJoy, and he mimics shooting him. With amused approval from one of the National Park Service employees, he carries on the joke: "Not that I'm violent or anything, just that certain species—or individuals within that species—sometimes have to be removed for the salvation of all the rest, right, Alma? Euthanized. There's a term I like. As long as it's got a .223-caliber slug attached to it." His suggestion is met with a round of laughter (Boyle 2011, 202). And in the discussion of the pig eradication, he declares, "This isn't a game. This is war. All-out war. And wave goodbye to the little piggies" (206). The easy hilarity with which Frazier includes humans in his eradication campaign and applies the terms of military conflict to an ecological restoration project are so disturbing because they seem precisely to confirm LaJoy's accusations and to hold up a mirror image to LaJoy's own hostility and aggression, possibly even more disturbing because they are disguised as humor.

But if the novel proves LaJoy right in many of his indictments, maybe more so than he himself is aware of, he also errs egregiously and proves himself as much of a hypocrite as Takesue on other occasions. His ardent engagement for animal welfare, for example, does not prevent him from trapping and capturing two raccoons who have torn up his newly planted lawn in search of grubs. Worse yet, his mixture of sentimentalism and bad judgment makes it impossible for him either to kill them or to relocate them to the hills where they might be forced to compete with raccoons who have already claimed the territory. Instead, he relocates them to Santa Cruz Island on one of his boat trips. If this introduction of yet another nonnative predator species to an already fragile island ecosystem is already proof of spectacular ecological ignorance, so is his final plan to take rabbits and rattlesnakes to the island after the pigs have been eradicated, this time in a deliberate attempt to sabotage the restoration. Even though his boat is hit by a tanker and sinks during the passage, killing him and all of the human passengers, some of the rattlesnakes make it to Santa Cruz swimming, just as the rats off the *Winfield Scott* did a century and a half earlier. Their escape presumably sets off another cycle of invasion, predation, and extinction. Worst of all, LaJoy's inability to think beyond individual animals and his complete ignorance of natural processes leads to the death of one of the young women who have joined his animal rights organization. On a clandestine trip to Santa Cruz Island to document the slaughter of the pigs, LaJoy is surprised to find that the heavy winter rains have transformed harmless creeks into dangerous rivers and moderately challenging hillsides into mud traps, even though such seasonal changes are entirely predictable. Forging on with his mission regardless, the team soon finds itself in trouble, and one of the college-age women falls off an overhang and drowns in the dangerous river below, all in the presence of a journalist, an incident that ends LaJoy's career as an activist.

By the end of the novel, LaJoy is dead, the Santa Cruz pigs are exterminated, and Alma Takesue is on her way to a celebration that will "declar[e] Santa Cruz Island free of invasive fauna" (Boyle 2011, 361). She herself, however, already knows at that moment that this victory may be temporary, since she has spotted a raccoon on the island three months earlier: "And that—the appearance of the raccoon as dusk fell on that June night—is either one of the greatest coincident finds in the history of island biogeography or a disaster in the making. Or both" (361–362). Frazier wants to exterminate the animal, pointing out its possible damage to some of the species that the National Park Service has just spent millions restoring. But Takesue resists: "I'm telling you, we're looking— probably, I mean, possibly—at the first natural transplant in what, sixteen thousand years? . . . this animal got here the way the skunks and the foxes and the mice and the fence lizards and all the rest did and we have a clear duty not to interfere with it. Tag it maybe. Collar it. But nature's got to take its course" (363).

The idea that anything like nature unaffected by humans could take its course on the island is triply ironic: because Takesue has just participated in a massive effort to rearrange its ecosystem, because she mistakes her archenemy David LaJoy's willful animal transfer for nature, and because she does not even know yet about the rattlesnakes, who in some sense do arrive at the island at their own initiative, even though they were taken part of the way on LaJoy's boat. The reader knows Frazier is right in suggesting that someone might have brought the raccoon to the island, but Takesue dismisses the idea, proving that her ignorance of human behavior equals LaJoy's ignorance of ecology.

More than anything, the ending of the novel highlights that neither conservationists' nor animal rights advocates' ideas about nature have adequate purchase on the complex interactions between humans and their natural environments. Takesue and, with her, the National Park Service and The Nature Conservancy prove incapable of distinguishing between species that have arrived on their own and those that have arrived by means of human agency—yet their taxonomy of native and introduced species and their management programs hinge on the ability to make this distinction. LaJoy's insight at the moment of his death, "He understands, for the first time, how wrong this is, how wrong he's been, how you have to let the animal—*the animals*—decide for themselves" (Boyle 2011, 358), is equally hollow, considering that he has already taken raccoons to Santa Cruz and that his boat this time carries rabbits and rattlesnakes to release on the island (though only the rattlesnakes make it to shore). Any approach to nature that seeks to draw a principled distinction between human and nonhuman agency and to establish taxonomies of value on that basis is doomed to failure in the plot of *When the Killing's Done.*

If the novel argues that attempts to sort out humans from environments they have interacted with are as futile as categorical distinctions between native and introduced species, it also invites readers to compare such distinctions to those that humans draw between different kinds of humans. The presence of Frazier, the hunter introduced from New Zealand to California to exterminate nonnatives, drives this point home rather unsubtly, as do the newspaper headlines that accompany his contract: "$7 Million Awarded to Foreign Hunters to Slaughter Santa Cruz Island Pigs" (Boyle 2011, 200), the implication being that nonnatives are being invited by natives to exterminate nonnatives. The history of Alma Takesue's family also points to this connection, as her mother's choice of Greg Takesue, a fifth-generation Japanese American, for her husband met with the dismay of her mother, who had lost her own husband in World War II in the battle against the Japanese. Histories of conflicts, migrations, and hybridizations characterize the social as well as the natural sphere in Boyle's novel, and attempts to sort out the elements they have mixed up are futile at best and lethal at worst. The shipwreck that led Alma Takesue's grandmother to Anacapa Island at the beginning of the novel is deliberately juxtaposed with the shipwreck that brought the rats to the island a century earlier, and with the shipwreck that kills Dave LaJoy and Anise Reed but takes rattlesnakes to Santa Cruz Island at the end. If neither conservationist nor animal welfare perspectives are ultimately able to account for humans' interactions with the more-than-human world, neither do they offer useful models for interpreting the social world. Both spheres, in *When the Killing's Done*, are structured in terms of distinctions whose logic is tenuous but nonetheless determines lives and deaths.

4. Re-Imagining Domestication

Boyle's goal in *When the Killing's Done* is not to reconcile conservationism and animal welfare advocacy, but to highlight the leaps in logic and the self-contradictions that inhere in each of them, and to show how they fall short of grasping the intricacies of humans' interactions with non-human species. My purpose here is not reconciliation either, as I indicated earlier, but rather to understand conservation and animal welfare advocacy as different perspectives on how modernization alters nature—how and with what consequences humans domesticate nonhuman species. Boyle paints a panorama of domestication that always falls short, in a sense: attempts to manage and control nature in the end prove they are not up to the task. I would argue, beyond Boyle, that the different approaches to domestication that conservationism and animal welfare advocacy take can become newly relevant to each other as environmentalists increasingly view nature as already pervasively domesticated.

Thom van Dooren's detailed and insightful study of whooping crane conservation provides a good example of how animal welfare and conservation might be considered together. Van Dooren points out that public stories about whooping cranes foreground the extraordinary effort of rearing them captively and guiding them on long migrations with light airplanes, all guided by humans dressed up as whooping cranes to keep the birds from imprinting on humans. What is usually omitted are the ethical questions that accompany keeping populations of birds in captivity for breeding purposes, the material circumstances of their captivity, artificial insemination, and the use of other species considered less important and valuable—in this case, sandhill cranes—as experimental subjects and "sacrificial surrogates" for the more valued species. Even successful conservation stories, in this light, turn out to require "an effort to navigate between the violence of conservation, with its various forms of sacrificial and captive life, and the violence of extinction" (van Dooren 2014, chap. 4). This choice of different types of violence is even more pronounced in cases when conservation of a particular set of species requires the actual killing of other species. Van Dooren argues:

> When presented with this situation, perhaps many of us would still choose the violence of a conservation grounded in captive breeding over that of extinction. But making this decision cannot be allowed to erase this genuine ethical difficulty: the violence of the care that is practiced here. Instead, making a stand for conservation must require that we actively take on this predicament, that we consciously dwell within it, in an effort to, wherever possible, work toward something better. . . . The point is not that we can never kill or cause suffering in the name of conservation, but that the decision to do so—no matter how rigorously we justify it and weigh our options—should never leave us comfortable and satisfied. (chap. 4)

Van Dooren warns that even if we decide, in certain cases, that the well-being of individual animals should be sacrificed for the well-being of the species—its own or another—the violence implicit in this decision needs to be openly acknowledged and become part of the ethics and imagination that frame conservation. This warning is particularly à propos in a context in which even wild nature is becoming increasingly domesticated in many respects.[15] As the notion of the Anthropocene and a planet pervasively reshaped by humans has gained influence over the past fifteen years, the idea that environmentalism might be able to return us to an earlier state of nature has lost a good deal of its persuasiveness. This fundamental shift amounts to seeing nature as globally domesticated rather than as still wild, as biologists Peter Kareiva et al. have argued in their essay "Domesticated Nature":

> Humans did not . . . stop with simply domesticating a few chosen species; we have domesticated vast landscapes and entire ecosystems. Moreover, just as domesticated plants and animals have predictable and repeatable traits among different species, domesticated ecosystems also reveal common traits. In particular, when humans tame nature they seek enhanced

---

15. For a related analysis, see Chrulew (2011).

productivity, convenient commerce, and protection from predators and storms. However, along with domestication, there is often
concurrent and inadvertent selection for maladaptive features
in either species or ecosystems. . . . Whereas plant and animal
breeders are well aware that domestication involves tradeoffs in
vigor, the notion of tradeoffs resulting from the domestication
of entire landscapes has only recently received serious scientific
attention. . . . Ours is a world of nature domesticated, albeit
to varying degrees, from national parks to high-rise megalopolises. . . . Under this paradigm, our challenge is to understand
and thoughtfully manage the tradeoffs among ecosystem services that result from the inescapable domestication of nature.
(Kareiva et al. 2007, 1866)

Adopting this perspective requires a new understanding of restoration
ecology, of wilderness areas, and of wildlife protection. If Mary Midgley
has argued that humans have quite different duties to wild animals than
to domestic ones (Midgley 1983, 112–124), this distinction may lose
some of its force in a world in which the survival of *all* species is directly
or indirectly dependent on human action.

But as van Dooren's work highlights, animal welfare and animal rights
considerations also point to the dangers of reconceiving environmentalism within a framework of global domestication.[16] Animal advocates'
protests against the incomplete or simply misguided forms of domestication to which humans have subjected animals highlight that domesticated nonhumans are vulnerable to different but in certain ways no less
dire risks than wild ones. Since the environmentalist sense of endangerment has so often translated into apocalyptic visions of devastated futures, envisioning the ecologies of the future as essentially domestic seems
to promise a welcome change of perspective. Yet a glance at the discourse
of animal welfare and animal rights movements suggests that such a shift
might bring with it different but no less dark tropes of endangerment:
environmentalists might move from tropes of apocalypse and the end of
nature to those of oppression, slavery, and holocaust. Rather than moving from a sense of environmental danger to one of ecological design
and management, in other words, the adoption of the domestication idea
might merely rearticulate the sense of endangerment in a way that reso-

16. I will explore the problems of envisioning the planet as pervasively domesticated
and the idea of human control that often accompanies it in more detail in chapter 6.

nates more closely with animal welfare discourse than it does at present. Seen from this perspective, it is the differences between the animal welfare and the environmentalist approaches to endangerment that could prove most useful for environmentalists as they rethink their own discourses of danger, domestication, and acceptable violence in the Anthropocene.

5 Biodiversity, Environmental Justice, and Multispecies Communities

"When foreign ecologists came to do research, I thought they were insensitive and just plain weird—well-fed, binoculared foreigners counting animals in countries where people were still trying to count their dead." With this blunt statement in a recent op-ed piece in the *New York Times,* ornithologist Trish O'Kane summarizes how she perceived conservationists during her earlier vocation as a human-rights journalist investigating the massacres carried out by the forces of Guatemalan dictator Efraín Ríos Montt in the early 1980s (O'Kane 2014). O'Kane's juxtaposition concisely summarizes an entire field of ideological and practical tensions between conservation biology and social justice. Questions of endangered species, extinction, and biodiversity developed from the 1970s to the turn of the millennium in a field of collaboration and conflict between the animal welfare movement, which emphasizes the survival and well-being of the individual animal, and environmental conservation, which focuses on the survival of species (see chapter 4). But if animal welfare advocates in a sense accused environmentalists of not caring enough about animals, environmental justice advocates at the same time attacked conservationists for caring too much about animals and not enough about people.

In the United States, the emergent environmental justice movement in the 1980s focused particularly on pollution and the siting of toxic waste dumps. As Robert Bullard's seminal *Dumping in Dixie: Race, Class, and Environmental Quality* ([1990] 2000) and other works showed, communities of color were disproportionately exposed to the risks of pollution and hazardous materials, following a pattern of what came to be called "environmental racism." In Africa and Asia, conflicts between environmentalists and social justice advocates often emerged around the establishment of wildlife reserves and national parks, and while they frequently involved elements of racial confrontation, the broader issue of contention was political and economic inequality.[1] Advocates for indigenous communities in Africa and Asia often charged that the creation of wildlife reserves entailed not so much the protection of endangered fauna and flora as a shift from one set of human uses to another, to the detriment of communities who had used the areas in question sustainably for centuries, sometimes millennia. Wildlife sanctuaries, they alleged, made the use of certain areas for work and subsistence—hunting, plant harvesting, agriculture—difficult or impossible for some people while at the same time enabling leisure uses for others. Or, worse yet, such sanctuaries disabled small-scale sustainable uses of an area's resources but opened them up to far more destructive uses by large corporations or international tourism. The Peoples Union for Democratic Rights, for example, excoriated the management of the Simlipal Tiger Reserve in the Indian state of Orissa in the early 1980s:

> The choice is not between no cultivation and cultivation but between large scale illegal denudation of forests and cultivation by tribals. . . . The choice is not between complete removal of human settlement and deforestation by tribals but between organized deforestation with the connivance of state agencies and limited deforestation by tribals. In the end the choice is not between an ecosystem without human interference and that with human interference but it is between interference by tribals and interference by smugglers, traders and pleasure-seekers. It is a choice

---

1. Some scholars use the term *environmental justice* to refer only to the movement in the United States, and *environmentalism of the poor,* the term coined by Ramachandra Guha and Joan Martínez-Alier, to refer to movements in the global south. This distinction is not made by all writers and debaters on the topic, however. I will use *environmental justice* here to discuss movements that seek to combine the fight for social justice with the struggle for the conservation of the natural environment, regardless of where they take place.

> between two sets of human beings. (*Simlipal Report,* quoted in
> Gadgil and Guha 1995, 92)[2]

In Tanzania, similarly, the German environmental pioneer Bernhard
Grzimek succeeded in creating Serengeti National Park but drew the enraged opposition of local communities by claiming in 1959 that "a National Park is a wilderness area and should remain that way, as in prehistoric times. Humans, even indigenous humans, should not live inside
it. . . . A National Park has to be empty of humans, neither Europeans nor
Africans belong there" (Ein Nationalpark ist ein Stück Wildnis und soll
es bleiben wie in Urzeiten. Menschen, auch eingeborene Menschen, sol-
len darin nicht leben. . . . Ein Nationalpark muss menschenleer sein, es
gehören weder Europäer noch Afrikaner hinein; Grzimek and Grzimek
[1959] 2009, 278–281; translation mine). By now, many studies have
highlighted the damaging consequences of this kind of "fortress conservation" and the displacements and refugees it has entailed.[3]

In some cases, the attempt on the part of European or North American conservation organizations to limit or terminate local communities'
uses of natural resources rested on mistaken ecological assumptions.
Grazing, for example, can cause grave damage to sensitive ecological areas. But in many places, including the United States, prohibitions of grazing have led to a proliferation of particular native plant species or even
nonnative ones that in the end reduce biodiversity.[4] In other cases, limits
on legal hunting on the part of local communities simply open the area
up to illegal and uncontrolled poaching by individuals from other areas.
Even granting, however, that certain uses of nature by local and/or indigenous communities would in fact not be sustainable over the long term,
given contemporary circumstances, the questions of who decides about
the fate of local or regional fauna, flora, water, and soil, and in whose
interest such decisions are made, remain. These questions continue to
be contested in many conservation areas today. For this reason, Ramachandra Guha and Juan Martínez-Alier have called for the recognition
of "the environmentalism of the poor," the care for nature that derives
from a community's dependence on local ecosystems for its life, health,
and work rather than from aesthetic appreciation and leisure experiences
(1997). In this view, biological conservation cannot be conceived apart

2. For analyses of the confrontations between wildlife advocates and social justice advocates in India, also see Lewis (2004, chaps. 5–8) and Rangarajan (2006).

3. For detailed analyses, see Brockington (2002), Chatty and Colchester (2002),
Adams and Hutton (2007), Agrawal and Redford (2009), and Dowie (2009).

4. For examples, see Gadgil and Guha (1995, 92).

from the social contexts in which destruction, maintenance, or improvement of natural resources takes place. Biodiversity, these scenarios highlight, is always a matter of socioeconomic context and cultural value first and foremost and a scientific issue second.

Considering biodiversity conservation in this context of social justice opens up a different set of issues from the ones I considered in chapter 4: not the question whether we should aim to conserve the welfare of individual animals or that of species, but how we can articulate human rights and human aspirations to a good life together with the claims of nonhuman species on our moral consideration. Theorists of posthumanism have argued that discrimination against other humans is structurally related to discrimination against nonhumans—put somewhat simplistically, that the same underlying logic informs racism and speciesism. It is the category of the animal, understood as another that does not have the same claim to moral consideration as a human and can therefore be killed or let die with impunity, that opens up the possibility of relegating other humans legally, ethically, and politically to that category.[5] In this vein, Cary Wolfe has argued that "the humanist concept of subjectivity is inseparable from the discourse and *institution* of speciesism, which relies on the tacit acceptance . . . that the full transcendence of the 'human' requires the sacrifice of the 'animal' and the animalistic, which in turn makes possible a symbolic economy in which we can engage in a 'noncriminal putting to death' . . . not only of animals, but other *humans* as well by marking *them* as animal" (2003, 43). Postcolonial critics Graham Huggan and Helen Tiffin have argued analogously that "if the wrongs of colonialism—its legacies of continuing human inequalities, for instance—are to be addressed, still less redressed, then the very category of the *human,* in relation to animals and environment, must also be brought under scrutiny. After all, traditional western constitutions of the human as the 'not-animal' (and, by implication, the 'not-savage') have had major, and often catastrophic, repercussions not just for animals themselves but for all those the West now considers

---

5. These issues obviously resonate with Michel Foucault's theorization of "biopolitics," his emphasis on the increasing administration of all aspects of life, reproduction, health, disease, and death by the modern state. But Foucault's framework seems to me too narrowly focused on state power to account for the current biodiversity crisis and conservation efforts, in which transnational organizations, NGOs, philanthropists, and local communities all play important roles. I therefore focus here on theories that in my view offer better grounds for understanding why individuals, communities, and institutions care or do not care about endangered species, and how they translate their concern into political practices and aesthetic forms. For an analysis of wildlife conservation that does use biopolitics as one of its theoretical foundations, see Braverman (2015).

human but were formerly designated, represented and treated as animal" (2010, 18–19).

But suggesting that racism and speciesism are systematically connected in the cultural logic of colonialism does not in and of itself answer the question of what to do when moral obligations toward oppressed humans conflict with moral obligations toward nonhumans, or what to do when the solutions that would theoretically satisfy both sets of obligations are not available in practice. Nor is it self-evident that such answers could be provided in the abstract, by way of general principles. But phrased in theoretical terms, the challenge that Wolfe as well as Huggan and Tiffin hold out is how we might reconcile the power differentials that lie at the core of postcolonial theory, of the environmentalism of the poor, and of environmental justice and human rights advocacies with the "flat ontologies," the leveling of categorical differences between kinds of beings, processes, and objects that accompanies many varieties of posthumanism. And not just posthumanism: in recent years, anthropologists in Australia, Europe, and North America have variously proposed "multispecies ethnography," "étho-ethnographie," or "zooantropologia" as new theoretical frameworks for thinking about the entanglement of nonhuman species in what have normally been considered simply human societies and cultures.

I will turn to these new theories in the concluding section of this chapter, after approaching the central questions they raise through the analysis of narratives. What stories do we tell about the relationship between colonialism, the oppression of humans, and the endangerment of animals and plants? How do these stories respond to the theoretical questions and ethical dilemmas that arise in the confrontation with the immiseration of humans and nonhumans? What dimensions do they highlight, which ones do they hide, and why? In exploring these questions, I will focus in section 1 on Cuban–Puerto Rican author Mayra Montero's novel *Tú, la oscuridad* (1995). Montero's fictionalization of the search for an endangered frog in Haiti associates the direct violence perpetrated on humans and the indirect violence that puts nonhuman species at risk through a divine call—a supernatural logic that one can read as an emphasis on the importance of local cosmologies or on the limits of science, or as a metaphor to highlight the magnitude of human and nonhuman suffering. *Virunga*, a graphic novel created by the Stanford Graphic Novel Project in 2009 and edited by Adam Johnson and Tom Kealey, also juxtaposes the risks that disenfranchised humans and endangered nonhumans are exposed to (see section 2). In a detailed portrayal of mountain gorilla conservation efforts in Virunga National

Park in the Democratic Republic of Congo, this novel shows how deeply conservation efforts, choices, and trade-offs are entangled in the military conflicts, economic inequalities, ethnic confrontations, sexual violence, and refugee crises in the region. Depending on whose viewpoint in this scenario of conflict one adopts, *Virunga* suggests, the meanings and functions of conservation efforts and of nature in general change radically, and the resulting differences are given visual shape through a variety of drawing styles in the novel. The privileging of the needs of charismatic animals over those of poor human populations that one character in *Virunga* questions also takes center stage in one of the best-known recent novels to have fictionalized questions of environmental justice and the nonhuman other, Amitav Ghosh's *The Hungry Tide* ([2005] 2006; section 3). Ghosh focuses on a scenario of confrontation between disenfranchised humans and endangered species in the Sundarbans, a vast area of tidal mangrove forests on the Bay of Bengal. But in addition, he juxtaposes two endangered species, tigers and dolphins, that foreground different kinds of competition between animals and humans for safety and protection, and that emphasize violence and reconciliation in conservation contexts, respectively. The chapter concludes in section 4 with a consideration of environmental justice in its convergences and tensions with "multispecies ethnography," the attempt on the part of anthropologists to rewrite analyses of human societies in terms of their relations with plants and animals. Any approach to what I would like to call *multispecies justice,* the claims of both human and nonhuman well-being on conservationists' consideration, I will argue, will need to consider not just biological but cultural species—that is, the distinctions that matter for science but also those that matter in cultural taxonomies. And it will need to be accountable not just to the ontological differences between species, but also to the cultural differences in divergent understandings of justice, which in part arise from different approaches to taxonomies of beings.

1. Frog and Ostrich: Violence and Domestication in Montero's Tú, la oscuridad

Cuban–Puerto Rican author Mayra Montero's *Tú, la oscuridad* may be "the Caribbean region's first avowedly environmentalist novel" (Paravisini-Gebert 2014, 350). The novel revolves around the journey of an American herpetologist, Victor Grigg, to Haiti to search for a specimen of an extremely endangered frog species, *Eleutherodactylus sanguineus* or "grenouille du sang" (blood frog; so named for its red color).

From November 1992 to February 1993, Grigg works with an aged Haitian guide, Thierry Adrien, who has already assisted a herpetologist of a previous generation, Jason Wilbur. "Daddy Toad" (Papa Crapaud), as Adrien had affectionately nicknamed Wilbur, taught him the fine points of frog identification. The story of the search for the elusive blood frog is told in alternating chapters narrated from the first-person viewpoints of Grigg and Adrien, and it is interspersed and overlaid with their memories and differing interpretations of the unfolding events. Grigg and a botanist whom he accidentally meets, herself on a parallel quest for a rare cactus, have no clear grasp of Haiti's political landscape and naively imagine that scientists who are just looking for frogs or plants could not possibly interfere with the bands of *Tontons Macoutes,* death squads who still claim Haitian territories after the demise of "Baby Doc" Jean-Claude Duvalier's dictatorship. But again and again, Grigg is forced to confront the realities: he finds corpses with cut-off limbs or unrecognizable faces that mark the power of a particular band, and he is threatened with death unless he abandons his search in a specific area. As the threats build up, he and Adrien escape from Haiti aboard a ship that eventually sinks in a storm and drowns them both, along with the last specimen of the *grenouille du sang.*

At first glance, the novel seems to juxtapose the direct, visible, and horrifying violence of political oppression with the more gradual, enigmatic, and saddening violence of ecological disappearance. Both seem to be caused by forces that are hard to understand, let alone manipulate, by individuals—to the point where they appear supernatural. Grigg and Adrien first explore the Mont des Enfants Perdus, a mountain whose ominous name derives from the gruesome and enigmatic disappearance of orphaned children years earlier. They quickly find themselves the target of threats by the commander of a band of *Tontons Macoutes*, Cito Francisque, who forces them to abandon the territory that he has reserved for his own exercises of power, including executions. The same process repeats itself later in the mountainous area of Casetaches, and along the way, bodies of people with cut-off hands or feet or mutilated faces signal the omnipresence of violence and death in Haiti as Adrien perceives and experiences it.

Grigg's and Adrien's perspectives on these events are intercut with apparently factual and detached observations on the disappearance of frogs in various parts of the world, such as the following:

> In 1992, four frog species disappeared from Cusuco National
> Park in Honduras.

Eleutherodactylus milesi, Hyla soralia, Plectrohyla dasypus, and *Plectrohyla teuchestes,* whose populations once abounded in the region, had given no prior indications of problems in the habitat, or signs of decline.

The frogs disappeared without a trace, and not a single tadpole of the four species could be found in any of the numerous bodies of water in the area.

Biologists have emphasized "the catastrophic, unexplainable nature" of these disappearances. (Montero 1997, 157)[6]

[En 1992 desaparecieron cuatro especies de ranas del Parque Nacional Cusuco, Honduras.

Eleutherodactylus milesi, Hyla soralia, Plectrohyla dasypus, y *Plectrohyla teuchestes,* cuyas poblaciones eran abundantísimas en la zona, anteriormente no habían dado señales de problemas de hábitat o de declinación.

Las ranas desaparecieron sin dejar rastro, y ni siquiera pudo ser hallado un solo renacuajo de las cuatro especies en ninguno de los numerosos cuerpos de agua del lugar.

Los biólogos subrayaron "la naturaleza catastrófica e inexplicable" de estas desapariciones.] (Montero 1995, 207)

Each of these intercalated passages adopts an apparently scientific tone but really foregrounds the shortfalls of science in accounting for the disappearance of the frogs. Montero here fictionalizes what was a genuine mystery in the 1980s and 1990s, the extinction of frog species in vastly different areas of the world. The enigma has since found a scientific explanation: many of the extinctions have been caused, and still are being caused, by chytridiomycosis, an infectious disease caused by a fungus, *Batrachochytrium dendrobatidis,* which was discovered in 1993 and has since been mapped in its global spread (see Olson et al. 2013; Kolbert 2014, chap. 1). Montero narrates what was, at the time she wrote *Tú, la oscuridad,* still a largely unexplained set of extinctions in such a way that

---

6. The English wording and page numbers follow Edith Grossman's 1997 translation.

inexplicable occurrences of violence and death seem equally to afflict
Haitian nature and society.

The *grenouille du sang,* by its very name, becomes the hinge of this
narrative translation. For Adrien, this particular frog has been associated with illness, misfortune, and death from his childhood:

> The last time I heard it I was a boy, and the very next day I got
> the fever and saw death coming for me. . . . Nobody in my fam-
> ily, not one of us, ever liked to hear the call of this frog. I swear I
> began to tremble. (Montero 1997, 30)

> [La última vez que lo había oído yo era un niño, y al otro día me
> cogieron aquellas fiebres, vi la muerte venir. . . . Ni a mí ni a na-
> die en mi familia nos ha gustado nunca oír el canto de esa rana.
> Le juro que empecé a temblar.] (Montero 1995, 50)

When Adrien sees one of the frogs in the rain as a young boy, he notes
that "with the gleam of the water, it seemed to me that yes, it did look
like it was covered in blood, it made you happy to see it, and it made you
afraid" (Montero 1997, 30–31) ("Con el brillo del agua me pareció que
sí, que estaba como bañada en sangre, daba gusto verla y daba miedo"
[Montero 1995, 51]). He routinely refers to it as "the devil" (Montero
1997, 169, 171, 174) ("la demonia" [Montero 1995, 225, 227, 233]).

Tellingly enough, Grigg and Adrien discover a live *grenouille du sang*
just at the moment when Grigg has desperately tried to think of a way to
explain the realities of Haiti to his elderly Australian colleague Vaughan
Patterson, the terminally ill scientist who sent him on the quest for *Eleutherodactylus sanguineus.* To Patterson, Haiti is nothing more than an
amphibian habitat, which makes it difficult for Grigg to come up with a
proper portrait of his own experiences of the country:

> How could I explain that Haiti wasn't simply a place, a name,
> a mountain with a frog that had survived? . . . What would I
> say about the way they threw live animals onto their bonfires,
> about the dust and the stink, that unbearable, unspeakable, un-
> fathomable stench? How would I describe the streets, the open
> sewers, the human shit in the middle of the sidewalk, the corpses
> at dawn, the woman whose hands were missing, the man whose
> face was missing? . . . God Almighty, how would I make him see
> that Haiti was disappearing, that the great hill of bones growing

before our very eyes . . . was all that would remain? (Montero 1997, 170–171)

[¿Cómo explicarle que Haiti no era un lugar a secas, un nombre solo, una montaña con una rana sobreviviente? . . . ¿Cómo hablarle de los animales que echaban todavía vivos a las hogueras, y del polvo y de las pestilencias, las abominables, impensables, desconocidas pestilencias? ¿Cómo describirle las calles, los albañales abiertos, la bosta humana en medio de la acera, los cadáveres del amanecer, la mujer sin sus manos, el hombre sin su rostro? . . . ¿Cómo meterle en la cabeza que Haití, gran Dios, se estaba terminando, y que esa loma de huesos que iba creciendo frente a nuestros ojos . . . era todo lo que iba a quedar?] (Montero 1995, 226–227)

Coming as it does right on the heels of this apocalyptic portrait of Haiti, the discovery of the last blood frog sums up all that Grigg—and, in a different way, Adrien—finds frightening, repulsive, or incomprehensible about Haiti. The endangerment of a particular species, in this narrative ordering, comes to stand as a synecdoche for the dangers that threaten Haiti as a whole, "the possibility of extinction . . . of a nation and its people" (Paravisini-Gebert 2014, 351).

One might object that such a reading of the *grenouille du sang* as a symbol of violence, oppression, and death in Haiti undermines both the ecological and the political substance of Montero's novel. It would seem to reduce the impending extinction of a species to nothing more than a metaphor, at the same time that poverty, oppression, and death squads seem to emerge from forces of evil—even of the satanic, since Adrien insists on calling the frog demonic—that are not susceptible to economic, social, or political analysis. I believe that this reproach is to some extent justified and pinpoints one of the weaknesses of the novel: Montero's emphasis on the supernatural and the satanic does indeed block any detailed social and political analysis. When one of Adrien's half-brothers joins the death squads, for example, it is difficult to make out any political or economic motivation—Julien seems in the grip of some evil force instead. In terms of ecological understanding as well, science at times gives way to mythology. The Haitian scientist Emile Boukaka, for instance, whom Grigg consults with during his stay, combines detailed observation and meticulous scientific record-keeping with an ultimate belief in a darker force at work in amphibian extinctions, the call of a voodoo deity: "The great flight has begun," he tells Grigg. "You people invent excuses: acid rain, herbicides, deforestation. But the frogs are disappearing from places where none of that has happened" (Montero 1997, 96) ("Ya empezó la gran huida. . . . Ustedes se inventan excusas: la lluvia ácida, los herbicidas, la deforestación. Pero las ranas desaparecen de lugares donde no ha habido nada de eso" [Montero 1995, 132]).[7] If almost all the documentary passages between chapters highlight the inability of science to account for the amphibian extinctions, this observation points to explanations in a supernatural realm, squarely beyond the grasp of ecology. Even more strikingly, it also seems to exonerate humans from any responsibility in the ongoing extinctions and to place the blame on cosmological processes of decline instead.

Although Boukaka remains a relatively minor character in the novel, Adrien sometimes suggests a similar perspective:

> You want to know where the frogs go. I cannot say, sir, but let me ask you a question: Where did our fish go? Almost all of them left this sea, and in the forest the wild pigs disappeared, and the migratory ducks, and even the iguanas for eating, they went too. (Montero 1997, 11)

> [Usted quiere saber adónde van las ranas. Yo no puedo decírselo, señor, pero le puedo preguntar, ¿adónde se fueron nuestros peces? Casi todos abandonaron este mar, y en el monte desaparecieron los puercos salvajes y los patos de temporada, y hasta las iguanas de comer, ésas también se fueron.] (Montero 1995, 26)

He segues from these observations to a panorama of general decline and death that anticipates almost verbatim Grigg's later thoughts on the state of Haiti:

> One day a man like you will come here, someone who crosses the ocean to look for a couple of frogs, and when I say frogs, I mean any creature, and he will only find a great hill of bones on the shore. . . . Then he will say to himself, Haiti is finished, God Almighty, those bones are all that remain. (Montero 1997, 11)

---

7. For a more detailed explanation of the voodoo myth of the animals' flight that Montero alludes to, see Paravisini-Gebert (2014, 352).

[Llegará el día en que venga un hombre como usted, alguien que atraviese un mar para buscar un par de ranas, quien dice ranas cualquier otro animal, y encuentre sólo una gran loma de huesos en la orilla. . . . Entonces se dirá: "Haití se terminó, gran Dios, esos huesos son todo lo que queda."] (Montero 1995, 26)

Because of its emphasis on violence and death of a kind that seems to defy rational explanation, *Tú, la oscuridad* has sometimes been compared to Conrad's *Heart of Darkness*.[8] This comparison accurately captures parallels between Marlow's and Grigg's travels to scenarios of colonial and postcolonial violence that they are at pains to understand. But the comparison also highlights crucial differences: there is no counterpart to Adrien's narrative in Conrad's novel, and more generally, Montero emphasizes the scientific perspective on a natural world in crisis even when she does not grant it definitive authority to understand and address that crisis. The passages between chapters that outline the global scope of amphibian extinction, which have no equivalent in Conrad's narrative, make it possible to read the novel against the grain of the supernatural explanations some of the characters invoke. If Boukaka believes scientific explanation obscures the true cosmological and theological significance of biodiversity loss, it is also possible to read the religious interpretation of species loss and of pervasive violence in Haiti as a metaphorical tool to grasp the magnitude of the crisis. Unnatural death inflicted on humans as well as nonhumans is so widespread and so destructive, in other words, that only the mythological imagination seems adequately equipped to describe it. From this perspective, Boukaka's invocation of Agwé Taroyo or Damballah as the ultimate cause of species disappearances becomes a way of thinking about the scope of human impacts on the natural world—impacts so complex that humans themselves have difficulty recognizing their own agency.

Whether one reads Montero's invocations of voodoo as an inappropriate diversion into the supernatural realm or as a complex metaphor for humans' own impact on other species, it remains that her novel posits social and ecological types of violence as part of the same continuum. The two kinds of violence and death are juxtaposed and compared throughout the novel and often become synecdochic extensions of each other, a connection implying that whatever solution might be found for

8. The title of Grossman's English translation, *In the Palm of Darkness*, foregrounds this parallel; literally, the Spanish title translates as "You, Darkness."

one crisis would also help mitigate the other. The novel does not spell out what such a solution might look like. But in an interesting counterpoint to Grigg's hunt for a rare frog, he also revisits in memory his father's ostrich farm in Indiana, which was at the time a new fashion in agriculture. These memories have nothing pastoral about them—Grigg remembers above all the way his mother dismissed the whole venture from the start and suspected his father of carrying on an affair with one of the employees. This marital alienation resonates in Grigg's own estrangement from his wife, Martha, who ends up consuming ostrich meat for the first time not with Grigg but with her lesbian lover. In spite of these conflictive memories, when Grigg's father passes away, Grigg's reaction is not to sell the farm as quickly as possible. On the contrary, he decides to keep it and the ostriches, which causes an amused dismissal on Martha's part that echoes his mother's earlier disdain for ostrich farming. While the novel does not spell out in detail Grigg's motivations in wanting to hold on to the farm, he does in this instance assume responsibility for the ambiguous relationship of care and violence for another species that his father began.

Thierry Adrien, as it happens, is deeply interested in Grigg's stories about the ostriches. The sketches Grigg draws for him to give him an idea of what the bird looks like echo the sketches various scientists in the novel draw of the frogs they are searching for, and they trigger in Adrien a plan for a quest of his own: " 'After we find the frog,' said Thierry, 'I'll save some money and go to see the birds. . . . First I'll see them, then I'll find out if I can bring one here. Nobody's ever seen anything like it in Haiti' " (Montero 1997, 139) ("Después que encontremos a la rana—dijo Thierry—voy a reunir dinero para ir a ver los pájaros. . . . Primero los veo, después averiguo si se puede traer alguno. En Haití eso no se ha visto nunca" [Montero 1995, 184]). This idea of introducing a new species to Haiti—short-circuited, of course, by Grigg's and Adrien's deaths at the end of the novel—functions as an imaginary counterpart to the disappearance of its native animals and as the only indication of Adrien's hopes and projects for the future. And if domestication comes with its own burdens of alienation and violence (a conversation about how an ostrich's head is cut off at the moment of slaughter is followed, in one of the novel's last chapters, by a botanist's frustrated outburst about the Haitians' habit of cutting parts off human corpses), it is also associated, in Montero's novel, with an acceptance of responsibility. While *Tú, la oscuridad* holds out no hope of a socially just, less violent, or more ecologically sustainable world, it does, through the motif of the ostrich farm, hint at a world in which humans manage and constrain the violence they perpetuate on nonhumans.

2. *Gorilla and Weaverbird: Virunga*

The question of how we might envision the relation between violence toward disenfranchised humans and violence toward nonhumans also motivates a story about conservation and endangered species in a different genre, the graphic novel. *Virunga*, edited by Johnson and Kealey, was collectively authored by a group of students who formed part of the Stanford Graphic Novel Project in 2009. The use of the comic book as a tool for reflection on serious and even traumatic events is of course not new. Comic strips and their long narrative variant, the graphic novel, have been used as media for storytelling about large-scale historical events from Hiroshima to the Holocaust as well as about personal histories in Japan, France, the United States, and Germany for decades. Many of these works grapple with the challenge of representing acts of mass and individual aggression responsibly in a medium that has traditionally tended to trivialize or glorify violence by turning it into visual spectacle. In fact, one could argue that it is precisely the readers' expectation of violence as the core of the comic book aesthetic that has made serious engagements with war, imprisonment, injury, rape, mutilation, and death in the genre so strikingly innovative over the past forty years, from Nakazawa Keiji's はだしのゲン (Hadashi no gen [Barefoot Gen], 1973) to Art Spiegelman's *Maus* (1991) and Joe Sacco's *Safe Area Gorazde* (2000). *Virunga* continues this tradition of experimentation but engages with violence that involves both humans and other species.

Virunga is set in the eponymous national park in the Democratic Republic of Congo, famous for Diane Fossey's seminal work with mountain gorillas, but also for its role as a destination for refugees during the Rwandan genocide and as a central area of military confrontation in the Kivu War between 2004 and 2008. As a narrative setting, it combines exceptional biodiversity with exceptional violence. The plot focuses on an eleven-year-old girl, Malika, who lives in a refugee camp in the park with her aunt and uncle after her parents have been killed. Herself a budding comic strip artist, she loves to watch and draw the gorillas, and in the process she comes to know some of the park rangers, including a woman ranger named Esther Illingo, who has lost her husband and been gang-raped in the conflict. Esther passes on to Malika some of her own drawing techniques as well as strategies for dealing with violence against a background of gradually increasing tension between the park rangers and two other groups, a rebel group led by Chairman Sakombi (perhaps modeled after Laurent Nkunda, the founder of the Congrès national pour la défense du peuple [National Congress for the Defense of the People]), and a militia group, the Mai-Mai.[9]

Malika, the orphaned refugee girl whose runs through the forest become the occasion for striking visual highlights of the natural world, also comes as close as the novel gets to an innocent character. All the other characters and groups, the novel is careful to show, are harder to judge unequivocally. Henry, Malika's uncle, a refugee like her, runs the camp's charcoal production, which is necessary for the refugees' daily needs but involves destruction of old-growth forest that the park rangers desperately try to prevent. Some of the charcoal is transported and distributed by Chairman Sakombi's men via the region's rivers and roads. At a certain point of the plot, the rangers strike a deal with Sakombi that runs counter to their large-scale goals: they agree no longer to interfere with his charcoal trade. But Sakombi commits himself in return not to hunt, capture, or kill the mountain gorillas, a more urgent conservation priority for the rangers. Rather than juxtaposing forces of good and evil, conservation becomes an arena of negotiations and trade-offs.

One of Sakombi's men, Njembe, however, does end up killing a whole gorilla family in a willful shooting incident that violates the deal with the rangers. Yet even he does not come across as a villain: Njembe was one of Malika's friends before he was drafted into Sakombi's rebel group as a boy soldier, and he is killed in a shootout with the rangers, more double victim than antagonist. Full hostilities between the rangers and Sakombi's group erupt when the rangers realize that the militia have kidnapped three young girls, friends of Malika's, to use as sexual and domestic slaves for the rebels. This abduction breaks the deal in the rangers' minds, and one of them dies in the ensuing confrontation.

These unexpected turns and difficult combinations of right and wrong defy any simple judgment of the novel's characters. Chairman Sakombi initially seems to be cast as the archvillain: in the first frame in which he appears, he is shown sitting thuggishly sprawled on a claw-footed chair in the midst of looted UNESCO supplies, wearing sunglasses and holding a cane with a an ominous-looking eagle's head, his enormous boots stretched out toward the observer—a classical way of representing evil guys in comic

9. Orlando von Einsiedel's documentary *Virunga* (2014) traces a more recent moment in the continuing intersections between conservation, military confrontation, displacement, and corporate exploitation of resources.

books (Johnson and Kealey 2009, 60–61). Some readers may cringe at the way he invokes God to justify keeping women from doing men's business and refuses to engage with the problem of endangered species. When one of the rangers points out that the gorillas are the last of their kind, he replies, "You are not their protectors. Only God chooses who will live and who will die" (62). But even Sakombi is far from irrational or devoid of motivations that readers might sympathize with. He points out that the rangers disrupt the trade in charcoal, without which people cannot cook or eat either locally or in Goma or Kivu, and in this context he directly raises questions of environmental justice: "You say you protect the animals from the people, but who protects the people from corruption and starvation and disease? I know that last year you inoculated the gorillas, but do the people get the shots? Where are the forces to protect the people? I will tell you. *We* protect the people. Without us, women and children have no meat for dinner and no fuel to cook with" (64–65). One of his soldiers similarly claims in an encounter with Malika, "*We* work against this corrupt government to return the land to the people" (28).

Virunga does not zero in on these arguments and the characters who articulate them enough to produce a genuine counterperspective to that of the rangers. But the counterpoints recur insistently enough to make it clear that the conservation projects associated with the national park are not above ethical questioning and are deeply embroiled in national politics. Neither are the rangers heroes beyond reproach: one of them, Aymar, was himself a poacher before he became a national park ranger.[10] The faculty leaders of the Stanford Graphic Novel Project, Adam Johnson and Tom Kealey, note in their afterword: "Our interest in the DRC began with the Virunga National Park in the North Kivu province. Virunga is the oldest national park in Africa and home to nearly half the world's 700 remaining mountain gorillas. . . . As we researched more about Virunga and the surrounding areas, we realized there were so many things that were interconnected that we could not justify leaving out, including the coal trade, child soldiers, sexual violence, and many rebel armies and militias. There are so many sides to every story, and we did our best to capture that" (2009, 216).

As they recount in broad strokes the history of armed conflict in the area, Johnson and Kealey place conservation efforts and the concern about charismatic primates into a context of violent international interventions to lay hold of resources such as diamonds, uranium, iron ore,

---

10. For a perceptive analysis, from an anthropologist's perspective, of conservation workers in Madagascar and their relationship to conservation, see Sodikoff (2012a, 2012b).

coal, and coltan (a mineral that is used in the production of electronics), as well as sustained military violence after the Rwandan genocide in "the world's deadliest conflict since World War II." Johnson and Kealey highlight, "Some 5.4 million people have died, and about 45,000 continue to die each month" (2009, 216).

While *Virunga*—or any other work of art of literature—could hardly be expected to do justice to all of the dimensions of this complex sociopolitical, economic, and ecological scenario, it does successfully suggest conflicting perspectives and story lines, including the negotiations and trade-offs that surround national-park-style conservation efforts focusing on species beloved by publics in the global north. Like the sketches of frogs that various characters draw in *Tú, la oscuridad,* different drawing styles in *Virunga* highlight how nonhuman nature reaches human perception through filters that vary according to culture, community, and individual. The pictures of gorillas in a rebel's digital camera (rendered as drawings, of course, in the graphic novel: Johnson and Kealey 2009, 31; fig. 9a), Esther's scientific drawing of them in her field journal (85; fig. 9b), and Malika's childlike sketches (80; fig. 9c) model mountain gorillas as objects of commerce, of scientific study, and of awakening curiosity—all this in addition to the more or less "realist" style that functions as default in *Virunga*. Esther's schematic drawings of individual gorillas' noses, which function as fingerprints of sorts by which the rangers identify them (81–82), visually resemble the characters of a foreign script and thereby suggest that gorillas might also be "read" as a sort of text, one susceptible to different interpretations and translations, to be sure. Malika's observation that the gorilla in one of Esther's drawings looks sad and her insistence that the gorillas are happy and at play (83) leads Esther to reflect: "Malika has never seen them suffer from tuberculosis or bleed out from ebola. She hasn't seen a new male kill all the infants and attack the juveniles. Or the way they all scatter when a silverback dies," memories accompanied by a black-framed image in which the gorillas appear drawn with pencil strokes that make them resemble stone figures (84). The question whether what the drawings show is the moods of the gorillas or those of their observers becomes undecidable at such moments.

At other moments, too, *Virunga* visually emphasizes the entanglement of politics and culture with any representation of nature. Faced with the threat that Sakombi's men will capture and sell off young gorillas, one of the rangers recalls a mythological story according to which humans were originally unable to speak, whereas gorillas possessed language. Humans, as they made fire, moved up to the volcanoes where the mountain gorillas lived, and they could not understand the gorillas'

FIGURE 9. Mountain gorillas depicted in the graphic novel *Virunga*, as seen through a camera lens (*a*), in Esther's scientific journal (*b*), and in Malika's childlike drawings (*c*). *Source*: Johnson and Kealey (2009, 31, 85, 80). Reproduced by permission of the authors.

command for them to go away. "A deal was made. The gorillas gave away their words and the humans promised never to return" (Johnson and Kealey 2009, 51). In the plot, the story does little more than inspire the idea of proposing a deal to Chairman Sakombi. But as a story about the origins of language, it also suggests that now that humans have broken their promise and returned to the gorillas' territory, language might be taken from them and go back to the gorillas—an interesting premise for the graphic novel as a potentially nonlinguistic genre as well as for its frequent representation of animals as speakers and agents.

In fact, a speaking animal appears only once in *Virunga,* in a sequence that ostensibly takes place only in Esther's mind. In this scene, the weaver-bird, who in other scenes appears as just a white or black silhouette against a contrasting black or white background, encourages Esther to leave her pain behind and engage anew with her life. The imagined bird here seems to take on a life of its own, whereas Esther has earlier called it up in her mind merely as a way of coping with rape and violence. In a scene in the novel's first "Act" or chapter, we see Esther suggesting to Malika that if anything horrible were done to her, she should not remember the people's faces but close her eyes and imagine a weaverbird instead. The bird then promptly appears in the next few frames, though in this instance without speaking. The sequence closes with Esther and Malika mirrored in the weaverbird's iris (Johnson and Kealey 2009, 37; fig. 10).

All encounters between humans and animals are overshadowed by memories or anticipations of violence, as emphasized through a similar foregrounding of animal eyes in the scene just before Esther meets Malika for the first time. Malika has gone on one of her usual runs through the forest and happens upon a mountain gorilla. A full-page image shows the gorilla in the foreground and Malika watching from among tall grasses in the background, relatively smaller than the gorilla in the distance. But a slender vertical panel embedded into this page-size drawing shows the right side of Malika's face and her wide-open right eye in close-up, a surrealist juxtaposition of different camera-zoom views that foregrounds her perception as well as a different view of both her and the gorilla that might represent someone else's gaze, including, possibly, another gorilla's (Johnson and Kealey 2009, 23; fig. 11).

The following page has a central, unframed image that shows the gorilla on the left and Malika on the right with a forest road between them (fig. 12). Overlaid on the top of the central panel, three smaller vertical panels echo the previous page by showing the right side of the gorilla's face, the animal's gaze alert and wary, and the left side of Malika's, her eye still open in surprise and astonishment, with a close-up of the gorilla's hand in between. At the bottom, the central panel is supplemented by four smaller horizontal panels that show the gorilla's and Malika's faces in their entirety but at a greater remove, and two views of the encounter scene from the central panel at different "zoom" positions. This intricate juxtaposition of different eyes, different gazes, and different viewing positions emphasizes the relativity of perspectives and precedes Malika's sitting down and drawing

FIGURE 10 Esther's imagination of the weaverbird. *Source*: Johnson and Kealey (2009, 37). Reproduced by permission of the authors.

the gorilla. But it is also followed, almost immediately, by the appearance of one of Sakombi's men, who has been taking photographs of the gorillas in preparation for "shopping" their images to potential buyers. This opens up the possibility that the zoomed-in and zoomed-out images on the previous pages were views captured with his digital camera. Even though the rebel, in this scene, intends no violence toward Malika and in fact converses with her casually about their mutual interest in the gorillas, the threat of poaching retrospectively hovers over what at first appeared to be Malika's

FIGURE 11 View of Malika and the mountain gorilla she observes. *Source*: Johnson and Kealey (2009, 23). Reproduced by permission of the authors.

one-on-one encounter with the primate. And since the rebel's camera also turns out to contain an image of the three friends of Malika's who end up with Sakombi's group later on, this also includes the threat of kidnapping and sexual violence. What appear at first sight to be some of the most striking and almost surrealist juxtapositions in *Virunga*, then, turn out in hindsight to have only too real implications of surveillance and violence.

One final example shows the range of varied strategies this graphic novel uses to reflect on the connection between perceptions of nature and political violence in the context of the Democratic Republic of the Congo and beyond. One of the images that starts out the novel in act 1 is a panoramic drawing of a river, its forested shores, and an island against a background of volcanic mountains with clouds drifting along and above them—a panoramic vista of undisturbed natural beauty and idyllic harmony (Johnson and Kealey 2009, 6). Exactly the same image reappears approximately 150 pages later, at the end of act 8 (171), with one small alteration that only a close examination reveals: two tiny human figures at one of the river bends, one lying down with a gun at his feet, the other one kneeling beside him and leaning over him in concern (fig. 13). This

FIGURE 12 Play of perspectives in Malika's encounter with the gorilla. *Source*: Johnson and Kealey (2009, 24). Reproduced by permission of the authors.

FIGURE 13A Repeated panels at the opening (*a*) and toward the end (*b*) of *Virunga*: landscape and violence. *Source*: Johnson and Kealey (2009, 6, 171). Reproduced by permission of the authors.

FIGURE 13B

panel functions as the tragic zoom-out conclusion of a fatal encounter between a ranger and one of Sakombi's rebels, both equally inexperienced young men. The dead man is Malika's friend Njembe, who had been drafted into Sakombi's group as a child soldier. He has just killed an entire gorilla family for no reason other than to prove his manhood and soldierly value to the other rebels, who had humiliated him in an earlier scene. In the act of killing the gorillas, he is surprised by ranger Pascal, himself an inexperienced rookie, who shoots Njembe when he sees him lifting up his gun. No two images in *Virunga*, echoing each other across much of the novel's plot, convey more forcefully than these two that any vision of nature and of conservation apart from humans and apart from the political violence that shapes the region is an illusion, and that violence will sooner or later intrude into even the most undisturbed and most majestic vistas of the landscape.

Malika, in the novel's last chapter, escapes to Kinshasa on a UN truck. In her new urban life, she develops her drawing skills and creates a comic, embedded into the main story, that presents an idyllic and perhaps utopian counternarrative to the pervasive deprivation, suffering, and violence experienced by both humans and nonhumans in the main plot. If this conclusion offers no realistic vision of what a political solution to the complications of the plot might look like (a tall order for any writer or artist, let alone a group of college undergraduates on their first creative venture!), it does affirm a dual role for the graphic novel as both a documentary genre for current crises and a medium for envisioning possible alternatives. But the main achievement of *Virunga* may not lie in what it envisions—or refuses to offer—as a political solution, but in its emphasis on the imbrication of endangered species conservation with political, sexual, and economic violence: direct violence and "structural" or "slow" violence, as Johann Galtung and Rob Nixon have respectively called it (Galtung 1969; Nixon 2011). This graphic novel therefore considerably complicates the alignment of violence against humans with violence against nonhumans and with species extinction that we saw in Montero's *Tú, la oscuridad*. In *Virunga* mythological stories make an appearance, but they play a very minor role compared to the complex political, economic, national, and ethnic conflicts and convergences that give rise to a range of different stories in the plot, none of which can simply be subsumed under or aligned with others. Whatever an environmentally just DRC might look like, *Virunga* suggests, this justice will need to be built from the different stories and different investments, cultural and economic, of local residents, refugees, rebels, militias, governments, and transnational organizations.

3. Tigers and Dolphins: The Hungry Tide

The conflicts between protection of the poor and conservation of endangered species, between protection of national park landscapes and their uses in local residents' survival that *Virunga* stages through its reflections on different ways of seeing and drawing become even more prominent in Indian-born novelist Amitav Ghosh's *The Hungry Tide*. But whereas *Virunga* features no non-African characters, *The Hungry Tide* takes its point of departure from a cast of characters that in some ways resembles that of *Tú, la oscuridad*. Set in the tidal mangrove forest of the Sundarbans in the Bay of Bengal in the early 2000s, the novel brings together three protagonists: Piyali Roy, an American biologist of Indian descent who visits the area to do research on a rare kind of river dolphin; Kanai Dutt, a Delhi businessman and translator who comes to pick up papers that his deceased uncle, Nirmal, has left for him; and Fokir Mandol, an illiterate fisherman who becomes Roy's guide in her search for *Orcaella brevirostris*, the Irrawaddy dolphin. Piya Roy and Fokir Mandol in some ways replay the dichotomies that also structure the relationship between Grigg and Adrien: the American scientist and the native guide, scientific expertise in its encounter with local knowledge, literacy and orality, personal histories whose social and erotic constellations open windows onto broader political and economic histories. Given Roy's and Mandol's complementary kinds of expertise on the sea and its creatures—Roy's cetological knowledge and Mandol's daily observations and experiences as a fisherman—one might expect that issues of environmental justice would emerge around the quest for the endangered dolphins in the novel's present in the early 2000s.

But they do not. Instead, the conflicts and convergences of biological conservation and social justice revolve around the Bengal tiger, another highly endangered species, and they unfold in part by way of memories. Kanai Dutt finds that the packet of papers his uncle has left for him does not contain poems or essays, as he expected, but instead a journal written in 1979, shortly before Nirmal's death. The journal recounts some of the events leading up to a massacre of refugees that took place on the island of Morichjhāpi in May 1979. In 1978 a group of refugees from Bangladesh who had been relocated to the Dandakaranya camp in Madhya Pradesh fled to the Sundarbans because of the camp's desperate conditions and the hostility of the surrounding communities. They arrived at the island of Morichjhāpi with the intention of settling there, cleared the land for agriculture, and began to fish and farm. But the area had been designated part of the Sundarbans Tiger Reserve in 1973 and as

a wildlife sanctuary in 1977. The Indian Left Front ministry saw the settlement as an alarming first encroachment on protected land that might
be followed by others, and it cracked down brutally on the refugees by
cutting them off from outside supplies and finally by evicting them. Approximately forty-one hundred families are believed to have been killed as
a consequence of the blockade and eviction, through starvation, disease,
accidents during the transit back to camps, or police shootings (Jalais
2005, 1759).

In Ghosh's fictionalization of the incident, as relayed through Nirmal's journal, it is Kusum, one of the refugees, who articulates clearly
the inhumanity she perceives in privileging the well-being of animals and
plants over that of humans:

> The worst part was not the hunger or the thirst. It was to sit here,
> helpless, and listen to the policemen making their announce-
> ments, hearing them say that our lives, our existence, were worth
> less than dirt or dust. "This island has to be saved for its trees,
> it has to be saved for its animals, it is a part of a reserve forest,
> it belongs to a project to save tigers, which is paid for by people
> from all around the world." Every day, sitting here with hunger
> gnawing at our bellies, we would listen to these words over and
> over again. Who are these people, I wondered, who love animals
> so much that they are willing to kill us for them? Do they know
> what is being done in their name? Where do they live, these peo-
> ple? Do they have children? Do they have mothers, fathers? As
> I thought of these things, it seemed to me that this whole world
> had become a place of animals, and our fault, our crime, was
> that we were just human beings, trying to live as human beings
> always have, from the water and the soil. No one could think
> this a crime unless they have forgotten how humans have al-
> ways lived, by fishing, by clearing land, and by planting the soil.
> (Ghosh [2005] 2006, 216–217)

The indictment of the international conservation movement along with
the national police force here combines with an invocation of sustainable uses of nature, including agriculture, which Kusum conceives of as
human universals. From this perspective, but framed more theoretically,
two biopolitical objectives on the part of the nation-state combine to
produce displacement and death for the poor: on one hand, the attempt
to contain and police refugee populations and, on the other, the goal to

maintain control of natural resources, including not just the Bengal tiger but also the plantations that had already been started on Morichjhāpi Island before refugees arrived.

Through Nirmal's account of the Morichjhāpi blockade and massacre, the reader is clearly invited to sympathize with Kusum. Her indictment of tiger conservation functions in counterpoint with another incident in the novel, located in the narrative present, in which the three protagonists witness how enraged villagers burn to death a live tiger that has attacked and killed two village residents. Roy is outraged by what she perceives as a meaningless act of destruction: "This is an animal. . . . You can't take revenge on an animal," she protests (Ghosh [2005] 2006, 242). Dutt and Mandol try to keep her from going into the fray to defend the tiger, and in the end they have to carry her physically off the scene to prevent her from becoming another object of the villagers' rage. The incident produces a break in Roy's emergent synergy with Mandol, since she is not just horrified by the burning itself, but also by what she perceives as his complicity in it. Dutt sympathizes with her emotions to some extent, but he also meditates on the problem of social justice that her outrage raises:

> I mean, aren't we a part of the horror as well? You and me and people like us? . . . That tiger had killed two people . . . and that was just in one village. It happens every week that people are killed by tigers. How about the horror of that? If there were killings on that scale anywhere else on Earth, it would be called a genocide, and yet here it goes almost unremarked: these killings are never reported, never written about in the papers. And the reason is just that these people are too poor to matter. We all know it, but we choose not to see it. Isn't that a horror too—that we can feel the suffering of an animal, but not of human beings? . . . Because we're complicit in this. . . . Because it was people like you . . . who made a push to protect the wildlife here, without regard for the human costs. And I'm complicit because people like me—Indians of my class, that is—have chosen to hide these costs, basically in order to curry favor with their Western patrons. It's not hard to ignore the people who are dying—after all, they are the poorest of the poor. (248–249)

Such a class-conscious indictment of elite indifference to the poor may sound a bit implausible from the mouth of Kanai Dutt, who stands out by a smug self-satisfaction and an embrace of class privilege that the novel associates with urban professionals—at least until his mind is changed later in the plot by his own encounter with tiger power. But from a different social and historical vantage point, Dutt's argument resonates with Kusum's perception that conservation and concern for animals are elite privileges that ignore the needs of the poor.

Roy responds to this attack on conservation by staking out a different perspective of political critique: "Just suppose we crossed that imaginary line that prevents us from deciding that no other species matters except ourselves. What'll be left then? Aren't we alone enough in the universe? And do you think it'll stop at that? Once we decide we can kill off other species, it'll be people next—just the kind of people you're thinking of, people who are poor and unnoticed" (Ghosh [2005] 2006, 249). Interestingly, this is not the argument one might have expected of the typical environmentalist from the global north: that top predators such as tigers matter crucially for the ecosystems they inhabit because they keep herbivores in check, who would otherwise proliferate and wreak havoc on the local plant life and in turn impoverish the ecosystems that humans in the region depend on. Instead, Roy follows the line of argument we saw in Wolfe and in Huggan and Tiffin, according to which the same structural logic underlies violence against poor humans and against nonhumans. The disdain for nonhuman life ultimately enables violence against human lives that can always be categorized as less than fully human, in this argument. Where Kusum and Dutt see conservation as pitted against the interests of the poor, Roy sees them as convergent in terms of their underlying political logic.

It is one of the strengths of Ghosh's novel that it presents both points of view with nuance, seriousness, and even passion, and that it does not invite readers easily to dismiss either viewpoint. My reading, in this respect, diverges from Upamanyu Pablo Mukherjee's, who sees Piya Roy as not much more than a mouthpiece of American environmentalism, Western science, and the disinterest of the global north in the fates of the southern poor.[11] If that were so, it would be hard to explain why so much of the novel is focalized through her and Kanai Dutt, whereas

11. "[Roy's] desire for an antiseptic, classificatory, limited relationship with the world is the paradigm for her scientific work—her intense submersion into the process of observing, recording and analysing marine life as data—and for her fierce desire to preserve the subjects of this exercise. Her world is a scientific 'field' rather than a place of habitation" (Mukherjee 2010, 131). Mukherjee grants Roy a sense of the human world beyond science only after her transformative experience of a cyclone (132).

Mandol, Kusum, and other inhabitants of the Sundarbans are presented only from the outside, through the eyes of the protagonists. It would be equally hard to account for the ending, which leaves Mandol dead in the cyclone but brings Roy back to the Sundarbans to pursue what she has identified as her life's task, the exploration of the Irrawaddy dolphin. Mukherjee sees this as her acquisition of a sense of place, and he may be right; but if the point of Ghosh's novel is "refugee migration, not some cosmopolitan boundary-crossing as *the* postcolonial event" (Mukherjee 2010, 132), it is surprising that the ending revolves precisely around Roy's and, to a lesser extent, Dutt's sociocultural boundary-crossing: not, in other words, the novel's refugees, but those who travel by choice from the metropolis.[12]

And what about the dolphins? Whereas the tigers move offstage at the end of the novel, it is Roy's dolphin research that opens up what perspectives for the future the novel offers. Why, one might ask, is Roy not presented as doing research on Bengal tigers in the first place, which would have easily connected the scientific and social justice themes in the novel? Or, to put it somewhat differently, why does the novel engage readers in the lives of two quite different endangered species? *The Hungry Tide* devotes an inordinate amount of time to the taxonomy and behavior of the Irrawaddy dolphin, as well as to the history of its discovery and identifications; in addition, a good deal of the first part of the novel, entitled *The Ebb/Bhata,* describes in great detail Roy's procedures for finding and studying the dolphins. If the episodes involving Bengal tigers give rise to some of the most spectacular and most violent conflicts in *The Hungry Tide,* dolphins generate a great deal more narrative material, and this material concerns ordinary details of history, science, and everyday work.

In unfolding these details, the novel gradually accretes symbolic meanings around the dolphins that are the opposite of those that cluster around the tiger. The history of the scientific study of Gangetic dolphins and Irrawaddy dolphins, the two species that inhabit the Sundarbans, is studded with misidentifications and misunderstandings, as Roy explains to Dutt. Dutt learns from her that Kolkata, his native city, played an important role in the development of cetology, a fact that he was not

---

12. Mukherjee refers only to Roy and Dutt as "cosmopolitans," which is fair enough. But recent theories of cosmopolitanism, which do not limit the term to privileged travel, would include refugees among cosmopolitans. For a reading of Ghosh in terms of such cosmopolitanisms, including eco-cosmopolitanism, see Weik (2006–7).

aware of (Ghosh [2005] 2006, 188). It was in Kolkata's Botanical Gardens that the first scientific article on the discovery of a river dolphin, the Gangetic dolphin, was written in 1801, though its scientific name had to be changed later because it already had been described by Pliny the Elder in the first century CE (188). A nineteenth-century scientist, John Anderson, kept a young Gangetic dolphin in his bathtub but never found out that the species has no eyesight and prefers to swim on its side (188–189). The English naturalist Edward Blyth called cetaceans of what he considered an unknown species *Globicephalus indicus,* though later investigation revealed them to be short-finned pilot whales (189), and several years later misidentified a specimen at a fish market as a juvenile of the same species he had named (190–191). Twenty-five years later, his mistake was rectified when scientists at the British Museum identified a related specimen as an entirely new species, the Irrawaddy dolphin, *Orcaella brevirostris,* a relative of the killer whale. Anderson also mistakenly distinguished two populations of *Orcaella brevirostris* with somewhat different behavior as two different species (191). Roy herself, in her research on the dolphins in various regions of Asia, shows local fishermen cards with drawings of different dolphin species to prompt them to identify which ones they might have seen and where, especially when she has no translator available. But one of her informants in the Sundarbans initially misunderstands the drawing of a dolphin as one of a bird: "Like an optical illusion, the picture seemed to change shape as she looked at it; she had the feeling that she was looking at it through his eyes. She understood how the mistake might be possible, given the animal's plump, dove-like body and its spoon-shaped bill, not unlike a heron's" (28–29).

The story of humans' encounters with cetaceans, as *The Hungry Tide* tells it, is one of changing perceptions, perspectives, images, understandings, and taxonomies, including misunderstandings and mistaken identifications. But it is also one of surprising symbioses and synergies. During a research trip to the Irrawaddy River in Myanmar, from which *Orcaella brevirostris* derives its common name, Roy observes how the dolphins help drive swarms of fish into the nets of local fishermen and in return eat the fish that the nets drive to the river bottom. "Did there exist a more remarkable instance of symbiosis between human beings and a population of wild animals?" Roy wonders (Ghosh [2005] 2006, 140). In exploring the Sundarbans aboard Mandol's boat, she notices unusual behavior patterns in the local *Orcaella* population that lead her to an innovative hypothesis about their interaction with the ebb and flow of the tide, and to the insight that her life's scientific work might lie in exploring this hypothesis: a task that would involve meticulous exploration of the water chemistry, sedimentation, and meteorology of the region along with the particulars of animal behavior and the variations among the Sundarbans' multiple microenvironments (104–105). To take a first few steps toward gathering data, she asks Mandol, with the help of gestures and drawings, to take her across a certain stretch of river in straight back-and-forth lines, a trajectory Mandol also uses to line-fish for crabs with his son. Another symbiotic work process ensues, this time between an American scientist and a Bengali fisherman who share no language between them:

> It was surprising that their jobs had not proved to be utterly incompatible—especially considering that one of the tasks required the input of geostationary satellites while the other depended on bits of shark bone and broken tile. But that it had proved possible for two such different people to pursue their own ends simultaneously—people who could not exchange a word with each other and had no idea of what was going on in one another's heads—was far more than surprising: it seemed almost miraculous. Nor was she the only one to remark on this: once, when her glance happened accidentally to cross Fokir's, she saw something in his expression that told her that he too was amazed by the seamless intertwining of their pleasures and their purposes. (148)

More indirectly, such a prospect of synergy opens up at the end of the novel, after Mandol's death, when Roy returns to the Sundarbans to stay and continue her scientific investigation with the help of funding from conservation organizations. The fund-raising will allow her, she proposes, to involve local fishermen as well as Mandol's widow, Moyna, to provide them with additional income and eventually to provide a college education for their son. "For me, home is where the Orcaella are," she declares (327), turning the dolphins into the anchoring point for a project that will combine science, conservation, and social justice in her vision.

Broadly speaking, then, the two endangered species in the novel, the Bengal tiger and the Irrawaddy dolphin, set up two divergent poles of ecological, social, and political meanings. The tiger scenes tend to be associated with violence between humans and nonhuman species and with scenarios of displacement, economic inequality, and political oppression, as well as with conflicts between conservation and social justice.

The activities and events surrounding the dolphins, by contrast, start out in serial mistakes and misunderstandings but eventually lead to real or projected scenarios of commitment, collaboration, homecoming, and community-building, and at least some redress to economic injustice. What *The Hungry Tide* suggests through this juxtaposition is that conservation efforts on behalf of endangered species and those meant to create and maintain social justice are neither inherently at odds with each other nor inherently synergistic. Rather, the novel invites readers to accept that some conservation scenarios throw up hard choices that environmentalists can only live up to by developing an ability to see them with the eyes of the community on the ground, whereas in other cases symbioses between conservation and social justice offer themselves up easily. It also encourages readers to reflect on what might convert scenarios of the first kind into those of the second: what might move conservation from tiger scenarios to dolphin scenarios.

4. Environmental Justice as Multispecies Justice

Similar questions animate all three of the otherwise quite different texts I have examined here: What are the connections and disjunctures between violence against disenfranchised communities and against endangered species? Whose risk perceptions determine conservation efforts, and what institutional shapes do these efforts take? Who protects, on what authority, and who is assumed to be in need of protection? What causes the kinds of situations in which the protection of nonhuman species works against the safety of local populations, and vice versa? How are local biodiversity protection projects shaped by regional, national, and international politics? As I have shown, the three narratives construe different answers to these questions, even as all of them draw on carefully researched political histories of the areas in which the plots are set. Montero, in this vein, focuses on a global pattern of extinctions whose scientific causes were not known when she wrote *Tú, la oscuridad* so as to stage the encounter of scientific expertise and local knowledge. Her novel concludes that pervasive violence against humans as well as against nonhumans in post-Duvalier Haiti derives from shared causes that involve either supernatural powers or political forces so inaccessible to individuals that they might as well be supernatural. The students in the Stanford Graphic Novel Project who created *Virunga* prominently feature Congolese refugees and mountain gorillas as vulnerable communities and highlight the multidimensional and constantly evolving political landscape in which they are alternately threatened and put under protection, with often difficult or ambiguous ethical choices for those who safeguard one or the other community. Ghosh, finally, stages the equally divergent interests of local residents, refugees, urban elites, national law enforcement, and international conservationists through two conservation scenarios, one surrounding the Bengal tiger, in which residents' and refugees' interests clash with national and international conservation efforts, and the other one surrounding the Irrawaddy dolphin, where they ultimately converge.

It is perhaps no accident that *The Hungry Tide,* the most detailed fictional exploration of conservation in the context of environmental justice, was written by an author with a degree in social anthropology. Anthropologists have recently been at the forefront of reenvisioning relationships between humans and animals in ways that directly touch upon issues of conservation and social justice. The annual convention of the American Anthropological Association in 2010 featured a "Multispecies Salon" art exhibit that the curators, anthropologists Eben Kirksey and Stefan Helmreich, took as the occasion for a manifesto-style essay, "The Emergence of Multispecies Ethnography" (2010). The exhibit, with different artists involved, was repeated in New Orleans and New York, and Kirksey published a revised version of this essay along with contributions by some of the artists in an anthology called *The Multispecies Salon* in 2014. Taking its point of departure from Anna Tsing's claim that "human nature is an interspecies relationship" (quoted in Kirksey, Schuetze, and Helmreich 2014), multispecies ethnography seeks to define the human itself: "Ethnographers are now exploring how 'the human' has been formed and transformed amid encounters with multiple species of plants, animals, fungi, and microbes. Rather than simply celebrate multispecies mingling, ethnographers have begun to explore a central question: Who benefits, cui bono, when species meet? To answer this question, multispecies ethnographers are collaborating with artists and biological scientists to illuminate how diverse organisms are entangled in political, economic and cultural systems" (Kirksey, Schuetze, and Helmreich 2014). Multispecies ethnography, therefore, aims broadly at reconstructing the understanding of "human" communities as in reality conglomerates of human and nonhuman species that shape each other.

Certainly, this idea is not entirely new, and multispecies ethnography is only beginning to define its own project and intellectual sources. It draws on Paul Rabinow's earlier concept of "biosocialities," Jennifer Wolch's call for a "transspecies theory" in the context of urban planning, Donna Haraway's meditations on "companion species," and Anna Tsing's investigation of the social uses of landscapes and nonhuman species in Indonesia and her work on matsutake mushroom culture (Tsing 2005, 2011, n.d.), as well as a long tradition of anthropological studies of animals, animal husbandry, agriculture, and symbolic functions of non-human species (see Kirksey and Helmreich 2010, 550–554). In France and Belgium, Dominique Lestel and Vinciane Despret have proposed "étho-ethnologie," "ethno-éthologie," or "anthropo-éthologie" as a new way of combining the study of human behavior with that of other animals (Lestel, Brunois, and Gaunet 2006; Despret 2006). In Italy, Roberto Marchesini's "zooantropologia" has pursued a related redefinition of the anthropological object of study (Marchesini and Tonutti 2007). Other theorists have pushed the boundaries explicitly beyond the question of the animal to other species. Matthew Hall and Eduardo Kohn have investigated the status of plants in *Plants as Persons: A Philosophical Botany* (2011) and *How Forests Think: Toward an Anthropology beyond the Human* (2013), respectively. Environmental philosophy has not yet figured quite as prominently in multispecies ethnography. The Australian philosopher Val Plumwood's reflections on "interspecies ethics" might offer another genealogy, although one less invested in ethnography and cultural differentiation (see Plumwood 2002, 167–194), as do ecofeminist theories and new materialisms that have addressed relations between species.

Multispecies ethnographers have so far been ambivalent in their reflections on Actor-Network-Theory as elaborated by Bruno Latour, John Law, and Michel Callon in the 1980s, although their thought clearly resonates with the core ANT claim that human societies function as networks of human and nonhuman actors who interact in both material and semiotic ways. Latour's coinage of the term *natureculture* in *We Have Never Been Modern* ([1991] 1993) as a way of thinking beyond what he considers the nature-culture dichotomy created by modernity, and his idea that nonhumans need to be represented in political decision-making by way of a "Parliament of Things" seem clearly useful for the elaboration of multispecies theory ([1991] 1993, 142–145; 2004, 231–232). Yet multispecies ethnographers have criticized Latour for taking the category of the human itself for granted and for not giving enough thought to the question how and under what circumstances particular humans can speak for nonhuman others (Kirksey, Schuetze, and Helmreich 2014). Anthropologists approach this issue with much caution, given decades of criticism of how they have spoken for human others in the past. Latour's suggestion of scientific "speech prostheses that allow nonhumans to participate in the discussions of humans, when humans become perplexed about the participation of new entities in collective life" has received particular critical attention in this context ([1999] 2004,

67). Yet it is not always clear how multispecies ethnographers envision an alternative.[13]

Multispecies ethnography also has many overlaps with philosophical approaches to the question of the animal, from animal welfare to animal rights and critical animal studies. The anthropologist and philosopher Deborah Bird Rose has most explicitly made this connection, especially to perspectives informed by continental philosophy, in *Wild Dog Dreaming: Love and Extinction,* her exploration of dogs and dingoes in Aboriginal and white communities in Australia (2011). The combination of environmental thinking, animal welfare thinking, and multispecies ethnography in Rose's approach makes clear that the multispecies perspective does not rest merely on the claim that it yields a better explanation of human societies. It also relies, implicitly or explicitly, on the claim that human observers owe nonhuman species inclusion in such descriptions for ethical reasons, and that inclusion might change relations between humans and nonhumans for the better. Rose makes these ethical implications explicit when she argues that multispecies ethnography ties humans and nonhumans together in cross-species genealogies that amount to an extended system of kinship, accompanied by the ethical obligations of family structures: "Life within a system of cross-species kinship is in dreadful peril at this time. The animals and plants that are dying out are not so much vulnerable, endangered, or extinct species, but more significantly are vulnerable and dying members of the family" (3–4).

As Rose's as well as Tsing's work makes clear, the normative dimension of multispecies ethnography puts it into the vicinity of environmental justice, since this anthropological approach seeks to articulate the claims of humans and nonhumans together. But this is not an unproblematic undertaking. The "flattening of ontologies" that comes with questioning the human subject and human-animal boundaries often makes it difficult to address head-on the uneven power distributions that environmental justice is centrally concerned with. Activists for social and environmental justice tend to be acutely conscious of the dangers in emphasizing proximities and kinships between humans and animals, since

13. Kirksey, in a lively analysis of various species in Costa Rica's Palo Verde National Park (2012), claims that he found no democratic agora in which the voices of these species might be heard (25) and that biology students' investigations of the calls of the fringe-toed frog amounted to a fragile speech prosthesis at best. Instead, his analysis aims at the hidden power flows that condition the comings and goings of species in the park. Yet it is difficult to see how his own account is not just such a prosthesis for the various Palo Verde species, being heard in a different agora—the scholarly community.

such kinships have historically often been called upon to legitimate the exclusion of certain groups of people from treatment as humans: "The power and terror [of white Australians' shooting of Aboriginal people's dogs as a prelude to other abuses] show us a darker porosity to the West's animal-human boundary: one in which humans are animalized so as to be killed with impunity," Rose points out (2011, 25). If Cary Wolfe argues that the human-animal distinction often enables the oppression of humans by other humans, and that questioning it will help to unsettle oppression, Rose poignantly highlights the dangers of questioning this boundary. Wolfe and Rose would agree that the definition of the animal as a being that *can* be mistreated without the consequences that would ensue in the mistreatment of a human is at the root of both processes. But where multispecies ethnography seeks to solve this problem by questioning the ontological differences between humans and other species, environmental justice and political ecology perspectives have typically sought solutions in disabling the power differentials that endow some humans with the authority to categorize others as belonging to the human species or not.[14]

   Pointing out this tension is not meant to imply that multispecies ethnography and environmental justice cannot speak to each other; rather, it is a way of exploring how their divergent theoretical commitments might become mutually productive. In colonial and postcolonial confrontations between indigenous societies and European settlers, divergent traditions and institutions governing humans' relationship to the land have been a recurrent object of conflict: European and North American models of private and public land ownership have been imposed on and contested by indigenous traditions of land stewardship and use in a variety of regions. A culturally aware approach to the conservation of endangered species similarly needs to take into account different traditions and institutions that shape humans' relationship to other species. In envisioning what "multispecies justice" in the context of biodiversity might look like, multispecies ethnography contributes to the aspirations of the environmental justice movement in two ways. On one hand, it shows how interactions with nonhuman species—from forest trees and seed cultivars to predators, pet animals, and viruses—have shaped particular cultures' way of life and sense of what a good or just life should look like. To the central preoccupations of environmental justice with

14. For a thoughtful discussion of the role violence needs to play in any redefinition of the human subject through relationality, see Yusoff (2012).

land use, resource exploitation, and differential exposure to technological risks, multispecies theory, in other words, adds interactions with nonhuman species and the moral claims these interactions are understood to imply in different cultural contexts. On the other hand, multispecies theory redefines what "justice" means with a view toward such specific social and cultural contexts: rather than assuming that "we" already know what humans owe other species, what other species owe humans, and how conservation serves the interests of both humans and nonhumans, multispecies ethnography alerts us to the way in which all of these questions might have different responses in different communities. In turn, environmental justice theory and activism highlight how interactions between species and ideas of justice themselves are constantly being reshaped and overwritten by economic interests and power structures. Indigenous ontologies, directly and via the studies undertaken by multispecies ethnographers, will no doubt play an important role in spelling out such ideas of justice, as the example of Bolivia demonstrates, which I discussed in chapter 3. As Marisol de la Cadena has highlighted, indigenous perspectives in Latin America and elsewhere have introduced nonhuman beings into the political sphere in unprecedented ways (2010, 340–344). Multispecies justice, then, is the kind of project that requires a more-than-human diplomacy—a project that pursues justice with both a sense of cultural differences and a sense of species differences.

In this context, again, it is clear that the problem of endangered species and biodiversity conservation is not ultimately a scientific one. While conservation biology has an important role to play in understanding how the lives of species are being reshaped by human actions, and sometimes in forecasting what the long-term consequences of human actions might be, it cannot be called upon to determine what our relationship to other species should ideally be—though it has often been misunderstood to do just that. While the insights of conservation biology are important and valuable in any discussion of what biodiversity we might want for the future, so are the insights of multispecies ethnography and of environmental justice: both of them ask who the "we" is and what ideas about desirable and undesirable species interactions, as well as about intended and unintended consequences, inspire different communities of "us." Indeed, the concept of biodiversity itself, which has become a shorthand for a variety of conservation issues since it began to be widely circulated in the 1980s, may well be both too abstract and too culturally rooted in a valuation of diversity that arose in some societies of the global north in the second half of the twentieth century. The idea of multispecies justice may come closer to serving as an umbrella for different cultures' ideas about what an ethically responsible relationship between different species should look like, provided that we keep in mind that species and kinship boundaries are also understood differently depending on the cultural context. The taxonomic distinctions of biology and culture—biological species and "cultural species," as one might call them—do not map onto each other neatly, and their relation is construed differently depending on the cultural community. Understanding such differences is one of the fundamental tasks of multispecies justice.

In this framework, the texts I have studied in this chapter, all of which take real-life conservation scenarios as points of departure for their fictional plots, stage different perspectives on multispecies justice. Unlike Trish O'Kane, who assumes in the op-ed column I quoted at the beginning of this chapter that individuals and communities caught up in violent conflicts have no attention to spare for endangered plants or animals, the authors of *Tú, la oscuridad*, *Virunga*, and *The Hungry Tide* assume that all their characters do have existing concerns about and relationships with nonhuman species, though these may take very different shapes. Thierry Adrien perceives endangered frogs and toads with a lifetime's worth of personal encounters and a cosmological perspective that aligns their disappearances with the violence experienced by Haitians during and after the Duvalier dictatorships. Malika and Esther both care deeply about mountain gorillas, and Esther devotes her life to their protection, even as both women experience displacement, sexual violence, and the loss of their closest family. Fokir Mandol knows the Irrawaddy dolphins from a lifetime of experience as a fisherman, not unlike the way Thierry Adrien knows frogs, and he also perceives tigers in the framework of cultural myths that condition his reaction to them as much as their physical threat to human lives. As these characters encounter militia leaders, members of the social elite, and Western scientists, their perceptions and relationships to endangered species are caught up in national and international scenarios of conflict. Neither *Tú, la oscuridad* nor *Virunga* suggests that there are any comfortable solutions to these conflicts or to the predicament of endangered animals or humans at risk; *The Hungry Tide* does, in an ending that one might be tempted to consider sentimental if it were not complicated by the tensions in the preceding plot. But all three texts use fictionalization itself as their main tool for exploring the shifting meanings and functions of endangered species in contexts of multicultural encounter, multispecies encounter, violence and power struggles, and attempts to create just societies—for humans and nonhumans. All of them are narrative invitations to imagine a world in which the scientific tasks of identifying organisms, counting species, and classifying them according to their risk status become part of the larger cultural enterprise of defining and enacting multispecies justice.

6   Multispecies Fictions for the Anthropocene

Concerns over biodiversity and efforts to conserve endangered species, as I have shown in chapters 4 and 5, have developed since the 1960s in fields of conflict and convergence with the animal welfare movement, on one hand, and the environmental justice movement, on the other. Conservationists, in this context, have seen themselves forced to justify their principles and practices against the accusation that they care for abstract entities such as ecosystems and species more than for actual animals, as well as against the accusation that they value the nonhuman lives of plants, animals, and landscapes over those of disenfranchised human communities whom conservation efforts have often disadvantaged or displaced. Understanding conservation in the context of these differently oriented social movements shows, as much as the analysis of conservation narratives, tropes, media, and institutions that I undertook in the first three chapters, that the valuation of biodiversity and efforts to protect it are profoundly cultural ventures, embedded in historical traditions and value frameworks that condition which lives are appreciated and conserved and which ones are disregarded, left to die out, or actively exterminated. The idea of multispecies justice, I have suggested, might prove a useful tool in thinking about biodiversity and conservation: it puts questions of justice for both humans and nonhumans front and center, even as it emphasizes that justice itself has to be imagined at the intersection of different cultural perspectives that may diverge in their conception of what is just. This is precisely the challenge for culturally attuned conservation efforts.

Over the past decade, the concept of the Anthropocene has emerged as a third context of debate in which the lives and deaths of species are considered. Based on the claim that humans' pervasive transformations of global ecosystems mark the beginning of a new geological "Human Age," the Anthropocene has been interpreted both pessimistically and optimistically. For pessimists, the Anthropocene signals the enormous scope of negative human impacts on the environment; for optimists, it opens up the possibility of reimagining the nature of the future not as a return to the past or a realm apart from humans, but as a nature reshaped by humans. Projects for "rewilding" and "de-extinction" in particular aim to undo extinction by reintroducing or even genetically recreating vanished species. As I profile these divergent approaches in section 1, I will highlight how they draw on tropes of speculative fiction, particularly the idea of terraforming.

The notion of the Anthropocene itself, section 2 goes on to show, is often accompanied by the transfer of tropes and narrative strategies from science fiction to mainstream fiction and environmental nonfiction. Its particular power, for this reason, resides not in its scientific definition as a geological epoch, but in its capacity to cast the present as a future that has already arrived—one of the quintessential functions of contemporary science fiction. Science fiction, as section 3 emphasizes, is also the literary genre that most explicitly deals with the planet and with humanity as a whole, and the Anthropocene in its humanistic dimensions has been variously understood as imposing the urgency of a new environmental cosmopolitanism or as glossing over continuing socioeconomic divides that make the postulation of any global "species being" no more than an ideological obfuscation. With its emphasis on the centrality of human agency, the Anthropocene idea also stands in tension with those varieties of posthumanism that have, over the past three decades, sought to emphasize the central importance of nonhuman agents in social networks.

But some of these posthumanisms, including the idea of multispecies justice, also offer the possibility of extending cosmopolitan models of thought beyond the human sphere without relying on the kind of "flat ontologies" that weaken the emphasis on differences within and beyond species boundaries. Section 4 focuses on a literary example, Orson Scott Card's *Ender* series of novels, to show how speculative fiction has staged the encounter of species that have not coevolved as an event with biological, cultural, and political ramifications. Section 5 concludes by highlighting how the planetary storytelling mode of speculative fiction might be useful for designing new narratives of biodiversity, conservation, survival, and multispecies justice.

1. Anthropo-Scenarios: Rewilding, De-extinction, and Science Fiction

In discussions about humans' transformations of global ecology and geochemistry, the concept of the Anthropocene has gained increasing importance over the past decade. The term was proposed in an article published in 2000 by the atmospheric scientist Paul Crutzen and the ecologist Eugene Stoermer, who postulated that humankind no longer inhabits the Holocene, the geological era that refers to the period from the last Ice Age—circa twelve thousand years ago—to the present day. Rather, they argued, we have entered a new epoch that they call the "Anthropocene" or "Human Age" because humans have transformed the Earth to such an extent that our impact will even be visible in the planet's geological stratification into the long-term future (Crutzen and Stoermer 2000). Processes such as population growth, fossil-fuel burning, nitrogen production, deforestation, biodiversity loss, and climate change, Crutzen and Stoermer argue, will be readable for future generations in the sediments that make up geological strata and will allow them to distinguish the current era from those that went before. They place the epochal threshold in the late eighteenth century, the beginning of the Industrial Revolution, and they argue that the changes that originated at the time of the invention of the steam engine have taken place at an even more rapid pace since World War II, the period they call the "Great Acceleration." Geologists, understandably wary about the introduction of a new geological epoch that has to date lasted only two hundred years, will decide in 2016 whether the evidence indeed warrants this change of nomenclature.

In the meantime, the Anthropocene has developed a cultural life of its own. Indeed, it is at this point doubtful whether the geologists' verdict will make much of a difference, considering the literature and debate the concept has already generated. Two journals, *Anthropocene* and *Anthropocene Review,* publish scholarship on the concept, and major research institutions and museums in Australia, Europe, and North America have organized conferences and exhibits around it. At least four full-length books, Christian Schwägerl's *Menschenzeit: Zerstören oder gestalten? Die entscheidende Epoche unseres Planeten* (2010; translated as *The Anthropocene: The Human Era and How It Shapes Our*

Planet, 2014), Jens Kersten's *Das Anthropozän-Konzept: Kontrakt-Komposition-Konflikt* (The Anthropocene idea: Contract-composition-conflict; 2014), Diane Ackerman's *The Human Age: The World Shaped by Us* (2014), and Jedediah Purdy's *After Nature: A Politics for the Anthropocene* (2015), explore the Anthropocene in its scientific, social, and cultural dimensions. For all of this attention, the idea of the Anthropocene is not entirely new: similar ideas about humans' decisive reshaping of the planet run all the way from Stoppani's "anthropozoic era" of 1873 and the idea of the "noösphere" as developed by Vernadsky, Le Roy, and Teilhard de Chardin between the 1920s and the 1940s to Andrew Revkin's 1992 "anthrocene" and Michael Samways's coining, in 1999, of the "homogenocene." But in recent years, it is the Anthropocene that has begun to circulate as a conceptual shorthand for describing a fundamental and global change in humans' relationship to the natural environment.

In a simple descriptive sense, Crutzen and his collaborators argue that the magnitude of ecological and climatological transformations invites a change of scientific terminology: "The term Anthropocene . . . suggests that the Earth has now left its natural geological epoch, the present interglacial state called the Holocene. Human activities have become so pervasive and profound that they rival the great forces of Nature and are pushing the Earth into planetary *terra incognita*" (Steffen, Crutzen, and McNeill 2007, 614). But the suggestion that a geological name change would be appropriate is, at a less descriptive and more political level, itself an attempt to wake up the scientific community as well as the general public to the scope of the human impact. There can be little doubt that Crutzen himself sees this impact as catastrophic:

> During the past three centuries, the human population has increased tenfold to more than 6 billion and is expected to reach 10 billion in this century. The methane-producing cattle population has risen to 1.4 billion. About 30–50% of the planet's land surface is exploited by humans. Tropical rainforests disappear at a fast pace, releasing carbon dioxide and strongly increasing species extinction. Dam building and river diversion have become commonplace. More than half of all accessible fresh water is used by mankind. Fisheries remove more than 25% of the primary production in upwelling ocean regions and 35% in the temperate continental shelf. Energy use has grown 16-fold during the twentieth century, causing 160 million tonnes of atmospheric sulphur dioxide emissions per year, more than

twice the sum of its natural emissions. More nitrogen fertilizer is applied in agriculture than is fixed naturally in all terrestrial ecosystems; nitric oxide production by the burning of fossil fuel and biomass also overrides natural emissions. Fossil-fuel burning and agriculture have caused substantial increases in the concentrations of "greenhouse" gases—carbon dioxide by 30% and methane by more than 100%—reaching their highest levels over the past 400 millennia, with more to follow. (Crutzen 2002, 23)

Stated as a series of sober facts, this catalog nevertheless defines the Anthropocene as the sum of all environmental havocs humans have wreaked on the planet. When the term is used in public discussions or in the media, it is often accompanied by connotations of global disaster. From this perspective, the Anthropocene is merely a new word to mark the endpoint of the typical environmentalist narrative of decline I discussed in chapter 1. That this decline will now be recorded even in geological strata just confirms how truly catastrophic humans' impact has been.

But the idea of a planet reshaped by human agency has also triggered the opposite interpretation—awed celebration of humans' expanded abilities. Most exuberantly, Diane Ackerman has claimed that "our relationship with nature has changed . . . radically, irreversibly, but by no means all for the bad" (2014, 14; original ellipsis). Even as she acknowledges the reality of ecological crises, she emphasizes technological innovation and social progress and in the end declares her faith in humans' ability to overcome catastrophes: "We're at a great turning, our own momentous fork in the road, behind us eons of geological history, ahead a mist-laden future, and all around us the wonders and uncertainties of the Human Age. These days . . . we control our own legacy. We're not passive, we're not helpless. We're earth-movers. We can become Earth-restorers and Earth-guardians. We still have time and imagination, and we have a great many choices. . . . Our mistakes are legion, but our talent is immeasurable" (311).

That much wide-eyed optimism and reliance on an unexamined global "we" may be hard to take seriously. But in between Crutzen's pessimism and Ackerman's optimism, the concept of the Anthropocene has become the staging ground for highly visible debates that cross the boundaries not only between the natural sciences, the social sciences, and the humanities, but also between academic and public debates. Most immediately relevant for my investigation of the cultural meanings of endangered species is the confrontation between old and new forms of conservation: conservation with an emphasis on the protection of wild areas and the creation of parks and reserves, as opposed to conservation with an emphasis on landscapes altered or even created by humans and the integration of human uses with species protection. In a broader framework, the Anthropocene has given rise to debates about optimistic and pessimistic constructions of the future in environmentalism, about management and unintended consequences, about the human species as a historical agent and the inequalities that divide humans, about geological and economic history, and about anthropocentrism and the posthumanisms that have transformed the humanities and parts of the social sciences over the past quarter century.

Among the natural and social scientists who see the Anthropocene as an opportunity to move from old to new ideas about conservation, the geographer Erle Ellis, together with varied collaborators over time, has proposed the notion of the "anthrome" as the humanly altered complement to the biome. "For the foreseeable future, the fate of terrestrial ecosystems and the species they support will be intertwined with human systems: most of 'nature' is now embedded within anthropogenic mosaics of land use and land cover," he argues (Ellis and Ramankutty 2008, 447).[1] This kind of emphasis on the ecosystems humans have altered or created is rarely just descriptive in debates about the Anthropocene, but often comes with a call for a new kind of environmentalist storytelling, as is explicit in an op-ed piece Ellis coauthored with the science writer Emma Marris and the biologists Peter Kareiva and Joseph Mascaro in the *New York Times*, titled "Hope in the Age of Man": "The Anthropocene does not represent the failure of environmentalism. It is the stage on which a new, more positive and forward-looking environmentalism can be built. This is the Earth we have created, and we have a duty, as a species, to protect it and manage it with love and intelligence. It is not ruined. It is beautiful still, and can be even more beautiful, if we work together and care for it" (Marris et al. 2011).

The environmental blogger Andy Revkin has echoed this perspective in his well-known *New York Times* blog *Dot Earth,* in a post called "Embracing the Anthropocene": "One clear reality is that for a long time to come, Earth is what we choose to make of it, for better or worse. Taking full ownership of the Anthropocene won't be easy. The necessary feeling is a queasy mix of excitement and unease. . . . That's a very different sensation than, say, mourning the end of nature. It's more a celebration, in a way—a deeper acceptance of our place on the planet, with

---

1. For a more specific argument about how conservation can be rethought on this basis as part of "agroecology," see Vandermeer and Perfecto (2014).

all of our synthetic trappings, and our faults, as fundamentally natural" (Revkin 2011).

For Revkin, as for Ellis, Kareiva, Marris, and Mascaro, the Anthropocene is a new environmentalist orientation toward the future rather than the past, celebration rather than mourning, and a new sense that humans are able to transform the planet—not just involuntarily, but following deliberate choices. The German science writer Christian Schwägerl echoes this sentiment in his book *Menschenzeit,* which ends on a note of hope, as does Emma Marris in the celebratory ending to her book *Rambunctious Garden: Saving Nature in a Post-Wild World:* "We've forever altered the Earth, and so now we cannot abandon it to a random fate. It is our duty to manage it. Luckily, it can be a pleasant, even joyful task if we embrace it in the right spirit. Let the rambunctious gardening begin" (Marris 2011, 171).

It is difficult not to sympathize with this future orientation and optimism, especially on the part of those who, like myself, are skeptical of the environmentalist tendency toward nostalgia, elegiac moods, and the latent misanthropy often found in the reverence for wilderness. But the bold confidence in statements such as these that humans will be able to manage the planet more successfully in the future than they have in the past is nevertheless surprising. It not only leaves out of consideration those large-scale natural processes over which humans have absolutely no control, which Nigel Clark has highlighted in *Inhuman Nature: Sociable Life on a Dynamic Planet* (2011): from the sunlight that we depend on to the earthquakes that endanger our cities, basic dimensions of nature remain resolutely nonhuman. It also glosses over the fact that some of the most fundamental human transformations of the planet took place outside our intention and control: climate change, toxification, ocean acidification, and biodiversity loss, to name four large-scale problems, were not planned or intended by anyone, but came about as side effects of other activities, many of them so distributed over millions of humans that they were not even perceptible for a long time.

These circumstances might incline one to dismiss the self-confident invitations to humans to go forth and manage Earth as wishful thinking, or as an earnest but ultimately misguided attempt to think about ways to deal with unintended ecological consequences. But one might also argue, with long-time environmental advocate Stewart Brand, that, joyous or not, humans may really have no choice but to manage the Earth. Brand, founding editor of the *Whole Earth Catalog,* notoriously quipped in his preface to the first issue in 1968, "We are as gods and might as well get good at it." But he has recently changed this slogan to "We are as gods and HAVE to get good at it" (2011, 1; cf. Ackerman 2014, 150), a wording that implies a different and more constrained but also more urgent sense of humans' eco-agency than the more playful quip from the beginnings of the modern environmentalist movement.

This sense of urgency has direct consequences for his vision of conservation. Brand, now a founding member of the Long Now Foundation, an organization dedicated to fostering thinking about the consequences of current human activities over the next ten thousand years, has become a champion of "de-extinction" projects (http://longnow.org /revive/). De-extinction is the umbrella term for various projects to recreate extinct species such as the mammoth, the aurochs, and the passenger pigeon with the help of genetic material found in fossils and museum specimens. Given the current state of biotechnology, the hope is that gaps in these genomes can be filled in with genes from currently existing species that are closely related to the extinct ones, or that key genes from extinct species might be inserted into closely related extant species. Elephant genes might be combined with mammoth genes, for example, or band-tailed pigeons' genes with passenger pigeons.' A provisional success in this endeavor was achieved in 2009 with the cloning of the Pyrenean ibex (*Capra pyrenaica pyrenaica*), or "bucardo" in Spanish, a subspecies of the Spanish ibex that had gone extinct in early 2000, from frozen cells of the last specimen. But the cloned kid, in what German science writer Lothar Frenz, with some bemusement, calls a "seven-minute Renaissance," survived only for seven minutes because of pulmonary problems, bestowing on this subspecies the dubious honor of going extinct not just once but twice (Frenz 2012, 61–62).

Brand, who considers this incident a mere temporary setback, sees de-extinction as a way to bring back vanished forms of biodiversity and to help currently dwindling populations of endangered species, but also as a way of changing the environmentalist storytelling template. In an e-mail to the biologists George Church and E. O. Wilson, he suggested:

> The environmental and conservation movements have mired themselves in a tragic view of life. The return of the passenger pigeon could shake them out of it—and invite them to embrace prudent biotechnology as a Green tool instead of menace in this century. . . .
>
> Wild scheme. Could be fun. Could improve things. It could, as they say, advance the story. (quoted in Rich 2014)

Brand here casts de-extinction not just as a conservation tool, but more broadly as a means of changing the tragic and elegiac stories environmentalists usually tell about species loss.

Does it change the story? One may grant that the technical difficulties in cloning animals, even though they are multiplied in cases where at least two different genomes have to be combined, will probably be overcome in due time. And one may also want to put aside, for the sake of argument, the pragmatic worry of some conservation biologists that such daring schemes will do nothing but divert much-needed funds from slower and less spectacular conservation efforts (Rich 2014). Even so, there are nagging ecological questions one may ask about the return of the passenger pigeon, let alone the woolly mammoth. Will such experiments ever lead to the creation of populations big enough to be released back into the wild? If so, what ecological consequences would ensue, given that, even in the case of the relatively recent extinction of the passenger pigeon, a century has gone by without it and its ecological niche has been occupied by other species? Would this in fact turn the de-extincted species into an introduced, possibly even invasive one (Rich 2014)? If, by contrast, only very small populations of de-extincted species can be created, they will remain zoo exhibits with no ecological significance—symptoms of our nostalgia for the nature of the past. Either way, de-extinction, especially of species like the woolly mammoth, which vanished millennia ago, seems like a curiously "retro" way of moving into the future. Rather than a change of story, it might strike one as just a different material reincarnation of the same impulse that has so often informed conservation—restoring species and ecosystems from some point in the past.

But the conceptual paradoxes of de-extinction are such that what emerges from this nostalgia might be something quite different from a reconstruction of the past. Would a de-extincted passenger pigeon be a passenger pigeon or an innovative product of biotechnology, a "Frankenpigeon" whose genome would actually combine two species, passenger and band-tailed pigeons, and whose first generation would have to be raised by band-tailed pigeons? The philosopher Ronald Sandler, who has highlighted this issue (2013a, 357–358), also raises the broader question of what moral claim de-extinction responds to—an obligation to the extinct species? To future generations of humans? Since neither of these groups is now alive, he argues, it is difficult to claim that the current cohort of humans morally owes them anything resembling de-extinction (355–357). Sandler concludes that the moderately persuasive justification for de-extinction is as an insurance policy if other conservation measures fail (359). The real attraction of de-extinction projects, he argues, lies in the awe at technological wizardry they generate (2013b).

If the likely conservation impacts of de-extinction are less interesting than the biotechnological achievement a revived species would represent, then the project does indeed move out from the elegiac to the science fiction mode on the model of Steven Spielberg's classic film *Jurassic Park* (1993), which Brand praises for its positive impact on the advancement of de-extinction (Rich 2014). *Jurassic Park* was itself based on a science fiction novel by Michael Crichton, and even though its plot revolves around the genetic resurrection of species that preexisted humans by tens of millions of years, its connection with contemporary biodiversity loss is evoked early in the film. When the visionary entrepreneur John Hammond presents his project of a theme park populated with dinosaurs that he plans to recreate from prehistoric DNA to an expert group of three scientists and a lawyer, only the lawyer reacts with enthusiasm, predictably because of its potential profits. The scientists voice reservations similar to those real-life conservationists have expressed vis-à-vis de-extinction, namely that the recreated dinosaurs would be introduced into an ecosystem dramatically unlike the one which they originally inhabited (including, in this case, one populated by humans). Hammond, a visionary more than an entrepreneur, grumbles disappointment that only the "bloodsucking lawyer" approves of his plans, and he observes with dejection and perhaps dismissal in his voice that if he were proposing to breed condors instead of dinosaurs, no doubt all the scientists would back him enthusiastically (though he may be wrong in this assumption, as current controversies over the potential of de-extinction show).[2]

The parallels with *Jurassic Park* foreground that the main attraction of de-extinction is precisely its proximity to science fiction and its exploration of how humans might create new kinds of nature. There is indeed potential here for a change of story—but perhaps more of a change than Stewart Brand would welcome. It depends on discarding the idea that de-extinction makes any significant contribution to restoring ecosystems of the past and welcoming it as a fascinating biotechnological experiment that might play a role in creating future ecosystems. De-extinction, if indeed it turns out to be feasible, might be one tool for the intervention ecology of the future (see Hobbs et al. 2011), whose success is not

2. For a more detailed discussion of *Jurassic Park*, see Heise (2003, 61–66).

defined by restoration of historical ecosystems but by the creation and maintenance of habitat for the species of the present and future.

"Rewilding" projects can be understood in a similar way—either as replays of the environmentalist impulse to restore the past or as interventions aimed at creating functioning ecosystems for the future. Rewilding seeks to return species to areas from which they have been locally extirpated—the reintroduction of the grizzly to California, for example, where it vanished between 1911 and the 1930s (Alagona 2013, 12–13). "Pleistocene rewilding" seeks to reintroduce species or their close extant relatives, in particular large vertebrates, that vanished in the Pleistocene: Donlan et al., for example, have suggested reintroducing camels, llamas, elephants, cheetahs, and lions to North America (2006; cf. Monbiot 2014). There is no doubt that the reintroduction of top predators can sometimes help to keep prey populations in check that are decimating their own food species. But in many cases, the habitats the predators are returned to are quite unlike what they were decades ago. How would grizzlies and people fare together, for example, in a state like California that is now home to almost 40 million people? "It is easy to embrace a story of ecological decline when you do not have to contend with thousand-pound omnivores in your daily life. When you do, things become more complicated," the environmental historian Peter Alagona quips (2013, 40). As in the case of de-extinction, rewilding may well turn out to be most useful when it is not mainly envisioned as a means of returning to the ecological past but as a tool in the creation of functional ecosystems for the future.

Recent environmentally oriented science fiction has taken up themes of de-extinction and rewilding as part of broader scenarios of terraforming, the shaping of global ecosystems at the hands of humans. Undoubtedly the most ecologically informed, culturally nuanced, and philosophically sophisticated scenario of terraforming in science fiction is Kim Stanley Robinson's trilogy *Red Mars, Green Mars,* and *Blue Mars* from the 1990s. How much Mars should be preserved in its original state, how much it should be transformed to accommodate humans' needs, and to what extent Earth should provide the template for its reengineering are central political and ethical questions around which the plot unfolds. The introduction of terrestrial species, some of them genetically altered so as to ensure their survival on Mars, is part of the more general terraforming project. The physicist Saxifrage Russell, one of the most energetic advocates of terraforming, encounters pika on one of his journeys across Mars, small white rodents that remind him of the lab rats he used to work with:

> He crouched and watched the little rodents until he got cold.
> There were greater creatures out on that plain, and they always
> stopped him short: deer, elk, moose, bighorn sheep, reindeer,
> caribou, black bear, grizzly bear—even packs of wolves, like
> swift gray shadows—and all to Sax like citizens out of a dream,
> so that every time he spotted even a single creature he felt star-
> tled, disconnected, even stunned; it did not seem possible; it was
> certainly not natural. Yet here they were. And now these little
> snow pika, happy in their oasis. Not nature, not culture: just
> Mars. (Robinson 1996, 679)

"Mars" here is, of course, a thought experiment to explore Earth's own
possible futures—including synthetic ecologies that feature (re)intro-
duced and genetically altered species from the past, with a view not toward recreating ecosystems of the past, but toward creating ecosystems
that provide new habitats for both humans and nonhumans.[3]

In a more recent novel, *2312* (2012), Robinson returns to scenarios of de-extinction and rewilding at even greater length. In this novel,
set in the early twenty-fourth century, humans have ingeniously terraformed planets, moons, and satellites across the solar system and have
reengineered their own bodies, which now range from froglike to pygmy-
like, incorporate animal genes and abilities, and oscillate across a wide
spectrum of gender identities. Planet Earth, meantime, continues to be
riddled with social crises from poverty to power struggles and ecological problems from climate change and sea-level rise to species extinction.
As a way of dealing with species loss on Earth, Robinson's posthumans
have created so-called terraria, or artificial habitats. A how-to manual
that is quoted in between the novel's chapters explains how to create a
terrarium DIY-style:

> Take an asteroid at least thirty kilometers on its long axis. . . .
> Hollow out your asteroid. . . . Begin with a light dusting of heavy
> metals and rare earths. . . . With a soil base cooked up, your
> biome is well on its way. . . . A lot of terraria designers start
> out with a marsh of some kind, because it's the fastest way to
> bulk up your soil and your overall biomass. . . . Over time you
> can transform the interior of your terrarium to any of the 832
> identified Terran biomes, or design an Ascension of your own

---

3. For a more detailed analysis of this and other synthetic ecologies in recent science
fiction, see Heise (2011).

making (Be warned that many Ascensions fall as flat as bad
soufflés). (Robinson 2012, 38–42)

Humorously styled as a kind of outer-space cookbook, this manual introduces twenty-first-century readers to the synthetic ecosystems of the
future, including "Ascensions" named after an island in the South Atlantic famous from Darwin's travels. Ascension Island's highly functional
ecosystems are almost entirely made up of introduced species (cf. Duffey
1964, Wilkinson 2004).

   Species that are endangered or extinct on Earth continue to be bred
in the terraria, either from surviving DNA or by means of captive populations, and these survivor populations become part of a global de-
extinction project far beyond anything Steven Spielberg and Stewart
Brand have imagined. The new humans from Mercury, Venus, Titan,
and Io seek to aid the Earth's immiserated populations and ailing ecosystems, though their efforts are often frustrated by Earth's large populations, long histories, and complex social structures. But one of their
projects, which comes to be called the "Reanimation," successfully re-
introduces species that have gone extinct on Earth from the terraria.
During the Reanimation, the animals are released by the thousands in
a surrealist kind of rain, in aerogel-filled bubbles that float down to the
Earth's surface. They are accompanied by activists such as the Mercury-
born Swan Er Hong, who are charged with helping the animals after
their landing:

> Swan looked around, trying to see everywhere at once: sky all
> strewn with clear seeds, which from any distance were visible
> only as their contents, so that she drifted eastward and down
> with thousands of flying wolves, bears, reindeer, mountain lions.
> There she saw a fox pair; a clutch of rabbits; a bobcat or lynx;
> a bundle of lemmings; a heron, flying hard inside its bubble. It
> looked like a dream, but she knew it was real, and the same right
> now all over Earth: into the seas splashed dolphins and whales,
> tuna and sharks. Mammals, birds, fish, reptiles, amphibians: all
> the lost creatures were in the sky at once, in every country, every
> watershed. Many of the creatures had been absent from Earth
> for two or three centuries. Now all back, all at once. (Robinson
> 2012, 396)

As a fictionalization of de-extinction and rewilding, this scene is about
as realist as René Magritte's *Giaconda* painting with its rain of bowler-

hatted men in dark coats. An unusual departure from Robinson's usually sober and science-based utopianism, it reminds one of Jon Mooallem's portrait of wildlife management as a kind of surrealist performance art (Mooallem 2013). Surely, whatever the solution to the biodiversity crisis might be, it will not look like this! But provoking the readers' half-amused and half-incredulous smile is arguably Robinson's point. He chooses an intentionally implausible solution to the real problem of biodiversity loss so as to foreground that the nature of the future will not be "natural" in the sense of any return to an originary past, but will be a readaptation, planned by humans so as to create ecosystems of their own design. In a deliberate counterpoint to the usually bleak visions of the environmental future in much contemporary science fiction, Robinson here develops a scenario that acknowledges the seriousness of Earth's ecological challenges over the next few hundred years but that resonates with the more optimistic interpretations of the Anthropocene concept.

2. The Anthropocene as Speculative Fiction

The affinities between the idea of the Anthropocene and the genre of science fiction—or more broadly, speculative fiction that focuses on the future without necessarily emphasizing science and technology as the engines of history—do not stop at visions of biodiversity loss and species reintroduction. One of the hallmarks of science fiction in many if not all of its manifestations has been the engagement with the fate of planet Earth as a whole, in far futures on Earth itself, in humans' migration to extraterrestrial habitats, or in their encounters with civilizations from other planets. In terms of literary history, indeed, it makes sense to think of science fiction as the genre that perpetuates the epic mode in the age of the novel, precisely in that it seeks to tell the story of the world as a whole.[4] Science fiction, one could argue, complements the database as another form of contemporary epic storytelling.

    It therefore makes sense—though it remains generically surprising—that science fiction motifs and structures keep cropping up in environmental nonfiction, books whose principal concern is to drive home the *reality* of current ecological crises, especially but not only the altered environments that will result from climate change. In this vein, the

---

4. Franco Moretti traces the genre of modern epic through texts of the past two hundred years (cf. chapter 2). Whereas he considers texts as varied as Goethe's *Faust II* and García Márquez's *Cien años de soledad*, he does not mention science fiction as the genre that in the twentieth century has most persistently sought to narrate at the grand scale of the planet, the human species, and beyond.

environmental nonfiction writer Alan Weisman uses the trope of the extinction of humankind in *The World Without Us* ([2007] 2008), a book designed to explore, in terms of science and engineering, what would happen to the natural, technological, and urban environments created by humans if humans themselves disappeared.[5] Similarly, Bill McKibben, in his book *Eaarth: Making a Life on a Tough New Planet* (2011), quite explicitly adopts the tropes of terraforming and humans on an alien planet:

> The world hasn't ended, but the world as we know it has—even if we don't quite know it yet. We imagine we still live on that old planet, that the disturbances we see around us are the old random and freakish kind. But they're not. It's a different place. A different planet. It needs a new name. Eaarth. . . . It still looks familiar enough—we're still the third rock out from the sun, still three-quarters water. Gravity still pertains; we're still earth*like*. But it's odd enough to constantly remind us how profoundly we've altered the only place we've ever known. (2–3)

McKibben here uses the conceptual vocabulary of science fiction to jolt his readers out of routine assumptions about the natural world and its future development. Seen from this perspective, Earth itself appears as a terraformed planet—a planet reshaped to suit the ideas and needs of humans and yet out of their ultimate control.

The appropriation of speculative fiction for environmental nonfiction goes even further in Naomi Oreskes and Erik M. Conway's *The Collapse of Western Civilization: A View from the Future* (2014), a short science-fiction-style text that developed from an essay on social-scientific perspectives on climate change Oreskes originally wrote for the journal *Daedalus*, as she explains in an interview that is included in the volume (63). The text purports to be the report of a historian located in the Second People's Republic of China in 2393 looking back on the "Period of the Penumbra" (1988–2093 CE), including what the historian calls the "Great Collapse and Mass Migration" (2073–2093 CE). Other than its future viewpoint, the text offers little in the way of narrative: there are no characters, and the plot consists of the gradual realization of the worst-case scenarios projected by climate-change scientists in the late twentieth and early twenty-first centuries. Indeed, neither the point in

---

5. For a detailed analysis of the motif of the disappearance of humans in Weisman's and other texts, see Greg Garrard's essay "Worlds without Us: Some Types of Disanthropy" (2012).

time nor the historical and cultural background of the narrator is even
specified in the text itself, but instead in a brief preface, where the authors explain: "Science fiction writers construct an imaginary future;
historians attempt to reconstruct the past. Ultimately, both are seeking to understand the present. In this essay, we blend the two genres
to imagine a future historian looking back on a past that is our present
and (possible) future" (ix). More than a genuine work of science fiction,
The Collapse of Western Civilization functions as a companion piece to
Oreskes and Conway's *Merchants of Doubt*. It simply transfers to the
future opinions that are currently held by advocates of rapid action to
mitigate climate change: it takes a dim view of climate-change denialism,
of neoliberal economics, and of natural gas as a bridge fuel. Its historical hindsight confirms most of the dire predictions of climate-change scientists: a temperature rise of 3.9 degrees Celsius by 2040, catastrophic
heat waves and crop failures, social unrest, disintegration of the West
Antarctic Ice Sheet and the Greenland Ice Sheet, an eight-meter sea-level
rise, and displacement of 20 percent of the global population. To this
apocalyptic scenario Oreskes and Conway add a few more speculative
ingredients: a geoengineering project that injects aerosols into the atmosphere starts in 2052 but is halted in 2063, when it turns out that it stops
monsoons in India and causes large-scale crop failures there; an out-
break of plague triggered by a new strain of the pest bacterium, which
kills half of humankind; and the genetic engineering and release of a li-
chenized fungus that rapidly consumes CO_2 by a Japanese scientist—the
only fictional character with a name in this text. The fungus, *Pannaria
ishikawa*, spreads rapidly around the globe and brings CO_2 levels back
under control in the last decade of the twenty-first century. In their interview, Oreskes and Conway indicate that in constructing their future
scenario, they were influenced by Kim Stanley Robinson's *Mars* and *Science in the Capital* trilogies. Since Robinson's *Mars* trilogy focuses on
a comprehensive vision of terraforming, Oreskes and Conway also rely
on the idea of a terraformed planet as their central inspiration. Yet they
short-circuit Robinson's distinctive cosmopolitan emphasis on cultural
differences: the twenty-fourth-century Chinese historian is simply a foil
onto which the opinions of a left-wing American historian of the early
twenty-first century are projected, as if neither cultural nor historical
distance mattered.

Whatever their achievements and shortfalls, McKibben's *Eaarth* and
Oreskes and Conway's *Collapse* enable an understanding of the Anthropocene itself as a trope of speculative fiction: the idea of a planet terraformed by humans in such a way that the traces of the process will be

perceptible in the geological strata to a putative far-future observer.[6]
Both works approach the idea of a planet pervasively transformed by
humans—a terraformed Earth—with the imaginative and rhetorical
tools of speculative fiction. If the Anthropocene, in these books, appears
itself as an offshoot of the speculative-fiction genre, this perspective is
helped by a shift in the way science fiction relates to the future. Fredric
Jameson famously argued that the function of science-fictional futures is
to make readers see the present anew as the past of societies yet to come:

> The most characteristic SF does not seriously attempt to imag-
> ine the "real" future of our social system. Rather, its multiple
> mock futures serve the quite different function of transforming
> our own present into the determinate past of something yet to
> come. It is this present moment—unavailable to us for contem-
> plation in its own right because the sheer quantitative immen-
> sity of objects and individual lives it comprises is untotalizable
> and hence unimaginable, and also because it is occluded by the
> density of our private fantasies as well as of the proliferating ste-
> reotypes of a media culture that penetrates every remote zone of
> our existence—that upon our return from the imaginary con-
> structs of SF is offered to us in the form of some future world's
> remote past, as if posthumous and as though collectively re-
> membered. . . . SF thus enacts and enables a structurally unique
> "method" for apprehending the present as history. (2005, 288)

This approach makes sense especially for works of science fiction set in a
future distant from us by at least a half century, which ask by their very
structure how we might achieve their utopias or prevent their disasters
and dystopias. Many recent climate-change novels and films fit into this
category, but also classics such as Edward Bellamy's *Looking Backward:
2000–1887* (1888) or Aldous Huxley's *Brave New World* (1932), as
well as novels that, like Oreskes and Conway's *Collapse,* feature future
observers looking back on the present: many of French novelist Michel
Houellebecq's novels, Margaret Atwood's *Handmaid's Tale* (1985),
George Turner's *The Sea and Summer* (1987), and Sheri S. Tepper's *The
Family Tree* (1998), for example. All of these novels quite explicitly his-
toricize the readers' present from the perspective of a far future.

6. I am indebted to Gerry Canavan for drawing my attention to this future observer in
accounts of the Anthropocene as a staple of science fiction.

Yet a good deal of recent speculative fiction no longer ventures into far temporal distances. The protagonists of recent science fiction quite often live not so much in anything that is readily identifiable as a future to the reader, but in a present that in the characters' own minds has undergone some momentous but not quite identifiable change. "Something has changed," the characters in Gibson's *Count Zero* (1986) keep pointing out, without detailed awareness of the merger of two artificial intelligences that the earlier volume *Neuromancer* (1984) described. The protagonist of Jonathan Lethem's *Amnesia Moon* (1995) travels through a North American landscape that everyone he meets agrees has been visited by some recent cataclysm, but just what that disaster was and how far back it took place is not clearly remembered by anyone. Gibson's trilogy *Pattern Recognition* (2003), *Spook Country* (2007), and *Zero History* (2010) is perhaps the most conspicuous example of this presentification of the future: it features a society that is barely distinguishable from that of the present day but presents it as if it *were* a speculative fiction. Gibson's often-quoted quip, "The future is already here—it's just not evenly distributed yet" (Kennedy 2012) might as well stand as an epigraph to McKibben's *Eaarth* or Oreskes and Conway's *Collapse*. Gibson himself was no doubt thinking of technological advances that would have seemed implausibly futuristic just a few decades ago—extremely powerful computers in every purse and pocket, global digital networks, cloned animals (perhaps even de-extincted ones!)—and the ways in which they have transformed the global north but not the south. But another kind of future is unevenly distributed the other way around: the consequences of climate change, pollution, and species loss that may yet seem distant to the average citizen of the global north are already all too manifest in the global south.

Contemporary speculative fiction, then—as a distinct literary genre and as a rhetorical mode that has spread far beyond narratives about future worlds or other planets to mainstream fiction and to environmental nonfiction—defines itself in the tension between two different approaches to the present. From one perspective, the present appears as the past of imagined futures, and from the other perspective as an already if incompletely materialized future that makes palpable the obsolescence of the present.[7] The Anthropocene, I would suggest, can usefully be understood as the second kind of speculative fiction, in that it focuses on the reality of a terraformed planet that the genre has long held out as a vision for the future of other planets, but which has already arrived

7. I have made this argument in more detail in the introduction to a special issue of the journal *Ecozon@* on "The Invention of Ecofutures" (Heise 2012).

in the present on our own planet. In adopting strategies of speculative fiction, environmentalist writers such as McKibben and Oreskes and Conway seek to open readers' eyes to the futures they already inhabit.

3. The Anthropocene and the Species Question

The long-term narrative associated with the Anthropocene casts humans as the protagonists of a plot that has unfolded over at least ten thousand years and has led to epochal change in the past two hundred. Or rather, as the protagonist, in the singular, since the main character here is the human species at large. This conceptual move tends to come easily to natural scientists, who often lump all humans together so as to highlight their differences from or interactions with other species and natural environments. It is a much more difficult move for social scientists and humanists, to whom historical, social, and cultural differences between communities tend to stand out much more sharply than they do to natural scientists. For the humanist, the primary given is a wide anthropological variety from which "the human" as a generalization can emerge only by way of slow and painstaking assembly. This is true of the humanities in general, but particularly of disciplines such as anthropology, history, art history, and comparative literature, which have traditionally specialized in tracing differences between moments in time, communities, cultures, and aesthetic forms.

Of course, this focus has not always prevented scholars in these disciplines from postulating human universals of various kinds or all-embracing kinships whose hypocrisies Roland Barthes brilliantly exposed in "The Great Family of Man" ([1957] 1972). In his footsteps, a wide range of theoretical paradigms in the humanities—from Neo-Marxism, feminism, and postcolonialism to New Historicism, Cultural Studies, critical race theory, queer theory, and some new materialisms—have exposed how claims to universality invariably rely on historically and culturally specific yardsticks of the "human," usually to the detriment of those who are judged to fall short of such measures of humanness. The interest in difference and the resistance to universalisms has also generated a wide variety of theories about how difference is undercut or overcome in particular circumstances of transcultural encounter: key concepts such as hybridity, *mestizaje,* diaspora, nomadology, borderlands culture, multiculturalism, pluralism, and cosmopolitanism, to name a few, all have sought to describe and sometimes to prescribe ways of transcending cultural difference, especially in the face of increasing economic and technological globalization.

The Anthropocene, by making the human species at large the agent of history, challenges traditions of thought that have relied, over the past half century, on the assumption of some foundational difference—whether it be gender, sexual orientation, class, or race. The postcolonial historian Dipesh Chakrabarty, in this context, has most forcefully proposed that the globally shared confrontation with climate change calls for a new theoretical approach to such differences. Chakrabarty readily admits that the main culprit of climate change has been industrial civilization such as it has evolved over the past two hundred years, and that the globalization of capitalism has accelerated the fast pace of climatic change. Yet critiques of capitalism, in his view, do not address the full temporal scale of climate change:

> Capitalist globalization exists; so should its critiques. But these critiques do not give us an adequate hold on human history once we accept that the crisis of climate change is here with us and may exist as part of this planet for much longer than capitalism or long after capitalism has undergone many more historic mutations. The problematic of globalization allows us to read climate change only as a crisis of capitalist management. While there is no denying that climate change has profoundly to do with the history of capital, a critique that is only a critique of capital is not sufficient for addressing questions relating to human history. (2009, 212)

Climate change threatens *all* modes of humans' inhabitation of the planet, in other words, and thereby highlights boundary conditions of humans' collective existence that are unrelated to capitalism. "The . . . crisis of climate change thus requires us to bring together intellectual formations that are somewhat in tension with each other: the planetary and the global; deep and recorded histories; species thinking and critiques of capital" (213). Contrary to the efforts of anthropologists, historians, and scholars of literature who have sought to detach the concept of humanity from its association with mere biological species or natural condition, Chakrabarty points out, the notion of the Anthropocene brings with it the idea that the human species is a collective with geological force, a natural condition for the rest of life on the planet (214).[8]

---

8. For the idea of humans as a geological force, see Chakrabarty's follow-up essay "Postcolonial Studies and the Challenge of Climate Change" (2012).

One might object that this conception of the human species as the agent of deep history, an essentialist misconception on the part of natural scientists, merely obfuscates the operations of economic power. "Why should one include the poor of the world—whose carbon footprint is small anyway—by use of such all-inclusive terms as *species* or *mankind* when the blame for the current crisis should be squarely laid at the door of the rich nations in the first place and of the richer classes in the poorer ones?" Chakrabarty asks (2009, 216). But in the end, he argues, all humans are now confronted with the consequences of climate change and the threat to so-called boundary conditions, ecological parameters outside of which human existence is not possible. Faced with this global challenge, we need a new universalism, even though it may be one that can be articulated only as a negative universalism if it is to avoid simply generalizing one particular perspective, like earlier universalisms (222).

Other theorists, particularly Marxist ones, have disagreed with this conclusion. The sociologist Jason Moore, who proposes that the current era should be called the "Capitalocene," indicts the Anthropocene concept for simply ignoring the "naturalized inequalities, alienation, and violence inscribed in modernity's strategic relations of power and production" and for focusing on environmental consequences rather than causes, like most environmental history (2014, 2, 4–5). Similarly, the philosopher Slavoj Žižek has challenged Chakrabarty's claim that capitalism is no longer the most decisive framework for analyzing the climate-change crisis.[9]

> Of course, the natural parameters of our environment . . . harbor a potential threat to all of us, independently of economic development, political system, etc. However, the fact that their stability has been threatened by the dynamic of global capitalism . . . has a stronger implication. . . . We have to accept the paradox that, in the relation between the universal antagonism (the threatened parameters of the conditions for life) and the particular antagonism (the deadlock of capitalism), the key struggle is the particular one: one can solve the universal problem (of the survival of the human species) only by first resolving the particular deadlock of the capitalist mode of production. . . . The key to the ecological crisis does not reside in ecology as such. (2011, 333–334)

9. For a detailed discussion of Chakrabarty, Žižek, and Marx's notion of "species being," see Dibley (2012).

One may agree with Žižek's claim that ecology as such does not hold the key to solving the problem of climate change without also accepting his argument that in order to resolve it, the capitalist mode of production has to be overcome. Climate scientists generally agree that even if emission of carbon dioxide and other greenhouse gases were to stop entirely tomorrow, the planet would still continue to warm up for several decades, so that the difference would become perceptible only to the current generation's grandchildren. But of course it will not stop tomorrow: even if a collective will to develop an alternative economic regime were to emerge in some of the planet's dominant nations, the transition to such a regime would almost certainly take decades (more likely, a century or more)—too late to affect the current climate crisis decisively. Žižek's assumption that overcoming capitalism is a prerequisite for addressing the climate crisis, in practice, simply denies the possibility of coming to terms with it.

In its substance, this debate is not quite as new as the emergent term *Anthropocene* might lead one to believe. The theory of a contemporary "risk society," first proposed by the German sociologist Ulrich Beck in 1986, already stipulated that the world was moving into a new kind of modernity characterized by pervasive uncertainty. Social stratification in the risk society, Beck argued, would be determined not so much by differences in wealth or control of the means of production as by differential exposure to technological and ecological risks. The old class society will soon reach its end point, to give way not to a classless society but to one whose classes will be defined in a fundamentally different way, in Beck's view. Activists in the environmental and climate justice movements as well as postcolonial theorists have tended to reject this hypothesis on the grounds that currently, environmental risks usually reinforce existing class divisions rather than cut across them. In this debate also, one of the crucial points of contention has been whether a Marxist-inflected critique of capitalism (or neoliberalism, now often the preferred target of attack) adequately captures the social structure of global environmental crisis.[10]

That this discussion has reignited around the Anthropocene pinpoints the recurring problem of conceptualizing collective agency in the context of global ecological crisis. For theorists such as Beck and Chakrabarty, "class" as the collective agent is no longer adequate, while newer entities such as the "multitude" proposed by Hardt and Negri have yet to

10. I have discussed Beck's approach in its confrontation with the environmental justice movement in chapter 4 of *Sense of Place and Sense of Planet* (Heise 2008).

prove their political relevance. The difficulty in conceiving of the human species as a historical agent, Chakrabarty argues, is that the category of "species" does not correspond to any register of our experience.

> When [the biologist E. O.] Wilson . . . recommends in the interest of our collective future that we achieve self-understanding as a species, the statement does not correspond to any historical way of understanding and connecting pasts with futures through the assumption of there being an element of continuity to human experience. . . . Who is the we? We humans never experience ourselves as a species. We can only intellectually comprehend or infer the existence of the human species but never experience it as such. There could be no phenomenology of us as a species. Even if we were to emotionally identify with a word like *mankind,* we would not know what being a species is, for, in species history, humans are only an instance of the concept species as indeed would be any other life form. But one never experiences being a concept. (2009, 220)

This is, according to Chakrabarty, the crisis in historical understanding that the Anthropocene and the postulation of species agency generate.

Chakrabarty's rejection of species as a concept that might ground collective identity resonates with Dale Jamieson's rejection of species as a relevant category in the interaction with nonhumans, which I quoted (and criticized) in chapter 4. Chakrabarty's skepticism toward species thinking leaves his argument, which is essentially a call for what in other theoretical discourses would be referred to as a kind of cosmopolitanism, with no positive content. What he imagines at the end is a "negative universalism" that cannot take on a concrete content that would always be less than universal, in that it would be bound to postulate some characteristics of a particular human community as the paradigm by which other communities should be measured.

Yet this argument is a curious one. Granted, humans may not normally be able to experience themselves as a species—any more than they are able to experience themselves as a nation: unless, that is, communities produce institutions, laws, symbols, and forms of rhetoric that establish such abstract categories as perceptible and livable frameworks of experience. A great deal of historical and cultural analysis over the past four decades, often building on Benedict Anderson's and Jürgen Habermas's seminal studies, has shown such political and cultural processes at work in the emergence of modern European nation-states in the

MULTISPECIES FICTIONS FOR THE ANTHROPOCENE

eighteenth and nineteenth centuries. The self-identification of particular communities as nations, these studies show, is historically specific and contingent. Theorists of cosmopolitanism have long argued that a different set of institutions, laws, symbolic markers, and rhetorical forms might make the framework of "humankind" experienceable in a similar way. And even the "species" framework might not forever remain as phenomenologically ungraspable as Chakrabarty makes it out to be. Surely what being a "species" means, from a biological and ecological as well as a social perspective, is to be situated in a network of lived, existential relations with other species and with the inanimate environment (soil, water, atmosphere, weather patterns). Multispecies ethnography, as I explained in chapter 5, focuses on some of these relations to develop new descriptions of human societies. Such ecological connectedness, especially for twenty-first-century citizens shaped by material and sociocultural structures that tend to make their own dependence on ecological networks invisible, may not be immediately perceptible or experienceable any more than the social embeddedness into class or nation; indeed, probably less so because there are fewer historical precedents for conceiving of "species" as a relevant social category. But there is no principled reason why it cannot be translated into the realm of perception, experience, and collective self-identification by means of its own set of rhetorical, symbolic, legal, social, and institutional structures.

An enormous amount of scholarship in anthropology, history, literary and cultural studies, philosophy, and political science over the past twenty-five years has investigated when and how models of cultural identification and political citizenship have emerged that transcend localisms and nationalisms, whether or not they have translated into cultural or political change, and with what consequences. Theories of cosmopolitanism, in particular, have analyzed the history of past attempts to assemble global concepts of humanity and the urgency and challenges of developing a contemporary vision of planetary identity that would be accountable to socioeconomic, racial, sexual, cultural, linguistic, religious, and other kinds of difference. Concepts such as "critical cosmopolitanism," "vernacular cosmopolitanism," and more generally the foregrounding of different coexisting cosmopolitanisms have moved cosmopolitanism beyond the elitist connotations it carried in the early twentieth century to a category that captures a broad spectrum of experiences and identifications across national, cultural, and linguistic borders.

My own attempt to think through the challenges of such differences and those of globally shared ecological crises have in the past led me to envision an "eco-cosmopolitanism" that is informed by deep knowledge

of at least one culture other than one's own, including a knowledge of
the ecology in which this culture is situated and of which it forms part
(Heise 2008, 50–62, 150–159). Eco-cosmopolitanism is not based on
the assumption that forming part of the biological species Homo sapiens
guarantees any far-reaching commonality or shared legacy that could
serve as the foundation for structuring a global political community.
On the contrary, eco-cosmopolitanism as I conceive it is shaped by an
awareness that very little commonality can be taken for granted and that
speaking about the human species, humanity, humanness, or the Anthropocene requires a patient and meticulous process of *assembly*—in
its most craftsmanlike and technological connotations. Speaking about
species is also an assembly in the political sense, the process of convening
a representative and democratic forum for deliberating and deciding on
courses of action that affect all: all humans, but also many nonhuman
species if the goal is some form of multispecies justice. This may sound
like a utopian scenario, and it is: not in the sense of a political vision that
is in practice unachievable, but in the sense of constructive, long-term
political goals that require an imagination reaching beyond what currently exists. Theories of cosmopolitanism share this intellectual task
with certain kinds of utopian fiction.[11]

4. Speculative Fiction and Multispecies Justice

Utopian scenarios have for a long time been shared between political
writing, philosophy, and science fiction. Considering the broad public
attention to species loss and to the broader transformations of nature
that the concept of the Anthropocene sums up, it is unsurprising that
recent speculative fiction has also taken up these issues. The idea of a
"Human Age" extends to us the invitation to think about the centrality
of human agency at the same time that it asks us to reflect on very long-
term futures (the hypothetical future geologist who might discover the
traces of Homo sapiens activities in the Earth's strata) and past geological epochs. But considering such long-term temporal frameworks can
of course also diminish the importance of human agency: measured with
the long yardsticks of geology and evolution, anthropogenic ecological
crises such as biodiversity loss or climate change might not matter as

11. I have discussed the descriptive and prescriptive aspects of recent cosmopolitanisms in some detail in *Sense of Place and Sense of Planet:* while descriptive theories analyze current forms of global identification, prescriptive cosmopolitanisms also seek to formulate ethical and political ideals, including certain kinds of utopia (Heise 2008, 57–58).

much as we currently imagine. The literary scholar Mark McGurl, in an essay called "The Posthuman Comedy," has suggested that thinking in terms of geological time intervals might make humans seem relatively unimportant and even laughable. Formally, this perspective on humans emerges most clearly in genres such as horror and science fiction: "Not only does genre fiction seem to violate the law of writing what you know from personal experience; not only does it bear 'formulaic' flatness on its grubby sleeve, catering to tastes unformed by the university, but its darkly dorky aesthetic unseriousness is an affront to the humanities— hell, an affront to humanity. Look at those characters, little more than the toys of allegory!," McGurl claims (2012, 550). Horror novels and science fiction, through their reduction of the human to certain types and their reduction of plot to encounters with the naturally or technologically other, portray humans in their entanglements with nature and technology, according to McGurl. This portrait is comedic in its basic thrust, not in the sense of being funny, but in the sense of not taking humans' grandeur or exceptionality very seriously.

One way in which science fiction rethinks and relativizes human exceptionality is through the confrontation with aliens, species with whom humans have not coevolved. Such "species fictions," as we might call them, plunge their readers head-on into questions of multispecies assemblies and multispecies justice. Humans' endangerment of other species and conservation efforts have resonated since the 1960s in science fiction texts that explore the emergence of new forms of human identity. Philip K. Dick's *Do Androids Dream of Electric Sheep?* (1968) and Kurt Vonnegut's *Galápagos* (1985) already considered the changing status of the human species in a world of diminishing biodiversity—a scenario that in both cases suggested an evolutionary phase change for humans themselves and required new answers to the search for justice among and beyond humans. Octavia Butler's *Xenogenesis* trilogy, *Dawn* (1987), *Adulthood Rites* (1988), and *Imago* (1989), traced the progressive gene mixing of the few human survivors of a global nuclear war with aliens, the Oankali, who are both saviors and oppressors with whom humans need to build a new kind of society. A similar challenge confronts the protagonists of Sheri S. Tepper's *The Family Tree* (1998) and Dietmar Dath's *Die Abschaffung der Arten* (The abolition of species; 2008), who coexist with intelligent animal species that have emerged from biotechnology. In a more apocalyptic vein, Paolo Bacigalupi's *The Windup Girl* (2009), set in Thailand, portrays a future world plagued by climate change, corporate exploitation, political conflict, epidemic disease, and agricultural disasters through mutating pests, in which new, genetically engineered plants and animals may have a better chance of survival than old ones. This might also apply to the "windups" or "New People," genetically engineered humans who are immune to many of the diseases that decimate the old humanity. All of these texts ask how humans need to reenvision their own identity so as to be able to live in societies populated by aliens who are at the same time intimately or even genetically related to humans—both self and other.

The most interesting among these texts are those that move beyond questions of individual identity to consider what a political order might look like that takes seriously the participation of its nonhuman citizens. Margaret Atwood's *MaddAddam* trilogy, for example, addresses this question through a threefold species encounter: the few remnants of Homo sapiens who have survived global genocide, the genetically engineered posthumans created by a biotech engineer, and genetically altered pigs with a partly human frontal cortex. The third volume ends with scenarios of reconciliation and shared futures between these three constituencies. The posthuman Crakers, whose genome combines human, animal, and even some plant genes, begin to hybridize with the remaining humans, suggesting a shared future for both species. And this human-posthuman community concludes a peace treaty with the highly intelligent "pigoons," who have often been their antagonists in the earlier volumes.

Some aspects of this emergent multispecies society remain disturbing, however—most obviously, its origins in and continued reliance on violent exclusion. Atwood's quasi-utopian society can come into being only because the overwhelming majority of humans has been eliminated through planetwide genocide, and the two remaining villains who are judged unredeemable are executed after a simple majority vote at the end. Somewhat surprisingly, Atwood here repeats one of the most troubling aspects of a good deal of postapocalyptic science fiction, including environmentalist science fiction: the tendency to do away with complicated mechanisms of democracy and justice until most of those who might disagree have exited the stage, and then symbolically to inaugurate a new society whose promise of freedom and peace almost inevitably appears like sleight-of-hand. Even the peace treaty with the pigoons remains unreassuring in this respect, since it is the pigoons' human-derived brain that bestows on them a kind of honorary citizenship in the new humanity, whereas more robustly unhuman species are not invited, and humans who are judged subhuman are put to death.

A more interesting vision of how a multispecies society might emerge from the life and death of very different species unfolds across the volumes of Orson Scott Card's *Ender* series, *Ender's Game* ([1985] 1991a), *Speaker for the Dead* (1986), *Xenocide* (1991b), and *Children of the Mind* ([1992] 1996). The first and most famous of these novels, *Ender's Game*, portrays humankind's initial encounter with an insectoid alien species. Humans construe the intentions of the insectlike "Buggers," as they are called, to be relentlessly hostile. They defeat the aliens through adolescents who are rigorously trained in simulated military games and who exterminate all of the insects in a battle that they themselves only learn afterward was not, after all, a simulation, but real war by means of virtual technologies. This "victory" leaves many humans plagued with guilt, especially the young battle commander Andrew Wiggin, whose childhood nickname "Ender" acquires a sinister literalness when he realizes that he has unwittingly led the effort to wipe out the only extraterrestrial species humans have ever known. His sorrow, mourning, and attempt to redeem his guilt by writing a book that presents the conflict from the point of view of an alien hive queen all eloquently speak to contemporary environmentalists' melancholy over humans' extinction of other species and to the almost compulsive urge to keep writing, filming, photographing, and painting the species we have lost.

In the second novel, *Speaker for the Dead*, humans discover another species of aliens three thousand years later, when a group of Brazilian-descended, Portuguese-speaking settlers land on a planet they call Lusitania. In rueful memory of the insect genocide, the institutions that govern human life in the new planetary colonies impose strict rules not to interfere with the intelligent Pequeninos or "Piggies," as the Lusitanian settlers call them, in Card's sly conflation of the Portuguese diminutive for "little ones" with the racist epithet "piccaninnies." As in the case of the Buggers, Card emphasizes the enormous difficulty of gaining access to the thought and culture of a truly alien community, especially since the "xenologists" (alien-specialized anthropologists) and xenobiologists are under strict orders to keep interspecies contact and knowledge exchange to a minimum so as to avoid a recurrence of the first xenocide.

But avoiding contact, exchange, and conflict turns out to be extremely complicated. *Speaker for the Dead* portrays an ecology some of whose most basic facts humans struggle to understand. The Pequeninos, for example, have individual names for the innumerable trees in the forest they inhabit—not, as it turns out, because of some quaint native custom, but because what looks to humans like two quite distinct species are in fact just different phases in the development of one species. At his death, a Pequenino male metamorphoses into one of the at least partly sentient trees, in the aliens' view an ascent to a higher order of being that makes murdering one of their own the greatest honor they can bestow. Needless to say, this "honor" is lost on the humans, two of whom are also submitted to this ritual, and violent interspecies conflict once again threatens to erupt.

Lusitania's ecology also confronts the xenobiologists with other vexing biodiversity riddles. The planet's extremely limited set of species, with mysterious methods of reproduction and gene transfer, raises urgent ecological questions according to one of the young xenobiologists, Elanora: "Evolution on this world was obviously well within the pattern that xenobiologists had seen on all the Hundred Worlds, and yet somewhere the pattern had broken down, collapsed" (Card 1986, 243). The xenobiologists trace this evolutionary breakdown back to a major disaster that occurred in the evolution of Lusitania's biological life within the past million years: the emergence of the "Descolada" virus. Named after the Portuguese verb "descolar," "to unglue," this virus undoes and randomly rearranges an organism's genetic materials and thereby caused the extinction of most of Lusitania's species. But the virus also enables genes to bond with foreign genetic material, which leads to an ecology in which the native species consist of plant-and-animal pairs (328–329).

Humans, to whom the virus adapted within ten years of their arrival on Lusitania, become permanent carriers and can ward off the genetic scrambling only by regularly ingesting a particular food additive. This epidemiological twist implies that humans become a potentially lethal threat yet again, this time to all human, animal, and plant life on other inhabited planets, because they would carry the virus with them if they traveled to other worlds. Politically, this danger is likely to lead to total quarantine of the Lusitanians in their colony and perhaps even the destruction of the planet. If and when governments on other planets come to recognize Lusitania as a source of potential disaster for biological life everywhere, a possible xenocide and genocide might ensue that is far more extensive than the one humans committed against the Buggers. Through this plot, riveting in its ecological and epidemiological detail, Card raises difficult questions of multispecies relationships and justice. Should the humans seek to exterminate the Descolada virus, but thereby almost certainly destroy all the life forms on Lusitania that depend on it? Should they let it live, but put the rest of humanity at risk if any of them ever leave the planet? What are the rights of the Pequeninos, who long to travel to other planets, in making these decisions?

Speaker for the Dead also traces an unfolding story of ecosystem alterations and cultural adaptations: not only do the humans reengineer Earthly plant stock so as to withstand the Descolada virus; some of them also pass seeds and agricultural techniques on to the Pequeninos, in flagrant violation of the rules of nonengagement. Even more incisively, when Ender—who, by virtue of the peculiarities of interstellar travel, is only a few decades old, even though several millennia have passed in objective time since his battle against the insects—journeys to Lusitania, he surreptitiously brings with him the cocoon of a Bugger hive queen he has secretly preserved. The insect queen decides in consensus with the Pequeninos that she will start a new colony on Lusitania and so resuscitate the species thought definitively extinct. This act of "restoration biology" or perhaps de-extinction, for Ender really an act of penitence for xenocide, ends up yielding an entirely new planetary ecosystem inhabited by three intelligent species—two of them, humans and insectoids, introduced.

This global multispecies society can, of course, as in many other works of science fiction, be understood allegorically to reflect the multiplicity of cultures on Earth. Yet if a futuristically transformed vision of multiculturalism indeed underlies Card's scenario, it relies on the awareness of and mutual respect for vastly different ways of inhabiting the same ecosystem, with particular emphasis on what might put other species at risk. And even though the term *Anthropocene* had not yet been coined in its current form when Card wrote the *Ender* novels, the multispecies society of Lusitania and other worlds that humans, Pequeninos, and hive queens colonize can also be understood as an anticipation of what came to be called the Anthropocene only a decade later. At the end of *Speaker for the Dead*, a carefully negotiated political pact between Buggers, Pequeninos, and humans suggests the possibility of a peaceful and democratic multispecies society that might serve as a thought model not only for relations between different groups of humans but of a differently structured relation of humans to nonhuman species on Earth.[12] Bruno Latour's vision of a "Parliament of Things," in which not only human but a variety of nonhuman agents might have a voice finds one possible instantiation in Card's science fiction world.

But *Xenocide*, the novel that follows *Speaker for the Dead*, makes it clear that Card envisions no easy utopia with unambiguous ethical choices. In this volume, the fate of two other agents involved in the Lusitanian

12. Card's long history of antigay rhetoric and his widely publicized opposition to same-sex marriage in 2013, which may derive from his lifelong commitment to Mormonism, stand in jarring opposition to this vision of mutual acceptance and painstaking political negotiation. In such blatant discontinuities between writers' lives and their works, not uncommon in the history of literature, it must be the literary critic's hope that the fiction will prove more enduring and powerful than the nonfiction.

plot moves to the forefront: that of an Artificial Intelligence who calls itself "Jane," and that of the Descolada virus itself. Jane's presence in both *Speaker for the Dead* and *Xenocide* pushes the reflection on cross-species justice beyond the biological realm to raise questions about technologically emergent forms of intelligence that have been the stuff of much science fiction since the 1940s. More importantly for questions of species conservation, humans seek to develop ways of eliminating or re-engineering the Descolada virus so as to protect themselves against it but at the same time to preserve the native Lusitanian life forms, all of which biologically depend on it. In the process, the nature of the virus itself as yet another alien life form begins to raise ethical questions. One of the scientists discovers that the viruses communicate with each other at a rudimentary level by means of genes, which implies that they might be considered another sentient species.

> "Does it matter?" asked Ender.
> "Matter!" said Quara.
> Ela looked at Ender with consternation. "It's only the difference between curing a dangerous disease and destroying an entire sentient species. I think it matters."
> "I meant," said Ender patiently, "does it matter whether we know what they're saying."
> "No," said Quara. "We'll probably never understand their language, but that doesn't change the fact that they're sentient. What do viruses and human beings have to say to each other, anyway?"
> "How about, 'Please stop trying to kill us'?" said Grego. "If you can figure out how to say that in virus language, then this might be useful."
> "But Grego," said Quara, with mock sweetness, "do we say that to them, or do they say that to us?" (1991b, 81)

As they are faced with the choice of exterminating either one alien species or another, and with either killing others or letting themselves be killed, the humans have to make decisions about what principles of justice are appropriate in a network of different human societies and different species. Instead of letting the species concept do any of the moral decision-making by default, one of the characters develops an intricate taxonomy of different kinds of humans, aliens, and their relations to each other. On this basis, the Brazilian scientists and the Pequeninos together reluctantly but successfully reengineer the Descolada virus, eliminating it in its old form but recreating it in a different shape that does not put other species at risk. Even as they preserve Lusitania's biology, in other words, they also alter its foundations and mode of functioning to create a new, hybrid ecology that includes both native and introduced species.

In Card's *Ender* series of novels, then, the imaginary planet of Lusitania functions as a scenario for staging some of the stark ethical choices humans confront in organizing their coexistence with other species on Earth. Since the few species on Lusitania are connected to each other in surprisingly tight ecological networks, with animal-like species and plant-like species functioning as different life phases of the same types of organisms, and all dependent on the operations of a particular virus, the human scientists and community leaders are left with no innocent choices. Whether they intervene or not, and no matter how they intervene in the planet's ecology, once humans have a colony on Lusitania, their choices shape the lives and deaths of sentient organisms. Card's imaginary ecology does not present a beatific vision of universal cross-species reconciliation or, on the contrary, a cynical view of environmental nihilism. Instead, it invites readers to conceive of their relations to other members of the ecological community and their ethical decisions about them not along simple species lines but through careful negotiations that take all participants' interests into consideration, even if not all can be honored in the end. In an age when humans shape nature, willingly or unwillingly, in many of its most fundamental dimensions, ethical and political decision-making needs to reach beyond species taxonomies toward a more complex and nuanced understanding of relatedness. When nature can no longer be separated from us, the *Ender* cycle suggests, questions of human justice become inextricably entangled with justice across species boundaries, and neither form of justice can be separated from the values and ideals of the involved communities. Decisions about biodiversity are in the end questions about value, about cultural frameworks of thought, and about historical traditions of social practice.

5. *Multispecies Fictions and Multispecies Futures*

The Anthropocene, at first sight, seems to rely on too simple an understanding of the human and too anthropocentric an approach to historical agency. But as the lively debates of the past decade have shown, if it is understood as a shorthand for the self-reflexive moment in which humans confront the pervasive intentional and unintentional transformations of planetary ecology and geochemistry they have brought about, it can serve both to complicate what we usually mean by "human" and to offer opportunities for redefining it. Card's parable of Lusitania seeks to capture some of these complications and opportunities: the Brazilian settlers decide to reengineer the foundations of the planet's biological life, but they do so in collaboration with the dominant native species and after their own biology has been reshaped by their new environment. Along with the political negotiations, this biological terraforming becomes the basis for a planetary multispecies society. The complications in our own case have been exposed in the multiple debates that have emerged around the Anthropocene: the implications of understanding humans as a species or even a geological force; the importance of socioeconomic and cultural differences; the constitution of human bodies and minds out of relations with other species, ranging from the microbiome in human guts to charismatic megafauna; and the human management or lack of control over risks ranging from environmental toxins to climate change.[13]

Precisely because the Anthropocene has generated a great deal of critical reflection on how what we used to consider "human" should be redefined in the context of a global ecological environment, few of whose parts and processes remain unaffected by humans' interventions, it has also led to conflicts over conservation. While some environmentalists seek to preserve natural areas with minimal human alteration, others have put a new emphasis on biodiversity in areas inhabited, used, and transformed by humans. In either scenario, complementing our thinking about species conservation with the idea of multispecies justice—or even replacing it with multispecies justice—will remind us that the values and principles that guide conservation decisions are political and cultural even when they are informed by scientific data. It will help to keep debates about conservation honest about these underlying values rather than hiding them behind biological or ecological arguments, and it will prompt discussions of competing valuations and uses of biodiversity and beliefs about it among the affected human communities. It will also encourage us to include what we see and know about other species' preferences and practices and to keep questioning our own projections of what these preferences and practices are and what they mean. With hindsight, it is easy to see the cultural projections and biases in biology and conservation of the past: attempts to see heterosexuality, the nuclear

13. The historian Julia Adeney Thomas, in this context, has argued that the three horizons of paleobiology, microbiology, and biochemistry offer incommensurable approaches to the human that are hard to reconcile with historians' conceptualizations of individual and collective agency (2014, 1589).

family, or male aggression as part of the natural order that could then be called upon to justify social arrangements, for example, or the colonial entanglements of early conservation with the interests of European and American big-game hunters. It is harder to spot how our own cultural perspectives shape the ways we think and talk about conservation. Reenvisioning conservation as a form of multispecies justice will help us make explicit the cultural values that underpin our conservation priorities and procedures.

These cultural foundations are perhaps easiest to see and to put to use when conservation turns to cities. As human-made environments from the start, cities lend themselves less than mountains, forests, or oceans to the idea that nature could be restored to an earlier state, or that humans could be kept apart from recovering ecosystems and species. They have traditionally been considered as biodiversity wastelands not worthy of conservationists' attention, but this perspective has begun to shift over the past decade. Cities are often quite rich in biodiversity because of the plants, animals, and microorganisms that a large human population cultivates and often imports from other places, but this is not the native biodiversity that is usually cherished by biologists and ecologists. For this reason, empirical studies of urban biodiversity are still a relatively small part of conservation biology.

But cities are in fact spaces that are shared by humans and other species, some brought intentionally, some introduced accidentally, some wanted and others not. The urban-planning scholar Jennifer Wolch, for this reason, began to call for a "transspecies theory" in her field in the 1990s (Wolch 1998), and multispecies ethnographers Thom van Dooren and Deborah Bird Rose have written eloquently about the way penguins and flying foxes co-inhabit the urban space of Sydney with its human inhabitants (van Dooren and Rose 2012). Whatever wealth or poverty of species biological and ethnographic studies may turn up in the future, decisions about what do with it will have to take into account the perspectives of diverse urban communities and the nonhumans' social and ecological agency and functions along with scientists' approaches. Who has access to what kinds of ecosystems and species? How are spaces and species used by humans, and how do microorganisms, plants, and animals use human-made structures? Which uses improve and which ones degrade the city, and by whose standard? What should be the institutions and principles to decide which species "we"—the urban communities—want around and which ones we do not? In Los Angeles, for example, should we track down and kill feral cats to protect birds and reptiles, or should we listen to the animal welfare advocates who resist putting them to death? Should we seek to get rid of feral cats and continue to ensure the welfare of P-22, the lone mountain lion who has made his way to Griffith Park? The first task, from the perspective of multispecies justice, is not so much to answer these questions as to build forums for conversation about what the principles for deciding such questions should be. Scientific principles will certainly be among these, but they will not be the only and may not be the decisive paradigms any more than they have been in many other conservation scenarios.

Urban multispecies justice can also productively inflect planning, architecture, and design. Health concerns and visions of the sanitary city led many urban authorities to displace some animals and animal-related activities out of the city in the nineteenth century, and new technologies helped to displace others as slaughterhouses were relocated to the outskirts and electric trams and cars replaced horse-drawn carriages. While health concerns continue to be important, of course, city authorities in a time of biodiversity loss find themselves facing the quite different challenge of how to make visible the nonhuman inhabitants of urban spaces and how to redesign urban spaces and architectural structures in such a way that they enhance rather than harm biodiversity. How can we plan traffic flows in such a way that they accommodate not just cars but also the movements of animals? How can we design buildings so that they become not death traps for birds but habitat for insects, reptiles, birds, and bats? Which rodents should we plan to include and exclude, in what numbers, and for what reasons? If we assume we will never get rid of rats, for instance—and it seems we won't, if we go by New York City's example! (Flegenheimer 2015)—how might we design sewers, gardens, and waste disposal procedures in such a way that the rats' behaviors become useful rather than harmful? How do we ensure that increased urban biodiversity does not increase health risks for the poor? By proposing multispecies justice as a framework for considering such questions, I am not suggesting that these questions will be easy to answer or that there will not be disagreement about them. The disagreements will no doubt in some cases entail different solutions for different places, both in cities and outside: rainforests, oceans, and national parks will call for other solutions than those appropriate for city parks or neighborhoods. But I am suggesting that the values, cultural perceptions, emotions, and traditions that inflect our perceptions and interactions with nonhuman species always have to be an explicit part of conversations about conservation, and that thinking about the construction of new, functional multispecies habitats may be a more productive and democratic goal to invest our energies in than the attempt to recreate the habitats of the past.

Taking a detailed look at the stories and images we use to think about conservation and endangered species is part of what it takes to achieve such a reorientation. The chapters of this book contribute to such a critical analysis of stories, photos, films, paintings, musical compositions, and other works of art, but also of the databases and legal texts in which collective concerns about endangered species express themselves in a range of cultures and societies around the world. The cultural meanings of endangered species and the values that are attached to biodiversity resemble each other across cultures in some respects and differ fundamentally in other respects, for reasons that I have outlined across the different parts of this analysis. While dedicated conservationists may wish that particular species as well as biodiversity at large might come to be valued purely for their own sake, I have tried to show that they usually come to matter when they become associated with stories that particular cultures tell about their own origins, history, modernization, and futures, as well as about their relation to a broader "humanity," to different humans, and to the species that form part of the understanding of human identity in particular cultural contexts. The movement to integrate conservation with multispecies justice has to build on a thorough understanding of how the cultural communities who are stakeholders in a particular ecosystem map their own species understanding and their relations to other species, and how other species might function symbolically in narratives that may not primarily be "about" animals, plants, or nature. The goal, then, is to understand how endangered species and extinctions mean—that is, to go beyond understanding *what* they mean ecologically toward understanding *how* they mean culturally. The future of endangered species and of biodiversity conservation is not, in the end, just a matter of science, but also and mainly one of histories, cultures, and values.

Coda: The Hug of the Polar Bear

In September 2010, the carmaker Nissan released a commercial to advertise one of its new products, the all-electric Leaf. The commercial starts with shots that had already become iconic by then: slabs of ice sliding off an arctic wall and a polar bear lying on a drifting ice floe, face and body posture suggesting deep melancholy. But then the bear swims to shore, walks through a boreal forest, traverses agricultural landscapes, passes under a highway, crosses an urban intersection at night, and in the morning walks through a suburban street up to a man who is just unlocking a Nissan Leaf in his driveway. Startled, the man turns around as the polar bear emerges from behind his car, stands up on its hind legs and puts its front paws around his neck in a warm ursine embrace, into which the eco-conscious commuter relaxes with a smile.

An appeal to green values in advertising is nothing new, of course, and manufacturers of all sorts have often appropriated environmentalist tropes to sell products that have a legitimate claim to sustainability or to distract attention from those that do not. But Nissan's polar bear ad did attract a considerable amount of attention over time, to the point where the carmaker has posted a "making of" video on its website to show how the commercial was filmed. What makes the ad interesting to watch even years after its first appearance is the way it upends familiar motifs of both car advertising and environmentalist portrayals of climate change. One of the most common fantasies car commercials sell is that a particular car will put its owners in touch with nature, which is why so many of these commercials feature a sleekly designed automobile rolling through stunning landscapes with no company, it appears, from other motorists—the handsome loner in the wilderness, only this time in a metallic shell. The Nissan Leaf ad, by contrast, never shows the car going anywhere. It simply sits in its suburban driveway until the most remote nature comes to join it all on its own—no doubt a humorous send-up of other carmakers on Nissan's part so as to shift the question of automobilists' connection to nature from the scenery they visit to the scenery they destroy and might preserve.

Melting Arctic ice and the polar bear drifting forlornly on an ice floe are staple elements of climate change discourse that Nissan takes up here to foreground just what and whom the burning of fossil fuels affects. And in fact these images at the beginning of the ad were taken from stock footage, according to the "making of" video. But in contrast to the more common portrayal in documentaries, the polar bear here takes agency and begins to walk south. The polar bear's purposeful journey, embarked on with consummate ease by the female bear Aggie, a veteran film actress, leads from wild to more and more human-made, technological, and urban settings. Not only does the bear know how to handle such artificial environments self-confidently—we see her resting after just having used a wildlife freeway underpass, she stays on the right as trucks pass her on a rural route, and she navigates an urban intersection using the pedestrian crossing—she also voices her opinions by roaring disapprovingly at passing trucks (presumably in protest at their fossil fuel burning). In the process, she metamorphoses from a wild to an urban animal and finally into an anthropomorphic sort of pet. During her night in the city, she exchanges quick glances with a raccoon who comes to drink at the same puddle—another wild animal, but one who has made urban environments its home. She spends some time enjoying the urban skyline by moonlight, like a visiting tourist. Walking along a rail line, she stands up on her hind legs and playfully greets a butterfly, looking a bit like an oversized cat, and of course she repeats this gesture in the climactic hug. We can read the bear's journey as an allegory of the Anthropocene, which "domesticates" animals in even the remotest areas by way of ubiquitous human impacts, or conversely of nature moving in on humans even in the most artificial environments, in the form of images and stories if not always in the flesh. The final hug self-consciously plays on clichéd linguistic tropes—the bear hug—as well as the stereotypical environmentalist reconciliation with nature. Only this time it is not humans who go to hug trees, but an Arctic predator who goes on a journey to hug a human right at his home.

That Nissan's playful and partly ironic send-up of familiar images would prominently feature a polar bear is in some sense no surprise. Perhaps no other species has received as much public attention over the past decade: polar bears have featured prominently in and on many environmental organizations' accessories, calendars, commodities, and promotional materials. With 20,000 to 25,000 individuals distributed over nineteen different populations around the Arctic, the polar bear has become one of the flagship species of conservation. Yet its symbolism differs from that of many of the other species I have discussed in this book in that it is not tied to a particular national or cultural community, but usually signals global ecological crisis. Starting with a campaign by the Center for Biological Diversity to have the polar bear listed as endangered under the U.S. Endangered Species Act in 2005 and its appearance—oddly, in an animated rather than a documentary sequence—in Al Gore's film *An Inconvenient Truth* in 2006, *Ursus maritimus* has featured as the charismatic animal spokesperson for climate change (Mooallem 2013, 53). And that is of course the reason for its appearance in the Nissan ad.

Polar bears split off evolutionarily from grizzly bears 150,000 to 200,000 years ago (Lindqvist et al. 2010) to become highly specialized carnivores who feed mostly on ringed and bearded seals. They typically prey on seals on sea ice, either at the breathing holes where the seals come up for air or on broken ice that seals climb onto. As a consequence of global warming, the periods with reduced sea ice are becoming longer and have led to feeding crises for polar bears and gruesome images of starving cubs. The image of the solitary polar bear on a shrinking ice floe, invoked at the beginning of the Nissan commercial, has become the icon of coming extinctions as one of the catastrophic consequences of climate change.

The polar bear, of course, fits well into the gallery of charismatic mammalian predators that generally dominate in representations of extinction. Beyond the photogenic appeal of adults majestically trotting across the ice and cuddly cubs playing in the snow around their mother, the white animal in a white landscape symbolizes an ideal vision of nature: pristine habitat, perfect adaptation. Jon Mooallem has brilliantly traced the evolution of the polar bear's cultural image from bloodthirsty predator in the 1980s to innocent victim of "the violence of climate change, which is otherwise slow and abstract" by about 2005, a change in public perception that has prompted conservation efforts and tourist interest that from Mooallem's perspective are both admirable and absurd (2013, 94). In the early twenty-first century, the polar bear as the symbol of climate change and the Anthropocene joins the dodo as the first species terminated due to modernization and colonization, and the oiled seabird as an icon of generalized environmental crisis (cf. Ross 1994, 166). The cultural meanings of all three species are not keyed to a particular community so much as to the planet as a whole.

But that the meaning of the polar bear is perceived as global by the European and American public does not imply that this perception is shared across cultural contexts. In 2010 the Nunavuk-based film director Zacharias Kunuk and his codirector Ian Mauro released the documentary *Qapirangajuq: Inuit Knowledge and Climate Change*, which presents an almost hour-long collage of conversations with Inuit men and women from different generations and communities. Without any editorial comment, the interviewees present their observations on recent changes in weather, wildlife behavior, and their own everyday practices. A sense of memory, worry, and anxiety pervades many of these comments—but, interestingly, not those referring to the polar bear. Several of the interviewees highlight that "bears are everywhere," according to their observations. Joanasie Karpik, one of the interviewees, comments: "When I was growing up, as a young man, there were no bears around. Today, the bear population is everywhere. We can now say that the polar bear population is expanding. The population is increasing everywhere. You can now see bears where you never saw them before." Another interviewee, Inookie Adamie, concurs that "the polar bear and raven populations have dramatically increased." Jaipitty Palluq points out what a European or American observer would likely consider the cause for what the Inuit perceive as an increase in total numbers: "Due to climate change, the floating ice is melting and bears are forced to come ashore. Bears are now visible everywhere on the land. Even inland. It was not like this before."

The new presence of polar bears is not something the Inuit welcome: as several of them point out, they have to travel armed, cache walrus meat near their cabins, and generally be wary of polar bears' presence during outdoor activities that used to be free of fear. But several of the interviewees make it clear that they do not consider climate change the root of the problem. Abraham Ulayuruluk reasons that "even with no ice, bears should be able to manage." An Inuit woman, Tagga Manik, similarly affirms: "We still have lots of ice, but even with open water, this has yet to be a problem for the bear and doesn't affect its hunting. In my opinion, climate change is not adversely affecting bears today."

And Noah Metuq, another interviewee, confirms: "Those who believe the polar bear population is declining, and place it on the endangered species list, they don't understand, in my opinion. Polar bears cannot be in danger. Even if at sea for a long time, they are not in danger. Because their natural environment is the sea." The Inuit knowledge the title alludes to here begins to diverge from what most polar bear specialists in the scientific establishments of Canada, Europe, and the United States assert—that diminished sea ice does present a significant threat to a highly specialized species whose environment, in the scientists' opinion, is changing too fast for them to adapt.

Instead of climate change, quite a few of the interviewees identify "Southerners" who meddle with the animals by anesthetizing, tagging, and collaring them as the real problem. Jamesie Mike, for example, argues that "bears that are tagged and handled act more aggressively. Bears that are tampered with will break into cabins and destroy snowmobiles. But it's not local hunters who handled them. . . . Sometimes, it is said they are few in numbers, but here in the Arctic many are out of sight in their dens." Inusiq Nashalik concurs: "They've been so disturbed and are going everywhere and starving. They are constantly tampered with, by Southerners, who only know them by what they read, and have never interacted with them. We know our wildlife intimately." Abraham Ulayuruluk pinpoints techniques of wildlife counting and tracking as the cause of the problem: "All the drugging, being put to sleep, ear tags affect their hearing. All this meddling is causing problems and making bears malnourished. They're no longer afraid of Inuit. I believe these issues are caused by wildlife biologists." Nathaniel Kalluk points to another technological cause for the bears' lack of food: "Wildlife biologists put radio collars on bears, the effects are horrible. Many times I've seen skinny bears, obviously starving to death, because of the radio collar. The polar bear's neck is long for a reason, it enables hunting seals at their breathing holes. When they are collared, they are unable to hunt properly." And Simon Idlout adds: "This tranquilizing and use of helicopters is terrible. Today bears are approaching and entering our communities. Why? They cannot hear. They inhabit a silent world and helicopters are damaging their hearing. It's the helicopters! . . . Polar bears grow up in near silence and their ears are very sensitive. . . . I'm not concerned about bears being harmed by climate change. Scientists often worry about polar bears, saying they will have difficulties. Bears hunt better in summer and gain more fat at this time. They can detect and hunt seals easier in water."

A risk perception quite different from that of the typical conservationist emerges here: what endangers the polar bears is not climate change and population decline but the constant interference of wildlife biologists who are newcomers to the region. "Scientists say with great authority: 'Polar bears are in decline and will go extinct,'" Metuq points out. "When I am out hunting, I never see these scientists. Not even one!" In comments such as these, indigenous firsthand knowledge of the local wildlife clashes with science, which quite a few of the interviewees see as secondhand knowledge gleaned from books and labs that has little traction in the real Arctic.

Some of these observations are uttered with a palpable sense of anger and impatience at outsiders who not only misdiagnose the local ecology and cause problems that would not arise or have only minor importance without their interference, but who also condescend to those who have always known and lived with polar bears. Rita Nashook, who identifies herself as an animal rights activist, explicitly expresses this indignation at being patronized: "Inuit are lectured: 'They're endangered animals, you must not hunt them!' Inuit do not endanger animals! It's Southerners, meddling with caribou, polar bears and whales that endanger wildlife! This handling and tagging is what harms animals! Wildlife biologists are the ones endangering wildlife! Then they suspect Inuit overharvesting as the cause. We are told: 'You must not touch protected animals.' Inuit do not endanger animals, nor do they cause needless suffering. We love our animals."

The polar bear's symbolic role as the paradigmatic victim of climate change vanishes in this comment. Instead, the bear turns into a symbol of struggle over cultural and political sovereignty. Who knows local wildlife? Who has the right to determine appropriate interactions with wildlife, and the authority to tell others how to live with it? From the Inuit perspective, the polar bear is not a symbol of global ecological crisis but of trouble caused by "Southerners"—Westerners and their ignorance and colonial intrusion into Inuit communities. The real species that is everywhere, out of place, and dangerously invasive is conservationists rather than polar bears, from this perspective, and the bears themselves are just symptoms of this intrusive white presence.

My point in highlighting this viewpoint in Kunuk's film is not to settle arguments like these but to foreground that such divergent cultural meanings are the stuff of living in multispecies communities. Multispecies justice has to define itself with these different cultural framings in mind. The species that, from a Euro-American perspective, most seems to transcend its local environment to signal the urgency of global ecological crisis turns out to have a quite different and far less transcendently planetary meaning in the local environment itself. What justice means to polar bears, to Inuit societies, to conservationists and scientists, and to publics far from the Arctic has to be negotiated with these different frameworks in mind.

Juxtaposing Inuits' view of the polar bear with the Nissan Leaf commercial foregrounds that, for all of the obvious striking differences between the two kinds of discourse about the plight of the polar bear, they share the motif of a species that is asserting a new presence in the human realm. In contrast to more conventional extinction narratives, in which the endangered species is harder and harder to find and see, the animal here makes its presence felt in the human space in a new way because of its endangerment. For the Inuit, the bears' visits to their villages are a cause for anxiety. The fact that the bears have changed their behavior patterns is in and of itself disturbing, and it poses palpable risks to humans. Jaipitty Palluq points out that the Inuit can no longer stash walrus meat far away from their cabins for fear that polar bears will find and eat it. An elderly Inuit woman, Evie Anilnilliak, indicates that the bears' omnipresence is frightening to her. And Anookie Adams mentions that he now always carries a gun when he travels anywhere. The Nissan commercial hints at such fears in the moment before the hug, when the Leaf driver looks momentarily startled and frightened at the appearance of the bear, only to turn the final embrace into a self-conscious and humorous symbol of new solidarity and conviviality between species. In either case, polar bears have come home—not to their own, but to humans'.

By pointing out this parallel, I do not mean to minimize the stark differences between an indigenous documentary and a corporate ad. But precisely by giving quite different meanings to a charismatic species' coming home to humans, these two perspectives on the polar bear highlight the difficulties and the potential of multispecies justice as a way of thinking about biodiversity conservation—a framework that foregrounds how cultural, political, and economic differences shape our thinking and talking about how species should live together as much as biological and ecological differences do. If stories about endangered species can bring them home in such a way that these differences can be expressed and negotiated with a view toward finding justice across different humans and different species, they will have accomplished their task.

Works Cited

Ackerman, Diane. 1995. *The Rarest of the Rare: Vanishing Animals, Timeless Worlds*. New York: Vintage.

———. 2014. *The Human Age: The World Shaped by Us*. New York: Norton.

Adams, Douglas, and Mark Carwardine. 1990. *Last Chance to See*. New York: Ballantine.

Adams, William M. 2005. *Against Extinction: The Story of Conservation*. London: Earthscan.

Adams, William M., and Jon Hutton. 2007. "People, Parks and Poverty: Political Ecology and Biodiversity Conservation." *Conservation and Society* 5:147–183.

Agamben, Giorgio. 1998. *Homo Sacer: Sovereign Power and Bare Life*. Translated by Daniel Heller-Roazen. Stanford, CA: Stanford University Press.

Agrawal, Arun, and Kent Redford. 2009. "Conservation and Displacement: An Overview." *Conservation and Society* 7:1–10. http://conservationandsociety.org/temp/ConservatSoc711 -7220861_200328.pdf.

Alagona, Peter S. 2013. *After the Grizzly: Endangered Species and the Politics of Place in California*. Berkeley: University of California Press.

Anderson, Elizabeth. 2004. "Animal Rights and the Values of Nonhuman Life." In *Animal Rights: Current Debates and New Directions*, edited by Cass R. Sunstein and Martha C. Nussbaum, 277–298. Oxford: Oxford University Press.

Angier, Natalie. 2009. "New Creatures in an Age of Extinctions." *New York Times*, July 26. www.nytimes.com/2009/07/26 /weekinreview/26angier.html.

———. 2014. "That Cuddly Kitty Is Deadlier Than You Think." *New York Times*, January 29. www.nytimes.com/2013/01/30/science/that-cuddly-kitty -of-yours-is-a-killer.html?_r=0.

Aridjis, Homero. 1990. "Nueva expulsión del paraíso." In *Imágenes para el fin del milenio & Nueva expulsión del paraíso*, 119–122. Mexico City: Joaquín Mortiz.

Atwood, Margaret. 2003. *Oryx and Crake*. New York: Anchor Books.

———. *The Year of the Flood*. (2009) 2010. Reprint, New York: Nan A. Talese/ Doubleday.

———. *MaddAddam*. (2009) 2013. New York: Nan A. Talese/Doubleday.

Auerbach, Eric. (1953) 2003. *Mimesis: The Representation of Reality in Western Thought*. Translated by Willard R. Trask. Reprint, Princeton, NJ: Princeton University Press.

Bailey, Col. 2001. *Tiger Tales: Stories of the Tasmanian Tiger*. Sydney, Australia: HarperCollins.

Baillie, Jonathan E. M., Craig Hilton-Taylor, and Simon N. Stuart, eds. 2004. *2004 IUCN Red List of Threatened Species: A Global Species Assessment*. Gland, Switzerland: IUCN.

Bakhtin, M. M. (1975) 1981. "Epic and Novel." In *The Dialogic Imagination: Four Essays by M. M. Bakhtin*, edited by Michael Holquist, translated by Caryl Emerson and Michael Holquist, 3–40. Reprint, Austin: University of Texas Press.

Balvanera, Patricia, Ilyas Siddique, Laura Dee, et al. 2014. "Linking Biodiversity and Ecosystem Services: Current Uncertainties and the Necessary Next Steps." *BioScience* 64:49–57. http://bioscience.oxfordjournals.org/content/64 /1/49.

Barrow, Mark V., Jr. 2009. *Nature's Ghosts: Confronting Extinction from the Age of Jefferson to the Age of Ecology*. Chicago: University of Chicago Press.

Barthes, Roland. (1957) 1972. "The Great Family of Man." In *Mythologies*, translated by Annette Lavers, 100–102. Reprint, New York: Noonday.

Beck, Ulrich. 1986. *Risikogesellschaft: Auf dem Weg in eine andere Moderne*. Frankfurt, Germany: Suhrkamp.

Beresford, Quentin, and Garry Bailey. 1981. *Search for the Tasmanian Tiger*. Hobart, Tasmania, Australia: Blubber Head Press.

Black, George. 2012. *Empire of Shadows: The Epic Story of Yellowstone*. New York: St. Martin's Press.

Bowker, Geoffrey C. (2005) 2008. *Memory Practices in the Sciences*. Reprint, Cambridge, MA: MIT Press.

Boyle, Thomas Coraghessan. 2011. *When the Killing's Done*. New York: Penguin.

Brand, Stewart. (2009) 2011. *Whole Earth Discipline: Why Dense Cities, Nuclear Power, Transgenic Crops, Restored Wildlands, and Geoengineering Are Necessary*. Reprint, New York: Viking Penguin.

Braverman, Irus. 2015. *Wild Life: The Institution of Nature*. Stanford, CA: Stanford University Press.

Brayard, Arnaud, Gilles Escarguel, Hugo Bucher, et al. 2009. "Good Genes and Good Luck: Ammonoid Diversity and the End-Permian Mass Extinction." *Science* 325:1118–1121.

Brockington, Dan. 2002. *Fortress Conservation: The Preservation of the Mkomazi Game Reserve, Tanzania*. Oxford: International African Institute.

Brower, David R. 1981a. "The Condor and a Sense of Place." In *The Condor Question: Captive or Forever Free?*, edited by David Phillips and Hugh Nash, 265–278. San Francisco: Friends of the Earth.

———. 1981b. "An Exchange with Russell Peterson." In *The Condor Question: Captive or Forever Free?*, edited by David Phillips and Hugh Nash, 251–264. San Francisco: Friends of the Earth.

Brower, Kenneth. 1981. "Night of the Condor." In *The Condor Question: Captive or Forever Free?*, edited by David Phillips and Hugh Nash, 29–35. San Francisco: Friends of the Earth.

Buell, Lawrence. 2001. *Writing for an Endangered World: Literature, Culture and Environment in the U.S. and Beyond*. Cambridge, MA: Harvard University Press.

Bullard, Robert D. (1990) 2000. *Dumping in Dixie: Race, Class, and Environmental Quality*, 3rd ed. Boulder: Westview Press.

Bundesamt für Naturschutz. 2015. *Artenschutz-Report 2015: Tiere und Pflanzen in Deutschland*. Edited by F. Emde, B. Jessel, R. Schedlbauer, et al. Bonn, Germany: Bundesamt für Naturschutz, 2015.

Burroughs, William. (1991) 2002. *Ghost of Chance*. Reprint, London: Serpent's Tail.

Butler, Judith. 2004. *Precarious Life: The Powers of Mourning and Violence*. London: Verso.

Callicott, J. Baird. 1989. *In Defense of the Land Ethic*. Albany: State University of New York Press.

Card, Orson Scott. (1985) 1991a. *Ender's Game*. Rev. ed. New York: Tor.

———. 1986. *Speaker for the Dead*. New York: Tor.

———. 1991b. *Xenocide*. New York: Tor.

———. (1992) 1996. *Children of the Mind*. Reprint, New York: Tor.

Cardinale, Bradley J., J. Emmett Duffy, Andrew Gonzalez, et al. 2012. "Biodiversity Loss and Its Impact on Humanity." *Nature* 486:59–67.

Carwardine, Mark. 2009. *Last Chance to See: In the Footsteps of Douglas Adams*. London: HarperCollins.

Ceballos, Gerardo, Paul R. Ehrlich, Anthony D. Barnosky, et al. 2015. "Accelerated Human-Induced Species Losses: Entering the Sixth Mass Extinction." *Science Advances* 1. http://advances.sciencemag.org/content/1/5/e1400253.

CEM-IUCN & Provita. 2012. *IUCN Red List of Ecosystems*. The Commission on Ecosystem Management (CEM) of the International Union for Conservation of Nature (IUCN) and Provita, Caracas, Venezuela. www.iucnredlistofecosystems.org.

Center for Biological Diversity. 2014. "The Endangered Species Act: A Wild Success." www.biologicaldiversity.org/campaigns/esa_wild_success/.

Chakrabarty, Dipesh. 2009. "The Climate of History: Four Theses." *Critical Inquiry* 35:197–222.

———. 2012. "Postcolonial Studies and the Challenge of Climate Change." *New Literary History* 43:1–18.

Challenger, Melanie. 2011. *On Extinction: How We Became Estranged from Nature*. London: Granta.

Chatty, Dawn, and Marcus Colchester, eds. 2002. *Conservation and Mobile Indigenous Peoples: Displacement, Forced Settlement and Sustainable Development*. New York: Berghahn.

Chrulew, Matthew. 2011. "Managing Love and Death at the Zoo: The Biopolitics of Endangered Species Preservation." *Australian Humanities Review* 50:137–157.

Clark, Nigel. 2011. *Inhuman Nature: Sociable Life on a Dynamic Planet*. London: Sage.

Coetzee, J. M. 2001. *The Lives of Animals*. Princeton, NJ: Princeton University Press.

———. (2003) 2004. *Elizabeth Costello*. Reprint, New York: Penguin.

Cohen, Michael P. 1988. *The History of the Sierra Club, 1892–1970*. San Francisco: Sierra Club Books.

Cokinos, Chris. 2000. *Hope Is the Thing with Feathers: A Personal Chronicle of Vanished Birds*. New York: Tarcher/Penguin.

Commission of the European Communities v. Federal Republic of Germany. 2006. Case C-98/03. http://curia.europa.eu/juris/liste.jsf?language=en&num=C-98/03.

Constitución política del Estado. 2009. In *Political Database of the Americas*, edited by Edmund A. Walsh School of Foreign Service, Center for Latin American Studies, Georgetown University. http://pdba.georgetown.edu/Constitutions/Bolivia/bolivia09.html.

Corwin, Jeff. 2009. *100 Heartbeats: The Race to Save the World's Most Endangered Species*. New York: Rodale.

Costello, Mark J., Robert M. May, and Nigel E. Stork. 2013a. "Can We Name Earth's Species before They Go Extinct?" *Science* 339:413–416. www.sciencemag.org/content/339/6118/413.full.

———. 2013b. "Response to Comments on 'Can We Name Earth's Species before They Go Extinct?'" *Science* 341:237-d. www.sciencemag.org/content/341/6143/237.4.full.

Council of the European Communities. 1979. *Council Directive 79/409/EEC of 2 April 1979 on the Conservation of Wild Birds*. http://eur-lex.europa.eu/legal-content/EN/TXT/?uri=celex:31979L0409.

———. 1992. *Council Directive 92/43/EEC of 21 May 1992 on the Conservation of Natural Habitats and of Wild Fauna and Flora*. http://eur-lex.europa.eu/legal-content/EN/TXT/?uri=CELEX:31992L0043.

Cowan, Edward. 1971. "Baby Seal Hunt Is On Again, and So Is Dispute." *New York Times*, March 18, 41, 43. http://timesmachine.nytimes.com/timesmachine/1971/03/18/82000256.html?pageNumber=41.

Crocker, Scott, director. 2009. *Ghost Bird*. Berkeley: Small Change.

Cronon, William. 1995. "The Trouble with Wilderness; or, Getting Back to the Wrong Nature." In *Uncommon Ground: Rethinking the Human Place in Nature*, edited by William Cronon, 69–90. New York: Norton.

Crosby, Alfred. (1972) 2003. *The Columbian Exchange: Biological and Cultural Consequences of 1492*. 30th anniversary ed. Westport, CT: Praeger.

Crutzen, Paul J. 2002. "Geology of Mankind." *Nature* 415:23.

Crutzen, Paul J., and Eugene F. Stoermer. 2000. "The 'Anthropocene.'" *Global Change Newsletter* 41:17–18.

Culler, Jonathan. 1981. "Apostrophe." In *The Pursuit of Signs: Semiotics, Literature, Deconstruction*, 135–154. Ithaca, NY: Cornell University Press.

Daszkiewicz, Piotr, and Jean Aikhenbaum. 1999. *Aurochs, le retour . . . d'une supercherie nazie*. Paris: H.S.T.E.S.

Davis, Karen. 2005. *The Holocaust & the Henmaid's Tale*. New York: Lantern Books.

Davis, Mark A., Matthew K. Chew, and Richard J. Hobbs, et al. 2011. "Don't Judge Species on Their Origins." *Nature* 474:153–154. www.nature.com /nature/journal/v474/n7350/full/474153a.html.

De la Cadena, Marisol. 2010. "Indigenous Cosmopolitics in the Andes: Conceptual Reflections Beyond 'Politics.'" *Cultural Anthropology* 25:334–370.

Derrida, Jacques. 2006. *L'animal que donc je suis*. Paris: Galilée.

———. 2008. *The Animal That Therefore I Am*. Edited by Marie-Louise Mallet and translated by David Wills. New York: Fordham University Press.

Despret, Vinciane. 2006. "Anthropo-éthologie des non-humains politiques." *Information sur les Sciences Sociales* 45:209–226. http://ssi.sagepub.com /content/45/2/209.

Deutscher Rat für Landespflege. 1961. *Grüne Charta von der Mainau*. www .landespflege.de/ziele/#charta.

De Vos, Ricardo. 2007. "Extinction Stories: Performing Absence(s)." In *Knowing Animals*, edited by Laurence Simmons and Philip Armstrong, 183–195. Boston: Brill.

Dibley, Ben. 2012. "'Nature Is Us': The Anthropocene and Species-Being." *Transformations* 21. www.transformationsjournal.org/journal/issue_21/article_07 .shtml.

Dillard, Carter. 2013. "Environmentalism as a Form of Animal Rights." Animal Legal Defense Fund: Winning the Case against Cruelty, http://aldf.org/blog /environmentalism-as-a-form-of-animal-rights/.

Domico, Terry. 2005. *The Last Thylacine*. Friday Harbor, Washington: Turtleback Books.

Donlan, C. Josh, Joel Berger, and Carl E. Bock, et al. 2006. "Pleistocene Rewilding: An Optimistic Agenda for Twenty-First Century Conservation." *American Naturalist* 168:660–681.

Doremus, Holly. 2010. "The Endangered Species Act: Static Law Meets Dynamic World." *Washington University Journal of Law & Policy* 32:175–235.

Dowie, Mark. 2009. *Conservation Refugees: The Hundred-Year Conflict between Global Conservation and Native Peoples*. Cambridge, MA: MIT Press.

Duffey, Eric. 1964. "The Terrestrial Ecology of Ascension Island." *Journal of Applied Ecology* 1:219–251.

Eco, Umberto. 2009. *The Infinity of Lists*. Translated by Alastair McEwen. New York: Rizzoli.

Ehrlich, Paul, and Anne Ehrlich. 1981. *Extinction: The Causes and Consequences of the Disappearance of Species*. New York: Ballantine.

————. 2004. *One with Nineveh: Politics, Consumption, and the Human Future*. Washington, DC: Island Press.

Ellis, Erle C., and Navin Ramankutty. 2008. "Putting People in the Map: Anthropogenic Biomes of the World." *Frontiers in Ecology and the Environment* 6:439–447. www.esajournals.org/doi/full/10.1890/070062. DOI 10.1890/070062.

Endangered Species Act of 1973. 1973. Public Law 93-205, December 28, 1973. www.gpo.gov/fdsys/pkg/STATUTE-87/pdf/STATUTE-87-Pg884.pdf.

Endangered Species Preservation Act of 1966. 1966. Public Law 89-669, October 15, 1966. http://uscode.house.gov/statutes/pl/89/669.pdf.

Estes, James A. 1991. "Catastrophes and Conservation: Lessons from Sea Otters and the *Exxon Valdez*." *Science* 254:1596. DOI: 10.1126/science.254.5038.1596.

European Commission. 2015. *The State of Nature in the European Union: Report on the Status of and Trends for Habitat Types and Species Covered by the Birds and Habitats Directives for the 2007–2012 Period as Required under Article 17 of the Habitats Directive and Article 12 of the Birds Directive*. Brussels: European Commission. http://eur-lex.europa.eu/legal-content/EN/TXT/?uri=COM:2015:219:FIN.

Faulkner, William. (1942) 1991. *Go Down, Moses*. Reprint, New York: Vintage.

Ferraro, Paul J., Craig McIntosh, and Monica Ospina. 2007. "The Effectiveness of the US Endangered Species Act: An Econometric Analysis Using Matching Methods." *Journal of Environmental Economics and Management* 54:245–261.

Fischer, Ludwig. 2003. "Die 'Urlandschaft' und ihr Schutz." In *Naturschutz und Nationalsozialismus*, edited by Joachim Radkau and Frank Uekötter, 183–205. Frankfurt, Germany: Campus.

Fitzpatrick, John W., Martjan Lammertink, M. David Luneau Jr., et al. 2005. "Ivory-billed Woodpecker (*Campephilus principalis*) Persists in Continental North America." *Science* 308:1460–1462.

Flannery, Tim, and Peter Schouten. 2001. *A Gap in Nature: Discovering the World's Extinct Animals*. New York: Atlantic Monthly Press.

Flegenheimer, Matt. 2015. "New York City Escalates the War on Rats Once Again." *New York Times*, June 24. www.nytimes.com/2015/06/25/nyregion/new-york-city-escalates-the-war-on-rats-once-again.html?_r=04.

Foer, Jonathan Safran. 2009. *Eating Animals*. New York: Little, Brown.

Francione, Gary. 1995. *Animals, Property, and the Law*. Philadelphia: Temple University Press.

————. 2008. *Animals as Persons: Essays on the Abolition of Animal Exploitation*. New York: Columbia University Press.

Frenz, Lothar. 2012. *Lonesome George oder Das Verschwinden der Arten*. Berlin: Rowohlt.

Fuller, Erroll. 1987. *Extinct Birds*. New York: Facts on File.

————. 2001. *Extinct Birds*. Rev. ed. Ithaca, NY: Comstock.

Gadgil, Madhav, and Ramachandra Guha. 1995. *Ecology and Equity: The Use and Abuse of Nature in Contemporary India*. London: Routledge.

Gallagher, Tim. 2005. *The Grail Bird: Hot on the Trail of the Ivory-Billed Woodpecker*. Boston: Houghton Mifflin.

Galtung, Johan. 1969. "Violence, Peace, and Peace Research." *Journal of Peace Research* 6:167–191.

Gammage, Bill. 2011. *The Biggest Estate on Earth: How Aborigines Made Australia*. Sydney, Australia: Allen & Unwin.

García Ureta, Agustín. 2007. "Habitats Directive and Environmental Assessment of Plans and Projects." *Journal of European Environmental Law* 2:84–96.

Gärdenfors, Ulf, Craig Hilton-Taylor, Georgina M. Mace, et al. 2001. "The Application of IUCN Red List Criteria at Regional Levels." *Conservation Biology* 15:1206–1212.

Garrard, Greg. 2004. *Ecocriticism*. London: Routledge.

———. 2012. "Worlds without Us: Some Types of Disanthropy." *SubStance* 41:40–60.

Gassner, Erich, and Michael Heugel. 2010. *Das neue Naturschutzrecht*. Munich: Beck.

Geden, Oliver. 1995. *Rechte Ökologie: Umweltschutz zwischen Emanzipation und Faschismus*. Berlin: Elefanten Press.

Gerber, P. J., H. Steinfeld, B. Henderson, et al. 2013. *Tackling Climate Change through Livestock: A Global Assessment of Emissions and Mitigation Opportunities*. Rome: Food and Agriculture Organization of the United Nations (FAO). www.fao.org/docrep/018/i3437e/i3437e.pdf.

Gettleman, Jeffrey. 2012. "Elephants Dying in Epic Frenzy as Ivory Fuels Wars and Profits." *New York Times*, September 3. www.nytimes.com/2012/09/04/world/africa/africas-elephants-are-being-slaughtered-in-poaching-frenzy.html?pagewanted=all.

Ghosh, Amitav. (2005) 2006. *The Hungry Tide*. Reprint, Boston: Houghton Mifflin Harcourt.

Gigon, Andreas, Regula Langenauer, Claude Meier, et al. 2000. "Blue Lists of Threatened Species with Stabilized or Increasing Abundance: A New Instrument for Conservation." *Conservation Biology* 14:402–413.

Glavin, Terry. 2006. *The Sixth Extinction: Journeys among the Lost and Left Behind*. New York: Thomas Dunne.

Gleich, Michael, Dirk Maxeiner, Michael Miersch, et al., eds. 2002. *Life Counts: Cataloguing Life on Earth*. Translated by Steven Rendall. New York: Atlantic Monthly Press.

Godfrey, Matthew H., and Brendan J. Godley. 2008. "Seeing the Past Red: Flawed IUCN Global Listings for Sea Turtles." *Endangered Species Research* 5:155–159.

Goodall Jane, Thane Maynard, and Gail Hudson. 2009. *Hope for Animals and Their World: How Endangered Species Are Being Rescued from the Brink*. New York: Hachette.

Gorke, Martin. 1999. *Artensterben: Von der ökologischen Theorie zum Eigenwert der Natur*. Stuttgart: Klett Cotta.

Green, Tim, Ben Southwell, and John Paul Davidson, directors. 2009. *Last Chance to See: Animals on the Verge of Extinction*. DVD. BBC Wales/West Park Pictures.

Greenberg, Joel. 2014. *A Feathered River across the Sky: The Passenger Pigeon's Flight to Extinction*. New York: Bloomsbury.

Greive, Bradley Taylor. 2003. *Priceless: The Vanishing Beauty of a Fragile Planet*. Kansas City, MO: Andrew McMeel.

Grenyer, Richard C., David L. Orme, Sarah F. Jackson, et al. 2006. "Global Distribution and Conservation of Rare and Threatened Vertebrates." *Nature* 444:93–96.

Gruhl, Herbert. 1975. *Ein Planet wird geplündert: Die Schreckensbilanz unserer Politik*. Frankfurt, Germany: S. Fischer.

Grzimek, Bernhard, and Michael Grzimek. (1959) 2009. *Serengeti darf nicht sterben: 367000 Tiere suchen einen Staat*. Reprint, Munich: Piper/Malik/National Geographic.

Guha, Ramachandra. 1989. "Radical American Environmentalism and Wilderness Preservation: A Third World Critique." *Environmental Ethics* 11: 71–84.

Guha, Ramachandra, and Juan Martínez-Alier. 1997. *Varieties of Environmentalism: Essays North and South*. London: Earthscan.

Guiler, Eric R. 1985. *Thylacine: The Tragedy of the Tasmanian Tiger*. Melbourne: Oxford University Press.

Hall, Matthew. 2011. *Plants as Persons: A Philosophical Botany*. Albany: State University of New York Press.

Haraway, Donna J. (1984) 1991. "A Cyborg Manifesto: Science, Technology, and Socialist-Feminism in the Late Twentieth Century." Reprinted in *Simians, Cyborgs, and Women: The Reinvention of Nature*, 149–81. New York: Routledge.

———. 2003. *The Companion Species Manifesto: Dogs, People, and Significant Otherness*. Chicago: Prickly Paradigm Press.

———. 2008. *When Species Meet*. Minneapolis: University of Minnesota Press.

Hargrove, Eugene, ed. 1994. *The Animal Rights/Environmental Ethics Debate*. Albany: State University of New York Press.

Hartnett, Sonya. (1999) 2007. *Stripes of the Sidestep Wolf*. Reprint, Cambridge, MA: Candlewick Press.

Hayles, N. Katherine. 2007. "Narrative and Database: Natural Symbionts." *PMLA* 122:1603–1608.

Hearne, Vicki. 1986. *Adam's Task: Calling Animals by Name*. New York: Knopf.

Hecht, Susanna, and Alexander Cockburn. (1990) 2010. *The Fate of the Forest: Developers, Destroyers, and Defenders of the Amazon*. Reprint, Chicago: University of Chicago Press.

Heinrich Balcazar, Freddy, and Mario Ricardo Eguivar, eds. 1991. *El medio ambiente en la legislación boliviana: Recopilación de disposiciones legales, con una introducción de las ordenanzas dictadas en la colonia, 1574–1991*. La Paz, Bolivia: Editorial Calama.

Heise, Ursula K. 2003. "From Extinction to Electronics: Dead Frogs, Live Dinosaurs, and Electric Sheep." In *Zoontologies: The Question of the Animal*, edited by Cary Wolfe, 59–81. Minneapolis: University of Minnesota Press.

———. 2008. *Sense of Place and Sense of Planet: The Environmental Imagination of the Global*. New York: Oxford University Press.

————. 2010. "Lost Dogs, Last Birds, and Listed Species: Cultures of Extinction." *Configurations* 18:49–72.

————. 2011. "Martian Ecologies and the Future of Nature." *Twentieth-Century Literature* 57:447–471.

————. 2012. "The Invention of Eco-Futures." *Ecozon@* 3.2 (Fall): 1–10. http://dspace.uah.es/dspace/bitstream/handle/10017/20417/invention_Heise_eco zona_2012_N2.pdf?sequence=1.

Hermand, Jost. 1992. *Old Dreams of a New Reich: Volkish Utopias and National Socialism.* Translated by Paul Levesque and Stefan Soldovieri. Bloomington: Indiana University Press.

Hill, Geoffrey E. 2007. *Ivorybill Hunters: The Search for Proof in a Flooded Wilderness.* New York: Oxford University Press.

Hilton-Taylor, Craig, Caroline M. Pollock, Janice S. Chanson, et al. 2008. "State of the World's Species." In *Wildlife in a Changing World: An Analysis of the 2008 IUCN Red List of Threatened Species*, edited by Jean-Christophe Vié, Craig Hilton-Taylor, and Simon N. Stuart, 15–41. Gland, Switzerland: IUCN. www.iucnredlist.org/about/publications-links#Other_Red_List _Publications.

Hindery, Derrick. 2013. *From Enron to Evo: Pipeline Politics, Global Environmentalism, and Indigenous Rights in Bolivia.* Tucson: University of Arizona Press.

Hobbs, Richard J., Eric S. Higgs, and Carol Hall, eds. 2013. *Novel Ecosystems: Intervening in the New Ecological World Order.* Oxford: Wiley-Blackwell.

Hobbs, Richard J., Lauren M. Mallett, Paul R. Ehrlich, et al. 2011. "Intervention Ecology: Applying Ecological Science in the Twenty-first Century." *BioScience* 61:442–450.

Hoffmann, M., T. M. Brooks, G. A. B. da Fonseca, et al. 2008. "Conservation Planning and the IUCN Red List." *Endangered Species Research* 6:113–125.

Holljesiefken, Anke. 2007. *Die rechtliche Regulierung invasiver gebietsfremder Arten in Deutschland: Bestandsaufnahme und Bewertung.* Berlin: Springer.

Hoose, Phillip. 2004. *The Race to Save the Lord God Bird.* New York: Farrar, Straus and Giroux.

Huggan, Graham, and Helen Tiffin. 2010. *Postcolonial Ecocriticism: Literature, Animals, Environment.* London: Routledge.

Hughes, Jennifer, Gretchen C. Daily, and Paul Ehrlich. 1997. "Population Diversity: Its Extent and Extinction." *Science* 278:689–692.

————. 2000. "The Loss of Population Diversity and Why It Matters." In *Nature and Human Society: The Quest for a Sustainable World*, edited by Peter Raven, 71–83. Washington, DC: National Academy Press.

Hyla, Lee. 2006. "Wilson's Ivory-Bill." In *Wilson's Ivory-Bill.* CD. New York: Tzadik.

Imboden, C. 1987. "Green Lists instead of Red Books." *World Birdwatch* 9:2.

Imort, Michael. 2005. " 'Eternal Forest—Eternal *Volk*': The Rhetoric and Reality of National Socialist Forest Policy." In *How Green Were the Nazis? Nature, Environment, and Nation in the Third Reich*, edited by Franz-Josef Brüggemeier, Mark Cioc, and Thomas Zeller, 43–72. Athens: University of Georgia Press.

IUCN Red List Committee. 2013. *The IUCN Red List of Threatened Species Strategic Plan 2013–2020*, Version 1.0. www.iucnredlist.org/documents/red _list_strategic_plan_2013_2020.pdf.

IUCN Red List of Threatened Species. 2015. "Conservation Successes Over-shadowed by More Species Declines—IUCN Red List Update." June 23. www.iucnredlist.org/current-news.

IUCN Species Survival Commission. (2001) 2012. *IUCN Red List Categories and Criteria: Version 3.1.* 2nd ed. Gland, Switzerland, and Cambridge, UK: IUCN. http://jr.iucnredlist.org/documents/redlist_cats_crit_en.pdf.

Jablonski, David. 1993. "Mass Extinctions: New Answers, New Questions." In *The Last Extinction*, edited by Les Kaufman and Kenneth Mallory, 47–68. 2nd ed. Cambridge, MA: MIT Press.

Jackson, Jerome A. 2006. *In Search of the Ivory-Billed Woodpecker*. New York: Harper.

Jalais, A. 2005. "Dwelling on Morichjhanpi." *Economic and Political Weekly* 40:1757–1762. www.epw.in/special-articles/dwelling-morichjhanpi.html.

Jameson, Fredric. 2005. *Archaeologies of the Future: The Desire Called Utopia and Other Science Fictions.* London: Verso.

Jamieson, Dale. 2002. *Morality's Progress: Essays on Humans, Other Animals, and the Rest of Nature.* Oxford: Clarendon.

Jasper, James M., and Dorothy Nelkin. 1992. *The Animal Rights Crusade: The Growth of a Moral Protest.* New York: Free Press.

Johnson, Adam, and Tom Kealey, eds. 2009. *Virunga: Africa's Oldest National Park.* Written and illustrated by the members of the 2009 Stanford Graphic Novel Project. Stanford, CA: Stanford University. http://web.stanford.edu /group/cwstudents/graphicnovel/virunga.html.

Johnson, Barbara. 1987. "Apostrophe, Animation, and Abortion." In *A World of Difference*, 184–200. Baltimore: Johns Hopkins University Press.

Juniper, Tony. 2002. *Spix's Macaw: The Race to Save the World's Rarest Bird.* New York: Atria.

Kareiva, Peter, and Simon A. Levin, eds. 2003. *The Importance of Species: Perspectives on Expendability and Triage.* Princeton, NJ: Princeton University Press.

Kareiva, Peter, Sean Watts, Robert McDonald, et al. 2007. "Domesticated Nature: Shaping Landscapes and Ecosystems for Human Welfare." *Science* 316:1866–1869.

Kennedy, Pagan. 2012. "William Gibson's Future Is Now." *New York Times*, January 13. www.nytimes.com/2012/01/15/books/review/distrust-that-particular -flavor-by-william-gibson-book-review.html?pagewanted=all.

Kersten, Jens. 2014. *Das Anthropozän-Konzept: Kontrakt-Komposition-Konflikt.* Baden-Baden, Germany: Nomos.

Kirksey, Eben. 2012. "Living with Parasites in Palo Verde National Park." *Environmental Humanities* 1:23–55. http://environmentalhumanities.org/arch /vol1/EH1.3.pdf.

———, ed. 2014. *The Multispecies Salon.* Durham, NC: Duke University Press. Kindle edition.

Kirksey, Eben, and Stefan Helmreich. 2010. "The Emergence of Multispecies Ethnography." *Cultural Anthropology* 25:545–576.

Kirksey, Eben, Craig Schuetze, and Stefan Helmreich. 2014. "Introduction: Tactics of Multispecies Ethnography." In *The Multispecies Salon*, edited by Eben Kirksey. Durham, NC: Duke University Press. Kindle edition.

Knight, John. 1997. "On the Extinction of the Japanese Wolf." *Asian Folklore Studies* 56:129–159.

Kohn, Eduardo. 2013. *How Forests Think: Toward an Anthropology beyond the Human*. Berkeley: University of California Press.

Kolbert, Elizabeth. 2014. *The Sixth Extinction: An Unnatural History*. New York: Henry Holt.

Körner, Stefan. 2000. *Das Heimische und das Fremde: Die Werte Vielfalt, Eigenart und Schönheit in der konservativen und der liberal-progressiven Naturschutzauffassung*. Münster: LIT.

———. 2003. "Kontinuum und Bruch: Die Transformation des naturschützerischen Aufgabenverständnisses nach dem Zweiten Weltkrieg." In *Naturschutz und Nationalsozialismus*, edited by Joachim Radkau and Frank Uekötter, 405–434. Frankfurt, Germany: Campus.

Kuhlmann, Walter. 1996. "Wildlife's Burden." In *Biodiversity and the Law*, edited by William J. Snape III, 189–201. Washington, DC: Island Press.

Kunuk, Zacharias, and Ian Mauro, directors. 2010. *Qapirangajuq: Inuit Knowledge and Climate Change*. N.p.: Igloolik Isuma Productions Inc. and Kunuk Cohn Productions. www.isuma.tv/inuit-knowledge-and-climate-change.

Latour, Bruno. (1991) 1993. *We Have Never Been Modern*. Translated by Catherine Porter. Reprint, Cambridge, MA: Harvard University Press.

———. (1999) 2004. *Politics of Nature: How to Bring the Sciences into Democracy*. Translated by Catherine Porter. Cambridge, MA: Harvard University Press.

Laurance, William F. 2013. "The Race to Name Earth's Species." *Science* 339 (March 15): 1275. www.sciencemag.org/content/339/6125/1275.1.full.

Lawton, John H., and Robert M. May, eds. 1995. *Extinction Rates*. Oxford: Oxford University Press.

Leakey, Richard, and Roger Lewin. 1995. *The Sixth Extinction: Patterns of Life and the Future of Humankind*. New York: Anchor.

Leigh, Julia. 1999. *The Hunter*. New York: Penguin.

Leopold, Aldo. (1949) 2001. *A Sand County Almanac: With Essays on Conservation*. Reprint, Oxford: Oxford University Press.

Lestel, Dominique, Florence Brunois, and Florence Gaunet. 2006. "Etho-ethnology and Ethno-ethology." *Social Science Information* 45:155–177. http://ssi.sagepub.com/content/45/2/155.

Lewis, Michael L. 2004. *Inventing Global Ecology: Tracking the Biodiversity Ideal in India, 1947–1997*. Athens: Ohio University Press.

Ley 71: Derechos de la Madre Tierra. 2010. In *LexiVox: Portal jurídico libre*. www.lexivox.org/norms/BO-L-N71.html.

Ley 300: Ley Marco de la Madre Tierra y Desarrollo Integral para Vivir Bien. 2012. In *LexiVox: Portal jurídico libre*. www.lexivox.org/norms/BO-L-300.xhtml.

Lin, Maya. 2010. What Is Missing? www.whatismissing.net.

Lindqvist, Charlotte, Stephan C. Schuster, Yazhou Sun, et al. 2010. "Complete Mitochondrial Genome of a Pleistocene Jawbone Unveils the Origin of the Polar Bear." *Proceedings of the National Academy of Sciences of the United States of America* 107:5053–5057.

Linse, Ulrich. 1986. *Ökopax und Anarchie: Eine Geschichte der ökologischen Bewegungen in Deutschland.* Munich: Deutscher Taschenbuch Verlag.

Loss, Scott R., Tom Will, and Peter Marra. 2013. "The Impact of Free-Ranging Domestic Cats on Wildlife of the United States." *Nature Communications,* January 29. www.nature.com/ncomms/journal/v4/n1/pdf/ncomms2380.pdf.

Louv, Richard. 2005. *Last Child in the Woods: Saving Our Children from Nature-Deficit Disorder.* Chapel Hill, NC: Algonquin.

Lowe, Celia. 2006. *Wild Profusion: Biodiversity Conservation in an Indonesian Archipelago.* Princeton, NJ: Princeton University Press.

Lukács, Georg. (1920) 1971. *The Theory of the Novel: A Historico-Philosophical Essay on the Forms of Great Epic Literature.* Translated by Anna Bostock. Reprint, Cambridge, MA: MIT Press.

Luck, Gary W., Gretchen C. Daily, and Paul Ehrlich. 2003. "Population Diversity and Ecosystem Services." *Trends in Ecology and Evolution* 18:331–336.

Lütkes, Stefan, ed. 2010. *Naturschutzrecht: Bundesnaturschutzgesetz, EG-Artenschutzverordnung, Bundesartenschutzverordnung, FHH-Richtlinie, Vogelschutzrichtlinie, Bundesjagdgesetz, Umweltschadensgesetz.* 11th ed. Munich: Deutscher Taschenbuch Verlag.

Maclaurin, James, and Kim Sterelny. 2008. *What Is Biodiversity?* Chicago: University of Chicago Press.

Maier, Donald S. 2012. *What's So Good about Biodiversity? A Call for Better Reasoning about Nature's Value.* Dordrecht: Springer.

Mann, Charles C. 2005. *1491: New Revelations of the Americas before Columbus.* New York: Vintage.

———. 2011. *1493: Uncovering the New World Columbus Created.* New York: Vintage.

Manovich, Lev. 2001. *The Language of New Media.* Cambridge, MA: MIT Press.

Marchesini, Roberto, and Sabrina Tonutti. 2007. *Manuale di zooantropologia.* Rome: Meltemi.

Marcone, Jorge. 2015. "Filming the Emergence of Popular Environmentalism in Latin America: Postcolonialism and Buen Vivir." In *Global Ecologies and the Environmental Humanities: Postcolonial Approaches,* edited by Elizabeth DeLoughrey, Jill Didur, and Anthony Carrigan, 207–225. New York: Routledge.

Marris, Emma. 2011. *Rambunctious Garden: Saving Nature in a Post-Wild World.* New York: Bloomsbury.

Marris, Emma, Peter Kareiva, Joseph Mascaro, et al. 2011. "Hope in the Age of Man." *New York Times,* December 7. www.nytimes.com/2011/12/08/opinion/the-age-of-man-is-not-a-disaster.html?_r=0.

Martin, Douglas. 1986. "Canada's Sealers Prepare for Reduced Hunt." *New York Times,* December 10. www.nytimes.com/1986/12/10/world/canada-s-sealers-prepare-for-reduced-hunt.html.

Marx, Leo. 2008. "The Idea of Nature in America." *Daedalus* 137.2 (Spring): 8–21.

Matthiessen, Peter. 2000. *Tigers in the Snow*. London: Harvill Press.

May, Robert. 1989. "How Many Species?" In *The Fragile Environment: The Darwin College Lectures*, edited by Laurie Friday and Ronald Laskey, 61–81. Cambridge: Cambridge University Press.

McGann, Jerome. 2007. "Database, Interface, and Archival Fever." *PMLA* 122:1588–1592.

McGurl, Mark. 2012. "The Posthuman Comedy." *Critical Inquiry* 38:533–553.

McIntyre, Sally. 2012a. *Collected Silences for Lord Rothschild*. http://every leafisanear.blogspot.co.nz/2011/04/collected-silences-for-lord-rothschild. html.

———. 2012b. *Huia Transcriptions*. http://everyleafisanear.blogspot.com/search ?q=huia+transcriptions.

McKibben, Bill. 1989. *The End of Nature*. New York: Anchor.

———. 2011. *Eaarth: Making a Life on a Tough New Planet*. New York: St. Martin's.

McKinnon, Dugal. 2013. "Dead Silence: Ecological Silencing and Environmentally Engaged Sound Art." *Leonardo Music Journal* 23:71–74.

McNee, Malcolm K. 2014. *The Environmental Imaginary in Brazilian Poetry and Art*. New York: Palgrave Macmillan.

Meeker, Joseph. (1974) 1997. *The Comedy of Survival: Literary Ecology and a Play Ethic*. 3rd ed. Tucson: University of Arizona Press.

Mérida, Gonzalo. 2004. "Estrategia boliviana de biodiversidad." In *Gobernabilidad Social de las Áreas Protegidas y Biodiversidad en Bolivia y Latinoamérica: Memoria del seminario realizado en Cochabamba del 26 al 29 de febrero de 2004*, edited by Freddy Delgado Burgoa and Juan Carlos Mariscal, 191–198. Cochabamba, Bolivia: AGRUCO Agroecología Universidad de Cochabamba.

Merwin, W. S. (1967) 2006. "For a Coming Extinction." Reprinted in *The Dire Elegies: 59 Poets on Endangered Species of North America*, edited by Karla Linn Merrifield and Roger M. Weir, 81. Kanona, NY: FootHills.

Middleton, Susan, and David Liittschwager. 1994. *Witness: Endangered Species of North America*. San Francisco: Chronicle Books.

———. (2001) 2003. *Remains of a Rainbow: Rare Plants and Animals of Hawaii*. Reprint, Washington, DC: National Geographic.

Midgley, Mary. 1983. *Animals and Why They Matter*. Athens: University of Georgia Press.

Miller, Rebecca, Jon Paul Rodríguez, Theresa Aniskowicz-Fowler, et al. 2007. "National Threatened Species Listing Based on IUCN Criteria and Regional Guidelines: Current Status and Future Perspectives." *Conservation Biology* 21:684–696.

Millet, Lydia. 2008. *How the Dead Dream*. Berkeley, CA: Counterpoint.

———. 2011. *Ghost Lights*. New York: Norton.

———. 2012. *Magnificence*. New York: Norton.

Mittelbach, Margaret, and Michael Crewdson. (2005) 2006. *Carnivorous Nights: On the Trail of the Tasmanian Tiger*. Reprint, New York: Villard.

Monbiot, George. 2014. *Feral: Rewilding the Land, the Sea, and Human Life.* Chicago: University of Chicago Press.

Montero, Mayra. 1995. *Tú, la oscuridad.* Barcelona: Tusquets.

———. 1997. *In the Palm of Darkness.* Translated by Edith Grossman. New York: HarperCollins.

Mooallem, Jon. 2013. *Wild Ones: A Sometimes Dismaying, Weirdly Reassuring Story about Looking at People Looking at Animals in America.* New York: Penguin.

Moore, Jason. 2014. "The Capitalocene, Part 1: On the Nature and Origins of Our Ecological Crisis." www.jasonwmoore.com/uploads/The_Capitalocene__Part_I__June_2014.pdf.

Mora, Camilo, Audrey Rollo, and Derek P. Tittensor. 2013. "Comment on 'Can We Name Earth's Species before They Go Extinct?'" *Science* 341 (July 19): 237-c. www.sciencemag.org/content/341/6143/237.3.full.

Morales Ayma, Evo. 2011. "Vivir Bien no es lo mismo que vivir mejor." Interview with Evo Morales Ayma in *Vivir Bien: Mensajes y documentos sobre el Vivir Bien, 1995–2010,* edited by Ministerio de Relaciones Exteriores [de Bolivia], 9–10. www.bivica.org/upload/diplomacia-vida_tres.pdf.

Moretti, Franco. 1996. *Modern Epic: The World System from Goethe to García Márquez.* Translated by Quintin Hoare. London: Verso.

Mortimer-Sandilands, Catriona. 2010. "Melancholy Natures, Queer Ecologies." In *Queer Ecologies: Sex, Nature, Politics, Desire,* edited by Catriona Mortimer-Sandilands and Bruce Erickson, 331–358. Bloomington: Indiana University Press.

Mrosovsky, Nicholas. 2003. "Predicting Extinction: Fundamental Flaws in IUCN's Red List System, Exemplified by the Case of Sea Turtles." Seaturtle.org. http://members.seaturtle.org/mrosovsky/.

Mukherjee, Upamanyu Pablo. 2010. *Postcolonial Environments: Nature, Culture and the Contemporary Indian Novel in English.* Houndmills, UK: Palgrave Macmillan.

Muller, Judy. 2013. "L.A.'s Proposed No-Kill Policy Raises Hackles on Both Sides." In *SoCal Connected,* broadcast by KCET, February 11. www.kcet.org/shows/socal_connected/content/animals/las-proposed-no-kill-policy-raises-hackles-on-both-sides.html.

Murchison, Kenneth M. 2007. *The Snail Darter Case: TVA versus the Endangered Species Act.* Lawrence: University Press of Kansas.

Myers, Norman. 1979. *The Sinking Ark: A New Look at the Problem of Disappearing Species.* Oxford: Pergamon.

Nazarea, Virginia D. 1998. *Cultural Memory and Biodiversity.* Tucson: University of Arizona Press.

Neuman, William. 2014. "Turnabout in Bolivia as Economy Rises from Instability." *New York Times,* February 16. www.nytimes.com/2014/02/17/world/americas/turnabout-in-bolivia-as-economy-rises-from-instability.html?_r=0.

Nettheim, Daniel, director. 2011. *The Hunter.* N.p.: Porchlight Films.

Nixon, Richard. 1972. "Special Message to the Congress Outlining the 1972 Environmental Program: February 8, 1972." In *The American Presidency*

Project, by Gerhard Peters and John T. Wolley. www.presidency.ucsb.edu/ws /index.php?pid=3731.

Nixon, Rob. 2011. *Slow Violence and the Environmentalism of the Poor*. Cambridge, MA: Harvard University Press.

Nordhaus, Ted, and Michael Shellenberger. 2011. "Evolve." *Breakthrough Journal* 2 (Fall): 13–20.

Normile, Dennis. 2010. "Counting the Ocean's Creatures, Great and Small." *Science* 330:25.

Nussbaum, Martha. 2004. "Beyond 'Compassion and Humanity': Justice for Non-human Animals." In *Animal Rights: Current Debates and New Directions*, edited by Martha Nussbaum and Cass Sunstein, 299–320. New York: Oxford University Press.

O'Kane, Trish. 2014. "What the Sparrows Told Me." *New York Times*, August 16. http://opinionator.blogs.nytimes.com/2014/08/16/what-the-sparrows-told -me/.

Olson, Deanna H., David M. Aanensen, Kathryn L. Ronnenberg, et al. 2013. "Mapping the Global Emergence of *Batrachochytrium dendrobatidis*, the Amphibian Chytrid Fungus." *PLoS ONE* 8.2: e56802. doi:10.1371/journal .pone.0056802.

Oreskes, Naomi, and Erik M. Conway. 2014. *The Collapse of Western Civilization: A View from the Future*. New York: Columbia University Press.

Owen, David. 2004. *Tasmanian Tiger: The Tragic Tale of How the World Lost Its Most Mysterious Predator*. Baltimore: Johns Hopkins University Press.

Paddle, Robert. 2000. *The Last Tasmanian Tiger: The History and Extinction of the Thylacine*. Cambridge: Cambridge University Press.

Palumbi, Stephen R. 2001. *The Evolution Explosion: How Humans Cause Rapid Evolutionary Change*. New York: Norton.

Paravisini-Gebert, Lizabeth. 2014. "Extinctions: Chronicles of Vanishing Fauna in the Colonial and Postcolonial Caribbean." In *The Oxford Handbook of Ecocriticism*, edited by Greg Garrard, 341–357. Oxford: Oxford University Press.

Patlis, Jason. 1996. "Biodiversity, Ecosystems, and Endangered Species." In *Biodiversity and the Law*, edited by William J. Snape III, 43–58. Washington, DC: Island Press.

Patterson, Charles. 2002. *Eternal Treblinka: Our Treatment of Animals and the Holocaust*. New York: Lantern Books.

Pearce, Fred. 2015. *The New Wild: Why Invasive Species Will Be Nature's Salvation*. Boston: Beacon Press.

Perlman, Dan L., and Glenn Adelson. 1997. *Biodiversity: Exploring Values and Priorities in Conservation*. Malden, MA: Blackwell Science.

Perry, Dan. 2004. "Animal Rights and Environmental Wrongs: The Case of the Grey Squirrel in Northern Italy." *Essays in Philosophy* 5.2, article 26. http:// commons.pacificu.edu/eip/vol5/iss2/26.

Philo, Chris. 1998. "Animals, Geography, and the City: Notes on Inclusions and Exclusions." In *Animal Geographies: Place, Politics, and Identity in the Nature-Culture Borderlands*, edited by Jennifer Wolch and Jody Emel, 51–71. London: Verso.

Plumwood, Val. 2002. *Environmental Culture: The Ecological Crisis of Reason.* London: Routledge.

Pollan, Michael. (2001) 2002. *The Botany of Desire: A Plant's-Eye View of the World.* Reprint, New York: Random House.

———. 2006. *The Omnivore's Dilemma: A Natural History of Four Meals.* New York: Penguin.

Price, Jennifer. 1999. *Flight Maps: Adventures with Nature in Modern America.* New York: Basic.

Purdy, Jedediah. 2015. *After Nature: A Politics for the Anthropocene.* Cambridge, MA: Harvard University Press.

Pyle, Robert Michael. 1993. *The Thunder Tree: Lessons from an Urban Wildland.* Boston: Houghton Mifflin.

Pyne, Stephen J. (1982) 1997. *Fire in America: A Cultural History of Wildland and Rural Fire.* 2nd ed. Seattle: University of Washington Press.

———. 2003. *Fire: A Brief History (Cycle of Fire).* Seattle: University of Washington Press.

Quammen, David. 1996. *The Song of the Dodo: Island Biogeography in an Age of Extinctions.* New York: Scribner.

Quint, David. 1993. *Epic and Empire: Politics and Generic Form from Virgil to Milton.* Princeton, NJ: Princeton University Press.

Rachels, James. 1999. *Created from Animals: The Moral Implications of Darwinism.* New York: Oxford University Press.

Ramazani, Jahan. 1994. *Poetries of Mourning: The Modern Elegy from Hardy to Heaney.* Chicago: University of Chicago Press.

Ramzy, Austin. 2015. "Australia Writes Morrissey to Defend Plan to Kill Millions of Feral Cats." *New York Times,* October 14. www.nytimes.com /2015/10/15/world/australia/australia-feral-cat-cull-brigitte-bardot-mor rissey.html.

Rangarajan, Mahesh. 2006. "Battles for Nature: Contesting Wildlife Conservation in Twentieth-Century India." In *Shades of Green: Environmental Activism around the Globe,* edited by Christof Mauch, Nathan Stoltzfus, and Douglas R. Weiner, 161–182. Lanham, MD: Rowman & Littlefield.

Raup, David M. 1991. *Extinction: Bad Genes or Bad Luck?* New York: Norton.

Regan, Tom. (1983) 2004. *The Case for Animal Rights: Updated with a New Preface.* Reprint, Berkeley: University of California Press.

Régnier, Claire, Guillaume Achaz, Amaury Lambert, et al. 2015. "Mass Extinction in Poorly Known Taxa." *Proceedings of the National Academy of Sciences of the United States of America* 112:7761–7766.

Reichholf, Josef H. 2005. *Die Zukunft der Arten: Neue ökologische Überraschungen.* Munich: Beck.

———. 2008. *Ende der Artenvielfalt? Gefährdung und Vernichtung von Biodiversität.* Frankfurt: Fischer.

Revkin, Andrew. 2011. "Embracing the Anthropocene." *New York Times/Dot Earth,* May 20. http://dotearth.blogs.nytimes.com/2011/05/20/embracing-the -anthropocene/.

Rich, Nathaniel. 2014. "The Mammoth Cometh." *New York Times Magazine,*

February 27. www.nytimes.com/2014/03/02/magazine/the-mammoth-cometh .html.

Robinson, Kim Stanley. 1996. *Blue Mars.* New York: Bantam.

———. 2012. *2312.* New York: Orbit.

Rodríguez, Jon Paul. 2008. "National Red Lists: The Largest Global Market for IUCN Red List Categories and Criteria." *Endangered Species Research* 6:193–198.

Rosaldo, Renato. 1993. *Culture and Truth: The Remaking of Social Analysis.* Boston: Beacon Press.

Rose, Deborah Bird. 2011. *Wild Dog Dreaming: Love and Extinction.* Charlottesville: University of Virginia Press.

Ross, Andrew. 1994. *The Chicago Gangster Theory of Life: Nature's Debt to Society.* London: Verso.

Roston, Tom. 2015. "Illuminating the Plight of Endangered Species, at the Empire State Building." *New York Times,* July 29. www.nytimes.com/2015/07/31 /movies/illuminating-the-plight-of-endangered-species-at-the-empire-state -building.html?_r=0.

Sakrison, David. 2007. *Chasing the Ghost Birds: Saving Swans and Cranes from Extinction.* Baraboo, WI: International Crane Foundation.

Sandler, Ronald. 2013a. "The Ethics of Reviving Long Extinct Species." *Conservation Biology* 28:354–360. http://onlinelibrary.wiley.com/doi/10.1111/cobi .12198/full.

———. 2013b. "The Ethics of Reviving Long Extinct Species." Presentation at "Thinking Extinction: A Symposium on the Philosophy and Science of Endangered Species," November 14–16. Laurentian University, Sudbury. Canada.

Sartore, Joel. 2009. *Rare: Portraits of America's Endangered Species.* Washington, DC: Focal Point.

Sax, Boria. 2009. *Animals in the Third Reich.* Mount Vernon, NY: Decalogue.

Sax, Dov F., and Steven D. Gaines. 2003. "Species Diversity: From Global Decreases to Local Increases." *Trends in Evolution and Ecology* 18:561–566.

Schaller, George B. (1993) 1994. *The Last Panda.* Reprint, Chicago: University of Chicago Press.

Schorger, A. W. 1955. *The Passenger Pigeon: Its Natural History and Extinction.* Madison: University of Wisconsin Press.

Schwägerl, Christian. 2010. *Menschenzeit: Zerstören oder gestalten? Die entscheidende Epoche unseres Planeten.* Munich: Riemann.

———. 2014. *The Anthropocene: The Human Era and How It Shapes Our Planet.* Translated by Lucy Renner Jones. Santa Fe, NM: Synergetic Press.

Scott, J. Michael, Dale D. Goble, and Frank W. Davis. 2006. "Introduction." In *The Endangered Species Act at Thirty: Renewing the Conservation Promise,* edited by Dale D. Goble, J. Michael Scott, and Frank W. Davis, 1:3–15. Washington, DC: Island Press.

Scott, J. Michael, Dale D. Goble, Leona K. Svancarra, et al. 2006. "By the Numbers." In *The Endangered Species Act at Thirty: Renewing the Conservation Promise,* edited by Dale D. Goble, J. Michael Scott, and Frank W. Davis, 1:16–35. Washington, DC: Island Press.

"Seal Hunters and Protesters Clash North of Newfoundland." 1976. *New York Times*, March 16. http://query.nytimes.com/mem/archive/pdf?res=F40B13F A3955127B93C4A81788D85F428785F9.

Seminoff, Jeffrey A., and Kartik Shanker. 2008. "Marine Turtles and IUCN Red Listing: A Review of the Process, the Pitfalls, and Novel Assessment Approaches." *Journal of Experimental Marine Biology and Ecology* 356:52–68.

Sepkoski, David. 2012. *Rereading the Fossil Record: The Growth of Paleobiology as an Evolutionary Discipline*. Chicago: University of Chicago Press.

Sibley, David A., Louis R. Bevier, Michael A. Patten, et al. 2006. "Comment on 'Ivory-billed Woodpecker (*Campephilus principalis*) Persists in Continental North America.'" *Science* 311 (March 17): 1555.

Simberloff, Daniel. 2013. *Invasive Species: What Everyone Needs to Know*. New York: Oxford University Press.

Singer, Peter. (1975) 2009. *Animal Liberation: The Definitive Classic of the Animal Movement*. Reprint, New York: HarperCollins.

Snyder, Noel F. R., David E. Brown, and Kevin B. Clark. 2009. *The Travails of Two Woodpeckers: Ivory-Bills and Imperials*. Albuquerque: University of New Mexico Press.

Sodikoff, Genese Marie. 2012a. *Forest and Labor in Madagascar: From Colonial Concession to Global Biosphere*. Bloomington: Indiana University Press.

———. 2012b. "Totem and Taboo Reconsidered: Endangered Species and Moral Practice in Madagascar." In *The Anthropology of Extinction: Essays on Culture and Species Death*, edited by Genese Marie Sodikoff, 67–88. Bloomington: Indiana University Press.

Songorwa, Alexander N. 2013. "Saving Lions by Killing Them." *New York Times*, March 17. www.nytimes.com/2013/03/18/opinion/saving-lions-by -killing-them.html.

Spargo, R. Clifton. 2004. *The Ethics of Mourning: Grief and Responsibility in Elegiac Literature*. Baltimore: Johns Hopkins University Press.

Spielberg, Steven, director. 1993. *Jurassic Park*. N.p.: Amblin Entertainment/ Universal.

Stearns, Beverly Peterson, and Stephen C. Stearns. 1999. *Watching, from the Edge of Extinction*. New Haven, CT: Yale University Press.

Steffen, Will, Paul J. Crutzen, and John R. McNeill. 2007. "The Anthropocene: Are Humans Now Overwhelming the Great Forces of Nature?" *Ambio* 38:614–621.

Steinberg, Michael K. 2008. *Stalking the Ghost Bird: The Elusive Ivory-Billed Woodpecker in Louisiana*. Baton Rouge: Louisiana State University Press.

Steinberg, Paul F. 2001. *Environmental Leadership in Developing Countries: Translational Relations and Biodiversity Policy in Costa Rica and Bolivia*. Cambridge, MA: MIT Press.

Stolzenburg, William. 2008. *Where the Wild Things Were: Life, Death, and Ecological Wreckage in a Land of Vanishing Predators*. New York: Bloomsbury.

Stone, Christopher D. (1972) 2010. *Should Trees Have Standing? Law, Morality, and the Environment*. 3rd ed. New York: Oxford University Press.

Sullivan, Robert. 2000. *A Whale Hunt.* New York: Scribner.

Takacs, David. 1996. *The Idea of Biodiversity: Philosophies of Paradise.* Baltimore: Johns Hopkins University Press.

Tanner, James T. (1942) 2003. *The Ivory-Billed Woodpecker.* Reprint, Mineola, NY: Dover.

Taylor, Martin F. J., Kieran F. Suckling, and Jeffrey J. Rachlinski. 2005. "The Effectiveness of the Endangered Species Act: A Quantitative Analysis." *BioScience* 55:360–367.

Techentin, Warren. 2009. "Tree Huggers Landscape." In *The Infrastructural City: Networked Ecologies in Los Angeles,* edited by Kazys Varnelis. Barcelona: Actar.

Terrazas Urquidi, Wagner. [1973]. *Bolivia: País saqueado.* La Paz, Bolivia: Camarlinghi.

Thomas, Claire. 2009. "Biodiversity Databases Spread, Prompting Unification Call." *Science* 324:1632–1633.

Thomas, Julia Adeney. 2014. "History and Biology in the Anthropocene: Problems of Scale, Problems of Value." *American Historical Review* 119:1587–1607.

Thompson, Ken. 2014. *Where Do Camels Belong? Why Invasive Species Aren't All Bad.* N.p: Greystone Books.

Timberg, Craig. 2008. "South Africa to Resume Elephant Culling." *Washington Post,* February 26. www.washingtonpost.com/wpdyn/content/article/2008/02/25/AR2008022500970.html.

Tockman, Jason. 2012. "Citizenship Regimes and Post-Neoliberal Environments in Bolivia." In *Environment and Citizenship in Latin America: Natures, Subjects and Struggles,* edited by Alex Latta and Hannah Wittman, 129–148. New York: Berghahn Books.

Toomey, Diane. 2012. "Maya Lin: A Memorial to a Vanishing Natural World." Interview with Maya Lin. *environment360,* June 25. http://e360.yale.edu/feature/maya_lin_a_memorial_to_a_vanishing_natural_world/2545/.

Tsing, Anna. 2005. *Frictions: An Ethnography of Global Connectedness.* Princeton, NJ: Princeton University Press.

———. 2011. "Arts of Inclusion; or, How to Love a Mushroom." *Australian Humanities Review* 50. www.australianhumanitiesreview.org/archive/issue-May-2011/tsing.html.

———. n.d. *Unruly Edges: Mushrooms as Companion Species.* http://tsingmushrooms.blogspot.com/.

Väliverronen, Esa, and Iina Hellsten. 2002. "From 'Burning Library' to 'Green Medicine': The Role of Metaphor in Communicating Biodiversity." *Science Communication* 24:229–245.

Van Aarde, Rudi, Ian Whyte, and Stuart Pimm. 1999. "Culling and the Dynamics of the Kruger National Park Elephant Population." *Animal Conservation* 2:287–294.

Vandermeer, John, and Ivette Perfecto. 2014. "Paradigms Lost: Tropical Conservation under Late Capitalism." In *The Social Lives of Forests: Past, Present, and Future of Woodland Resurgence,* edited by Susanna B. Hecht, Kathleen D. Morrison, and Christine Padoch, 114–128. Chicago: University of Chicago Press.

Van Dooren, Thom. 2014. *Flight Ways: Life and Death at the Edge of Extinction.* New York: Columbia University Press. Kindle edition.

Van Dooren, Thom, and Deborah Bird Rose. 2012. "Storied-Places in a Multi-species City." *Humanimalia* 3.2:1–27.

Varner, Gary E. 1998. *In Nature's Interests? Interests, Animal Rights, and Environmental Ethics.* New York: Oxford University Press. Kindle edition.

Verschuuren, Jonathan. 2004. "Effectiveness of Nature Protection Legislation in the European Union and the United States: The Habitats Directive and the Endangered Species Act." In *Cultural Landscapes and Land Use: The Nature Conservation–Society Interface*, edited by Martin Dieterich and Jan van der Straaten, 39–67. Dordrecht, Netherlands: Kluwer.

Vesna, Victoria, ed. 2007. *Database Aesthetics: Art in the Age of Information Overflow.* Minneapolis: University of Minnesota Press.

Von Einsiedel, Orlando, director. 2014. *Virunga.* N.p: Appian Way Productions/Grain Media.

Walker, Brett L. 2005. *The Lost Wolves of Japan.* Seattle: University of Washington Press.

Walters, Mark Jerome. 2006. *Seeking the Sacred Raven: Politics and Extinction on a Hawaiian Island.* Washington, DC: Island Press.

Watson, Robert N. 2014. "Protestant Animals: Puritan Sects and English Animal-Protection Sentiment, 1550–1650." *English Literary History* 81:1111–1148.

Weidensaul, Scott. 2002. *The Ghost with Trembling Wings: Science, Wishful Thinking, and the Search for Lost Species.* New York: Farrar, Straus and Giroux.

Weik, Alexa. 2006–7. "The Home, the Tide, and the World: Eco-Cosmopolitan Encounters in Amitav Ghosh's *The Hungry Tide.*" *Journal of Commonwealth and Postcolonial Studies* 13.2–14.1:120–141.

Weisman, Alan. (2007) 2008. *The World without Us.* Reprint, New York: Picador.

Wheeler, Quentin D. 2008. "Introductory: Toward the New Taxonomy." In *The New Taxonomy*, edited by Quentin D. Wheeler, 1–17. Boca Raton, FL: Taylor & Francis.

White, Richard. 1996. "'Are You an Environmentalist or Do You Work for a Living?': Work and Nature." In *Uncommon Ground: Rethinking the Human Place in Nature*, edited by William Cronon, 171–185. New York: Norton.

———. 2011. "Bill McKibben's Emersonian Vision." *Raritan* 31.2 (Fall): 110125.

Wilcove, David S., and Margaret McMillan. 2006. "The Class of '67'." In *The Endangered Species Act at Thirty: Renewing the Conservation Promise*, edited by Dale D. Goble, J. Michael Scott, and Frank W. Davis, 1:45–50. Washington, DC: Island Press.

Wilkins, John S. 2009. *Species: A History of the Idea.* Berkeley: University of California Press.

Wilkinson, David M. 2004. "The Parable of Green Mountain: Ascension Island, Ecosystem Construction and Ecological Fitting." *Journal of Biogeography* 31:1–4.

Williams, Raymond. 1973. *The Country and the City.* New York: Oxford University Press.

Wilson, Alexander. 1808–14. *American Ornithology; or, The Natural History of the Birds of the United States*. Philadelphia: Bradford and Inskeep.

Wilson, Edward O. 1992. *The Diversity of Life*. Cambridge, MA: Harvard University Press.

———. 2002. *The Future of Life*. New York: Vintage.

Wöbse, Anna-Katharina. 2003. "Lina Hähnle und der Reichsbund für Vogelschutz: Soziale Bewegung im Gleichschritt." In *Naturschutz und Nationalsozialismus*, edited by Joachim Radkau and Frank Uekötter, 309–328. Frankfurt, Germany: Campus.

Wolch, Jennifer. 1998. "Zoöpolis." In *Animal Geographies: Place, Politics, and Identity in the Nature-Culture Borderlands*, edited by Jennifer Wolch and Jody Emel, 119–138. London: Verso.

Wolfe, Cary. 2003. *Animal Rites: American Culture, the Discourse of Species, and Posthumanist Theory*. Chicago: University of Chicago Press.

———. 2012. *Before the Law: Humans and Other Animals in a Biopolitical Frame*. Chicago: University of Chicago Press.

Worster, Donald. 2008. *A Passion for Nature: The Life of John Muir*. New York: Oxford University Press.

Yaffee, S. L. 1982. *Prohibitive Policy: Implementing the Federal Endangered Species Act*. Cambridge, MA: MIT Press.

Youatt, Rafi. 2015. *Counting Species: Biodiversity in Global Environmental Politics*. Minneapolis: University of Minnesota Press. Kindle edition.

Yusoff, Kathryn. 2012. "Aesthetics of Loss: Biodiversity, Banal Violence and Biotic Subjects." *Transactions of the Institute of British Geographers* 37:578–592. http://onlinelibrary.wiley.com/doi/10.1111/j.1475-5661.2011.00486.x/abstract.

Žižek, Slavoj. 2011. *Living in the End Times*. Rev. and updated ed. London: Verso.

Zwanzig, Günter W. 1989. "Wertewandel in der Entwicklung des Naturschutzrechtes." In *Naturschutz braucht Wertmassstäbe: Seminar 3.–5. November 1987, Laufen an der Salzach*, edited by Josef Heringer, Kurt Oeser, and Alois Glück, 15–29. N.p.: Bayerische Akademie für Naturschutz und Landschaftspflege.

Index

Page numbers in italic refer to figures.